The American Jewish Woman,
1654-1980

BOOKS ON AMERICAN JEWISH HISTORY
BY JACOB RADER MARCUS

Early American Jewry (in 2 volumes)
Memoirs of American Jews, 1775–1865 (in 3 volumes)
American Jewry - Documents, Eighteenth Century
On Love, Marriage, Children . . . And Death, Too
Studies in American Jewish History: Studies and Addresses
The Handsome Young Priest in the Black Gown
The Colonial American Jew (in 3 volumes)
An Index to Scientific Articles on American Jewish History
The American Jewish Woman: A Documentary History
The American Jewish Woman, 1654–1980

BOOKS ON AMERICAN JEWISH HISTORY DEDICATED
TO JACOB RADER MARCUS

Essays in American Jewish History. To Commemorate the Tenth Anniversary of the Founding of the American Jewish Archives under the Direction of Jacob Rader Marcus
A Bicentennial Festschrift for Jacob Rader Marcus

The American Jewish Woman, 1654-1980

by JACOB R. MARCUS

KTAV Publishing House, Inc. · New York
American Jewish Archives · Cincinnati
1981

Library of Congress Cataloging in Publication Data
Marcus, Jacob Rader, 1896-
  The American Jewish woman, 1654–1980.

  Bibliography: p.
  Includes index.
  1. Women, Jewish—United States—History.
2. Jews—United States—History. 3. Women—
United States—History. 4. United States—Ethnic
relations. I. Title.
HQ1172.M37   305.4'8   81-1720
ISBN 0-87068-751-4   AACR2

Manufactured in the United States of America

For
Nettie and Merle

Contents

List of Illustrations

(following page 90)

Rebecca Gratz (1781–1869)
Abigail Minis (1701–1794)
Select Boarding School for Young Ladies
Purim Ball (1877)
Elizabeth Friedlander
Eugenia Levy Phillips (1820–1902)
Ladies United Hebrew Benevolent Society
Women's *Landsmanshaft*
Jewish Women's Religious Congress (1893)
Hannah G. Solomon (1853–1942)
Carrie Simon (1872–1961)
The *Deborah* (1855)
The *American Jewess* (1895)
The *American Hebrew*
The *Hebrew Standard*

(following page 152)

The Henry Street Settlement
Amalgamated Clothing Workers on strike (1915)
Alla Nazimova (1879-1945)
Helena Rubinstein (1871-1965)
Judge Caroline K. Simon (b. 1900)
Anna M. Rosenberg (b. 1902)
Beatrice Sanders (b. 1900)
Bess Myerson (b. 1924)
Roberta Peters (b. 1930)
Hannah Arendt (1906-1976)
Golda Meir (1898–1978)

Preface

WHY did I write this book? Actually I was pressured into it by colleagues and associates, and now that this monograph is completed I am grateful to them. The Jewish woman has been ignored in the standard chronicles of this country's Jewry. There are exceptions, of course, but the few women included can be counted on the fingers of one hand. There can be no question: there is an American Jewish woman's history that goes back to September 1654. All American Jewish annalistic works deal with men, a numerical minority among the Jews; there has been no full-length, scientifically conceived, source-based book retailing the lives and adventures of American Jewesses. They were, they still are, a majority of all Jews in this land.

Women were conscious of themselves as a group with a history of their own not later than the early 1890's. There is every reason to believe that they were thinking of themselves consciously, as a distinct community, decades earlier. And how does one define a Jew? Anyone is a Jew—so I have always maintained in my writings—who has one Jewish parent. Admittedly there are some "half-Jews" who are indifferent, even hostile, to the peoples whose "blood" courses through their veins. For my historiographical purposes, defection or hostility is not determinative. I have not sat down to write a book about committed or happy Jews.

Nor is this study of the American Jewish woman another feminist liberation narrative. Its intent is to describe the American Jewish woman from 1654 to 1980 as she emerges from the documents, the letters, the memoirs, the congregational minutes, and a large assortment of memorabilia. It is obvious that such a book will not only record her activities but also the "disabilities" under which she has labored for at least three thousand years in a patriarchial religious society. This is not a hearts-and-flowers panegyric of the Jewish housewife; it is an attempt to recapture the past "as it actually was."

Ten years from today, another history of the American Jewish woman will have to be written . . . I hope. A new school of Jewish historians is now rising; many of them are women; they will do justice to their sex. Books on the Jewish woman will appear; they must be written. They, the writers of tomorrow, will produce a monographic literature that is not in existence today. I deem it a privilege, with the limited resources at hand, to present a history that will serve—if for nothing else—as a point of departure. The periodization, I believe, is grounded on solid data. One may well cherish the hope that future writers of American Jewish history will give American Jewesses their due as sentient human beings, as women, as Jews.

This book has not been fortified by individual marginal notes. The necessary documentation—almost for each line—would be overwhelming and distracting. Yet every statement in this study has been based on data which I deem authentic. However, to substantiate the basic statements that I have made, a very detailed bibliography has been appended for the use of students and scholars. In addition, I have not hesitated to offer suggestions for further studies in this very inviting field. Much of the history, too, encompassed in this book is reflected in the substantial documentary I have edited to accompany this introductory monograph. I refer to Jacob R. Marcus, *The American Jewish Woman: A Documentary History*.

I find it necessary to make a somewhat detailed comment about the use of the word "Jewess." It carries no pejorative connotation in the *Oxford English Dictionary* and in *Webster's Third New International Dictionary* (1961). Many Jews today deem it a "dirty word" and avoid it. I believe it is a neutral descriptive noun and I use it constantly. If for some it has become a term of contempt, it is because Judeophobic Gentiles have made it so. I refuse to bow to their prejudice.

In my opinion there is a perfect analogue. For centuries non-Jews used the word "Jew" as a term of reproach. Jews in the United States, deferring to public opinion, avoided its use. Thus it was that throughout the nineteenth century we have the resurrection of the "Hebrews" and the "Israelites." We witnessed the rise of the Board of Delegates of American Israelites, the Union of American Hebrew Congregations, the Hebrew Union College, Maimonides College, and a host of Hebrew Benevolent Societies. Among the well-known newspapers of the last century were *Israel's Herold*, the *Asmonean* the *American Israelite, Deborah, Sinai*, the *American Hebrew*, and the *Macabaean*.

By the turn of the century, however, self-respecting Jews ceased to lower their voices when they used this three-letter word. For them it was no longer a badge of infamy. I see no reason why Jews today should blush when they refer to a Jewish woman as a "Jewess." Here in the United States there were dozens of distinguished Jewish females who were leaders in the non-Jewish communities which they graced, who were admired for their intellignece, their courage, their integrity, who were honored because they reflected in their lives the highest ideals of their millennial traditions. They have invested the word "Jewess" with respect and dignity.

And now there remains for me the very pleasant task of thanking all those who have helped me in the preparation of this work. I am particularly grateful to my friend and colleague, Dr. Stanley F. Chyet, Dean of the Graduate School of the Hebrew Union College—Jewish Institute of Religion, Los Angeles, California, for his most careful reading of the manuscript and for the innumerable changes he has recommended. His was a labor of love for which I cannot begin to thank him. My colleague at the American Jewish Archives, Abraham J. Peck, has been most helpful. Indeed he is one of those who urged me to write this book. Faedra Lazar Weiss, Rabbi Kurt Stone, and Professor Jonathan Sarna of the Hebrew Union College—Jewish Institute of Religion, Cincinnati, have "vetted" this manuscript and made many helpful suggestions. The staff workers of the American Jewish Archives have pitched in to make this book possible. They will forgive me if I do not mention them all by name; I do not wish to offend by an inadvertent omission. They know how grateful I am. Professor Herbert C. Zafren, the Librarian of the Cincinnati Hebrew Union College–Jewish Institute of Religion, and his staff have always gone out of their way to ease my task. This is an act of supererogation which I appreciate more than I can express. Without adequate tools, historians—craftsmen—are helpless. The authorities of the Cincinnati Public Library have been very helpful. I hasten to acknowledge my indebtedness particularly to Mr. Jacob Epstein for his many gracious courtesies.

I wish to express my gratitude to the Freudenthal Foundation of Trinidad, Colorado. The trustees, dear friends of mine, have never failed to evince an interest in my work. Their generosity has helped make this volume possible. My colleagues in the Alumni Association of the Hebrew Union College–Jewish Institute of Religion, devoted disciples and affectionate friends, have given me a substantial grant in order that this volume might see the light of day. To them, and "the saving remnant in Trinidad," my most heartfelt thanks. I would be remiss if I did not mention my copy editors Mr. and Mrs. Robert J. Milch for their expertise and unremitting efforts. For their concern and interest I am grateful. And finally I find it difficult to express adequately my gratitude to my personal secretary, Mrs. Etheljane Callner, who has labored side by side with me for thirty years. For her the production of this history and the accompanying documentary has been a sacred task to which she has dedicated herself. Thank you, thank you, Mrs. Callner.

Jacob R. Marcus

American Jewish Archives
On the Campus of the
Hebrew Union College–
Jewish Institute of Religion,
Cincinnati, Ohio.
January 1981

· 1 ·

The American Jew: His Story, 1654—1980

The Colonial Period, 1654—1775

JEWRY today in these United States numbers about 5,800,000 men, women, and children. These wanderers first made their appearance as a group in North America in late August or early September of 1654, when twenty-three Jews landed in Peter Stuyvesant's New Amsterdam. They were refugees fleeing from Dutch Brazil; they could no longer remain in that colony after its reconquest by the Portuguese. Coming to Dutch North America may well have been a voluntary act, for they could have returned to Amsterdam itself. Most Jews who settled in New Netherland under the Dutch, or who came in later under the English, did so because of their hope for larger economic opportunities. These newcomers, who arrived here in relatively small numbers in the seventeenth and eighteenth centuries, settled in the tidewater country, from Newport south to Savannah. Before 1720, most of them were of Spanish-Portuguese stock; after that date the majority were Central Europeans with a sprinkling of Slavic Jews from Eastern Europe. They accepted and adopted the Sephardic rite as their own. In the 1700's, the wealthiest family was an Anglo-American clan of army purveyors who helped the British drive the French out of North America; the few American Jewish businessmen who were to achieve success were coastal and overseas merchants, candle manufacturers, and, on occasion, slave importers. After the French were driven out of the transallegheny lands, a handful of these businessmen engaged in the fur industry—not as traders, but as major entrepreneurs. Most Jews were petty shopkeepers and artisan-retailers.

The Jews were never fully emancipated under the rule of the Dutch, which lasted until 1664, or the British, who relinquished authority in 1783. Some of the British North American colonies granted Jews the franchise; none of them allowed Jews to hold honorary office. Politically, they were better off than any group of European Jews. Relatively speaking, the British colonies were lands of almost unlimited opportunity. The English made no attempt to curb the colonial Jews in their worship services; freedom of conscience was absolute. Prayer groups were established in the larger towns, and religious functionaries of lesser status and authority were employed. No rabbi officiated in what is now the United States until 1840. For a talmudist, the colonies were exile. In turn the worshippers made no effort to bring learned spiritual leaders here; they had no intention of submitting to religious authority. These settlers were devotees of traditional Judaism, who nonetheless adapted their age-old faith to this westernmost Atlantic frontier by tacitly adopting a policy of salutary neglect. Parochial schools of a sort dragged out a desultory existence; the synagogue made every effort to provide for the needs of local Jews and itinerants who petitioned for relief. By 1775, the twenty-five hundred Jews in the fourteen British North American colonies had succeeded in creating six communities with synagogues, schools, and charities—the transatlantic crossing had been successfully accomplished.

The American Jew in the Early Republic and in the Age of Expansion, 1775—1865

At the time of the Revolution, which began in April 1775, most American Jews were Whigs, Continentals, whose hope for political equality was being frustrated by the conservatism of the sovereign states. It was not until 1876—77, a century after the Great Promise—the Declaration of Independence—that New Hampshire emancipated its Jews politically. It was the last of the original thirteen states to accord Jews equality. As early as the 1790's, Jews were entering state legislatures, and it was not long before many of them assumed office in the towns, where they were frequently numbered among the leading citizens. The federal government was more liberal than the state commonwealths. Simon Magruder Levy of Baltimore graduated with the first class at West Point; there were all of two men commissioned that year. Mordecai M. Noah, American Jewry's antebellum stormy petrel, was appointed consul to Tunis; Major Alfred Mordecai of the Warrenton, North Carolina, Mordecais, was one of the country's most distinguished ordnance experts. Uriah P. Levy, Noah's seafaring cousin, was court-martialed six times, hauled before a board of inquiry twice, but ended his career in a blaze of glory as "commodore" of the Mediterranean fleet. By 1841, David Levy Yulee was already serving in the House of Representatives as Florida's territorial delegate; in 1845 he was elected senator.

Yet by the middle 1840's there were still less than thirty thousand Jews in the country. It was not until the late 1830's that economic distress and political disabilities in Europe, and the hope for a better life in America, induced many Central Europeans to sail for these shores. They came with the German Gentiles, but there was never to be a mass German Jewish migration to the United States. Urban German Jews with some means hesitated to leave; Germany itself was on the way up. Many of those Jews who arrived here in antebellum days struck out for the Western frontier. Before 1840, a young native American adventurer had opened a store in Yerba Buena, California, the town that in the next decade was to call itself San Francisco.

The new Jews who were to come here before the Civil War, mostly Central Europeans, were peddlers, artisans, shopkeepers, merchants, land speculators. A handful had even become manufacturers. Enterprising businessmen in small numbers turned to banking, transportation, and insurance; ambitious young men became physicians, dentists, and lawyers. White-collar workers began to abound. When the tiny Jewish communities began to expand, in the early days of the republic, the synagogue found it difficult to serve as the only Jewish charity. Autonomous and semi-autonomous charities and mutual-aid societies had begun to make their appearance in the last years of the Revolution. Gradually, these organizations disassociated themselves from their religious sponsors; yet they were never anti-religious. America's Jewish social-welfare agencies now moved closer to secularization, the pattern that was to prevail. All types of relief associations were to dot the landscape by 1890; national Jewish mutual-aid lodges, benevolent societies, orphan asylums, and finally combination hospitals and homes for the aged were set up to make provision for young peddlers and clerks who had no one to look after them when they fell ill. The evangelically-minded Christian hospitals were no place for a Jew who dreaded the thought that if he fell into a coma he might recover only to find that he had been baptized by a zealous nurse. Most Jews in the antebellum period remained loyal to traditional European Orthodoxy, but it would be wrong to infer that they visited the synagogue regularly.

In Jewish cultural terms, American Jewry moved ahead, though its scholarly contribution was inconsequential. Congregational after-noon schools were opened; all-day or "parochial" schools and private institutions of learning for the children of the affluent were established. Sunday schools flourished, for they were typically "American." The Jews were happy to have religious schools on Sunday just like their Christian neighbors. A permanent English Jewish press rose in the 1840's; German-language weeklies catered to the immigrants. Textbooks, translated liturgies, apologetic works, and pamphlets attacking the Christian missionaries were produced. Jewish booksellers and publishers began to appear in the larger towns.

The most important Jewish cultural figure in antebellum America was the German immigrant Isaac Leeser (1806—1868). This man, who served as hazzan, actually rabbi, of the Sephardic congregation Mikveh Israel in Philadelphia, wrote textbooks and apologies vin-dicating Judaism, and introduced regular English preaching into the synagogue; it was he who edited the first successful Jewish periodical in this country. Acting as his own publisher, he issued translations of the Sephardic and Ashkenazic prayer books, and prepared both America's first vocalized Hebrew Bible and its first complete English translation of the Old Testament. It was Leeser who made possible the first American Jewish Publication Society and the first American rabbinical seminary. He was the country's most effective champion of traditional Judaism, and though he had but little support from his congregation, with which he was constantly feuding, he—more than any other individual of that day—made it possible for Jewry to come to terms religiously with the challenge of American modernism.

The lodges of the 1840's were not only mutual-aid societies, they were social centers; by the 1840's, clubs, eating and drinking and cardplaying societies, were founded. The successful immigrant could now afford to relax; the worst was over. The youth established "Young Men's" associations where literary pursuits were cultivated and social goals stressed. The Jews preferred to be by themselves; as immigrants and sons of immigrants, they were not welcomed in Gentile circles. Congress and the President made a commercial treaty with Switzerland which ignored the rights of American Jewish citizens, and when a Jewish youngster was taken from the arms of his mother in papal Italy to be reared as a Christian, the American authorities saw no reason to protest. Apprehensive, therefore, because of governmental disregard for Jewish rights and sensitivities, a number of synagogues united to form a national civic defense organization, the Board of Delegates of American Israelites.

The Board and other would-be champions found ample scope for their activities during the Civil War. Although there were thousands of Jewish soldiers—even a number of brevetted generals—no Jewish chaplain was tolerated before 1862. General U. S. Grant expelled Jews from some of the Mississippi River towns in his army department because a number were trading with the enemy. (So was his father, Jesse Grant.)

In the Confederacy, where anti-Jewish prejudice was never absent, Jews were nonetheless honored with the posts of quartermaster general, surgeon general, attorney general, secretary of war, and secretary of state. The last three portfolios were successively held by Judah P. Benjamin, a former United States senator from Louisiana and one of the country's most brilliant and successful lawyers. Eminent Southern Jews reflected an advanced humanistic culture that centered in Charleston, South Carolina. It is estimated that in 1865, when the war came to an end, there were some 150,000 Jews in the United States. This was a far cry from the 2,500 men, women, and children who had hugged the coastlands in 1776. The pioneering American Jewish community was now to be counted one of the world's larger Jewries.

The American Jew and the New Industrial Society, 1865—1980

American Jews, most of whom were of Central European provenance, had played very little part in the new industrialism of the pre—Civil War period. Mainly peddlers and petty bourgeois storekeepers, they had no capital, no training, and no industrial traditions. They were latecomers; nevertheless in the next generation, by the year 1900, they had made rapid headway in several areas of commerce and manufacturing: in meat packing, leather, tobacco, liquor, jewelry, banking, and garment production. Individuals had begun to make names for themselves in medicine and law; there were even a number, not many, who had gained recognition in the natural and social sciences.

While the German immigrants and their children were forging ahead in trade and industry in the 1880's and 1890's, they were confronted by hundreds of thousands of East Europeans who poured into this country. Many came to escape Russian and Rumanian tyranny and poverty; most had come here in the hope of building new lives for themselves. They brought a Russian and Polish type of Orthodoxy with them, liturgies and rituals of their own, an undeviating adherence to the dietary laws, and an insistence on retention of the ancient Hebrew language in the synagogue. Bethels and conventicles of an East European type sprang up in every corner of the country. By the early 1900's there were at least two thousand of them. The newcomers spoke Yiddish, published numerous Yiddish dailies and weeklies, and established a Yiddish theatre that catered to the needs of a people who were desperately struggling to effect a transition from an agrarian Russia to an industrial America. Unlike their German predecessors, very few of them were hostile to

Zionism, the new Palestine nationalism; Jews, they believed, were entitled to a land of their own where every man could live idyllically under his own vine and fig tree. Thus, turn-of-the-century America sheltered two coeval active Jewish communities: the so-called German and the so-called Russian. They worked together—after a fashion—though hostilities 'were ever-present. The older migration felt threatened by the uncouth newcomers; by 1920 the new arrivals outnumbered the old-timers at least five to one. For their part, the East Europeans resented the patronizing attitude of the "Germans," whose acculturated form of Judaism was damned as assimilation.

American Jewry moved forward politically in the days after the Civil War. There were Jews appointed as consuls, ministers, and ambassadors; they were elected congressmen and governors, and finally a distinguished lawyer was appointed to the Supreme Court in 1916. Most newcomers were too busy keeping their heads above water to concern themselves with politics. They voted with their neighbors; that was the American way. Whether they were Democrats or Republicans, they were equally hostile to the socialists. There were as yet very few independent voters. Among the Germans were men of wealth and standing who were interested in political reform; among the Jewish workers in the garment industry were many who were socialists or anarchists preaching the gospel of change and utopia. There is no question that most of the workers' leaders and the Jewish union stalwarts were committed Marxists; the Jewish masses were not, though they too rallied around Meyer London, a socialist, and sent him to Congress in 1915. They respected him for his integrity.

The United States was to witness radical changes in traditional Judaism. Influenced by American culture and the subconscious (sometimes fully conscious) desire to pattern themselves at least superficially on their Gentile neighbors, Jews began turning to the left religiously. They felt the need to develop a symbiosis of Judaism and Americanism. This process began as early as 1824 in Charleston; it reached its height in the 1870's. The leader of this acculturationist effort was the Bohemian immigrant Isaac M. Wise (1819—1900). With the help of devoted laymen, he built the Reform movement through a union of congregations, a rabbinical seminary, and a national association of rabbis. In 1885, a group of his disciples and colleagues met in Pittsburgh and adopted a radical religious program. They rejected, at least implicitly, the authority of rabbinism, of Orthodoxy, threw overboard those customs and practices tending to separate the Jew from his Gentile neighbor, and emphasized the moral and ethical teachings of the Bible and the rabbinical sages. The Pittsburgh Conference went too far even for Wise—a moderate Reformer still rooted in the old ways—but the Pittsburgh Platform, except for its rejection of Jewish nationalism centered on Palestine, still reflects the thinking and the theology of the Reform movement.

Reacting to this sharp break with tradition, the Americanized Orthodox in 1886 created their own denomination. Ultimately they called themselves Conservatives. Their followers included American- and German-born Jews. By the early 1900's they began to make substantial progress; today they outnumber the Reformers. The latter at no time constituted a majority of American Jews; in the 1870's, at the zenith of their power and influence, these religious left-wingers could never muster more than 40 percent of the country's synagogues. The East European Orthodox, the masses, would have nothing to do with the Reformers or the Conservatives. As late as 1920, the synagogues of the Orthodox, the Reformers, and the Conservatives were still American Jewry's basic institutions. Jews who flocked to the sanctuaries, especially on the High Holydays, did so not only for religious, but also for social and ethnic reasons; going to shul was an important act of faith—they identified with their people.

Jewish tradition maintains that Judaism is a composite of three elements: worship, philanthropy, and education. Even before the Civil War, exemplars of all later social-welfare institutions had already made their appearance. After the war, these agencies increased numerically. Then, almost every town, even the smaller ones, could boast of a Hebrew Benevolent Society. In the larger cities, the federation process had already set in no later than the 1850's, and by the early 1900's most communities had established federations that were soon to be almost all-inclusive. With the gradual decline of Europe's Jewish communities after World War I, these federations turned to the task of raising huge sums, particularly for the impoverished Jews of Eastern Europe.

Most of the philanthropic dollar was allocated for American Jewish and European Jewish charities. As realists, Jews believed—as did the patriarch Jacob—that nothing was more important than "bread to eat and a garment to wear." Very little was left for Jewish cultural purposes, but there was always a saving remnant, a handful of men who pleaded for Jewish education, for books. A second Jewish Publication Society was organized in the 1870's; and when that failed to survive, the present Jewish Publication Society of America was established in the 1880's. Dozens of different titles have been published by the Society; among its important publications is a five-volume English translation from the German of the *History of the Jews* by Heinrich Graetz. It was followed by a scholarly English translation of the Bible, a series of bilingual Hebrew classics, and the seven-volume *Legends of the Jews* by America's most distinguished rabbinic scholar, Louis Ginzberg. In the early 1900's the monumental *Jewish Encyclopedia* made its appearance. American Jewry was clearly on the way to cultural autonomy; by the 1920's it had become one of the world centers of Jewish scholarship.

Scientifically conceived Hebrew and Judaic studies owed much to a Jewry that had embraced a methodology acquired in the colleges and universities of the country. Few native Jews, however, were drawn to specific Jewish disciplines in the early twentieth century; their interests were almost totally centered on the secular sciences. Children of the natives were emerging as researchers, scholars, lawyers, doctors, and journalists. Children of the East European émigrés flocked to the colleges in large numbers; in the next generation many would win Nobel Prizes, especially in the natural sciences. Most Jews opted for a life of trade and industry. By 1920, a number were notable for their achievements as department store owners and garment manufacturers. By providing American men and women with good mass-produced garments at reasonable prices, they helped break down the distinctions between gentry and commoners and thus furthered democratic patterns. At least all Americans could dress alike.

By the third decade of the new century, American Jewry had

grown to some three and a half to four million souls. Its leadership was found in New York City, where the Jewish national organizations were housed, where Jewish bankers extended credit, and the most important traders and manufacturers displayed their wares. A very substantial proportion of the city's population, about 25 percent, was Jewish. It was here that American Jewry was preparing itself to exercise hegemony over the world's Jewries. By 1914, the Jews of East European stock were ready to challenge the dominant "Germans" for leadership in American and in World Jewry. The attempt failed; what resulted was a compromise. The anti-alien immigration acts of the 1920's closed the gates of the United States to further mass migration of East Europeans. Perforce, the Jews here had to intramarry; there was mutual assimilation. The "Germans" and the "Russians" disappeared; the new Jew to emerge was an "American"; all other ethnic labels were gradually discarded. In this Jewish melting pot neither Germans nor Russians succeeded in imposing their way of life on the new generation; the new cultural pattern which appeared was unique, though it did bear traces of its origins.

Late-twentieth-century American Jewry is very probably the country's most affluent group. This is by no means to imply that America's most wealthy citizens are Jews; they are not. The real wealth lies with the Gentiles, like the Mellons, the Fords, and the Rockefellers. In proportion to their numbers, the Jews as a body are very generous; their gifts to Israel are fabulous and over the years have probably amounted to billions. Yet possibly as many as 15 percent of all American Jews live on a level not far removed from poverty. These are the older immigrants and natives who, without savings or other resources, are compelled to subsist on social security grants in an age of rapidly advancing inflation. Employed Jews are petty tradesmen, clerical and kindred workers, sales personnel, managers, and professionals.

Following World War II, for reasons difficult to determine, Jews in this country began to receive academic appointments in relatively large numbers. Did the launching of the *Sputnik* satellite by Russia in 1957 impel frightened Americans to forgo the luxury of prejudice and employ Jews on the basis of merit? Increasingly, Jews are today making a name for themselves in the arts, the sciences, and literature. Politically, they have come into their own in the large cities, though their percentages in the urban centers are constantly diminishing. The last two mayors of New York City have been Jews; at least two politicians with national ambitions have offered themselves as candidates for the presidency. This is indeed an advance—in tolerance if not in equity—when it is recalled how relatively recently New Hampshire prohibited its Jews from holding office.

Jews are probably the most urbanized of all American citizens. Most of them are found in six large metropolitan areas: New York, Los Angeles, Philadelphia, Chicago, Miami, and Boston. In reality, their settlements comprise two megalopolises: the one extends from Baltimore to the borders of New Hampshire; the other begins at San Diego and stretches to the northern suburbs of San Francisco. Jews cluster together in towns because they are apprehensive, because they want the culture and the comfort of their own synagogues, their own charities, and their own particularistic institutions. Their sense of kinship, heightened by instantaneous communication and rapid transportation, has become even more intense through Jewish education and Zionist influence—the trauma of the German Holocaust. Their sectarianism is protected by American constitutional guarantees and statutory law.

The Local Jewish Community, 1775—1980

A structured local Jewish community is slowly becoming a reality. Changes are taking place in the three basic Jewish religious denominations. The Orthodox, resolute in their determination to observe every jot and tittle of the Law, have radically declined in numbers but, conscious of the inroads of the assimilatory environment, are gallantly fighting—with some success—in a highly intelligent holding operation. Where they can, they accommodate themselves to the acculturative demands of the time. But Orthodoxy is no longer of one piece; there are numerous variations and degrees of observance in traditional practices, ranging from "Modern Orthodoxy" to Satmar Hasidism. Over on the left, the Reformers are equally fragmented. In principle they all reject the authoritarian character of Jewish law (halakah); many of them, however, moving to the right in ceremony and ritual, are inclined to genuflect in the direction of the Law. The Conservatives, occupying the center between Orthodox and Reform, still profess allegiance to the rabbinic code; in actual practice they disregard virtually all laws and customs which are out of joint with the times. This opportunistic approach is their strength; they can boast that they enjoy the best of both worlds, the rabbinical and the modern. Despite the differences between all of these coreligionists, a common American Judaism is in the making. English in the service is not unusual; English prayers are interlarding the Hebrew texts; the wearing of headgear during services is no longer frowned upon even by left-wingers; the organ, the male-female choir, art music, bar and bat mitzvah and confirmation are making inroads on all sides. It is true that the Hebrew particularistic texts tend to remain unchanged, but the English paraphrases on the facing page stress the common ethical and universalistic teachings of Judaism.

Sabbath and Sunday school education has improved markedly. Afternoon synagogue Hebrew schools are found in every town of some size; all-day schools with religious and secular courses have now recruited a very substantial minority of American Jewish youth. Whether education of this type will make for more Jewish loyalty and provide the leadership for the next generation is still moot. Many Jewish parents favor day-school education not only because of its capacity for Jewish indoctrination but as a refuge against what they feel to be the declining standards of the public schools. All towns have Jewish centers, well-equipped social and leisure locales for youths and adults; the wealthy flock to their country clubs and, where social lines are drawn between the elite and the aspiring, the clubs are graded according to the decade in which ancestors emerged from the steerage.

The organized Jewish community of post—World War II has established vocational guidance and employment centers, a federated collection of hospitals and of health and welfare groups, a community-relations committee to cope with prejudice and to maintain liaison with the larger civic community. To tie all agencies together, the federation either subsidizes or publishes a community newspaper which goes into practically every Jewish home. Despite the fact that coverage for the United States is inadequate and cultural life is slighted, the news service tends to be good; however, a free editorial policy is notably absent; a monolithic communal mind-set seems inevitable. To counteract the complete domination of the community by the all-powerful federation of philanthropies, a Jewish Community Council has been established in many towns. It is ineffective against the communal oligarchy: the 5 or 10 percent of "big givers" in the federation make the important decisions. The old Yiddish proverb cannot be gainsaid: The man with the pay has the say.

The National Jewish Community, 1790–1980

A formal, structured national Jewish community has never existed in the United States, though since 1790 several attempts have been made to unite American Jews through common projects. This lack of one authoritative voice or body does not prevent the host of autonomous national agencies from working together in periods of crisis. Inasmuch as crises are never absent, Jews do pull together. Thus the present-day separate religious agencies do maintain a common umbrella organization, as do the federations, the civic defense associations, the community center groups, and the Zionists. The Jewish cultural agencies are on their own and, mayhap, this is good. There are numerous publishing houses, a scholarly press, and a national publication society whose membership roster is in no sense commensurate with America Jewry's large population. Of considerable significance is the fact that, in addition to the many Jewish schools and academies, there are literally hundreds of general colleges and universities that offer courses of a critical nature in Judaic studies. Thousands of students are enrolled; there has never been anything like this in all Jewish history.

Though no single agency can speak for American Jewry as a whole, though some frequently attempt to do so, there is de facto a national Jewish community. It has no offices, no perceptible policy, no elected or appointed leaders, and yet its existence is implied in the consensus that demands that every Jew somehow document his identity in one form or another. The determining optional criteria are synagogue membership, sympathy for Russian Jewry, aid to Israel, a spontaneous vigorous identification with all fellow-Jews when the Body of Jewry, here and abroad, is threatened. This community of sentiment and emotion is a very real one.

As there is a national community, there is also an international one; it is dominated by American Jewry. It is a Pax Americana Judaica. The only rival the Americans have is Israel, and this in the area of Hebraic studies. Overtly, American Jews with few exceptions passionately and emotionally acknowledge the spiritual primacy of the Third Jewish Commonwealth, but actually hegemony over World Jewish life in the 1970's is exercised by American Jewry. It is very doubtful whether Israel could continue as a sovereign entity without American Jewish economic and political support. Israel lives through the breath of the American Jew. American Jews, politically a reflection of the Imperium Americanum, are overwhelmingly predominant over the World Jewish scene because of their numbers, their advanced secular culture, their burgeoning Hebraic and Judaic studies, their political power, their wealth, their generosity, and their total commitment to Israel.

Who then is this American Jew, this man of the oncoming twenty-first century? He is completely and utterly Americanistic; he is completely and utterly Jewish in his sympathies. All told there are less than 6,000,000 Jews in the United States; this body of men and women constitutes less than 3 percent of the country's population, yet they are one of the most productive, most respected American religio-ethnic-cultural groups.

·2·

The American Jewess
Her Story, 1654—1980

Introduction

I T seems to be only too true that the history just epitomized is *his* story. Very little is said of women in the one-volume chronicles of American Jewry. In the 1888 *Hebrews in America* of Isaac Markens, there are about twenty entries referring to women out of a total of about four hundred. In the 1972 edition of Rufus Learsi's *The Jews in America*, women are mentioned in the index less than forty times; here there are about twenty-four hundred entries. Why is this? Why is it that women are so invisible? Did they do nothing to merit notice? This omission of women was unwitting, for it is patent that if American Jewish history is the record of its communities, its institutions, and its achievements, it owes almost everything to the family, and the family is the wife, as well as the husband and children. Without the American Jewess there is very little American Jewish historical experience. The following brief account is therefore an attempt to redress the imbalance; once this has been done a new chronicle will have to be written. It will be neither *her story* nor *his story*, but *their story*.

The Colonial Period, 1654—1775

In 1654, by the terms of the Dutch capitulation in Brazil, the Jews, as non-Catholics, had to leave the country. There was no place for them in this Portuguese dependency. The women who finally reach-ed New Amsterdam had suffered with their menfolk. The im-poverished émigrés who finally succeeded in reaching New Amster-dam were mistreated by Governor Peter Stuyvesant; it was his hope that they would leave. Conditions in the tiny Jewish community were exacerbated by internal feuds; within a few days after their ar-rival, men and women were suing one another for debts incurred on the long voyage. The community that was established was not viable; in less than a decade New Amsterdam Jewry no longer had a quorum of worshipers. Most of the men and women returned home to Holland, or sailed for either the West Indies or Surinam, where larger opportunities beckoned.

Under the English, who assumed control of Dutch North America in 1664, the Jews did better. It took time, but after two long genera-tions the reconstituted New Amsterdam—New York community, the only Jewish one on the continent, finally succeeded in building a house of worship. The women helped make this possible, for they gave money to erect the structure; they subscribed funds to buy a Scroll of the Law, and with loving care they sewed and embroidered the decorative cloth trappings which do so much to enhance the beauty of the synagogue interior. More than two centuries later the "Spanish and Portuguese Jewish Synagogue" of New York City still invokes God's blessings on those pious women of old who did what they could to help establish the continent's first Jewish sanctuary.

Notable among these women was Abigail Franks, wife of the country's wealthiest Jewish merchant and army purveyor. Though in a large measure self-taught, she had become a woman of culture who was at home in the best English writings of her generation. She was not uncritical of the Orthodox rituals and practices of her day, but she remained both loyal and observant. Her devotion to her faith did not in any degree diminish her social standing; she was at all times a welcome visitor at the governor's mansion. Reluctantly, she sent two of her boys to London in the hope that they would do well financially with the clan and marry within the fold. Three children remained behind in the colonies. Two, a boy and a girl, married out of the faith, the third, another girl, never married. She knew that if she chose a Gentile her parents would be utterly distraught; ap-parently there were no Jewish beaux who were her social peers.

The Revolutionary Period and the Early Decades
of the Nineteenth Century, 1776—1819

If the Jewish women of the Revolutionary period thought at all of the privileges and immunities inherent in the Great Promise, the Declaration of Independence, then they knew that the land was indebted to them, and that they too had earned the right to equality. When the Continentals had the upper hand, the Loyalists among the Jews, men, women, and children, were driven into exile; the husband of one woman, a prominent merchant, was brutally murdered. Some of these Loyalists fled the country, moving north to Canada or south to the British West Indies. The Whigs among them—and most Jews sided with the rebels—often fled their homes too, for every major "Jewish" town in the United States fell at one time or another into the hands of the British. Frances Sheftall's husband and son had both been captured and imprisoned by the English. Alone and with a large brood to support, this Savannah Jewess managed to keep her family together by working as a seamstress. When the British besieged and bombarded Charleston, South Carolina, she was more fortunate than others, for one of the Jewish families lost a child and a nurse during the cannonade.

Frances Sheftall's fellow-townswoman, Abigail Minis, ran into trouble during the war. She had a great deal to lose, for though a widow she had managed to salvage her husband's estate and to increase it. She ran a small plantation, owned fifteen or twenty slaves, and operated a tavern and a shop. When the Whigs occupied Savannah she supplied them with goods; but after the town was captured by the British this remarkable woman went into exile, taking her five daughters with her. None of her daughters married during her lifetime, and even her son Philip, a businessman and Revolutionary commissary officer, did not take a wife until he was forty. Despite the fact that he was a warden of the city and president of the local congregation, his late marriage would seem to indicate that, like his sisters, he was under mama's thumb. She lived to be over ninety. She was indeed a "mother in Israel" and a virago in the best Italian tradition.

Abigail was obviously a successful businesswoman. Business was alien to very few Jewish helpmates. The typical Jewess of that day was the wife of a craftsman-retailer or a storekeeper. The women, the wives and the growing girls, knew something about the family business; it was not unusual for them to clerk for the head of the house when he was absent. After the Revolution, when the economy was finally stabilized, a number of women—widows and spinsters—opened shops of their own; their number, however, was small.

The occasional woman who ran a shop of her own probably had a servant in the house. As early as the seventeenth century, when the Jewish community was young, the butcher and merchant Asser Levy had to go to court to recover a servant whom a neighbor had stolen from his wife. In the South the servants were black slaves; in the North, maids were either white indentured servants or black bondsmen. Mrs. Meyer Josephson, of Reading in Pennsylvania, had a female slave and was eager to get rid of her. The servant drank and was rebellious; the mistress dared not say a word to her. It is not known whether Mrs. Jonas Phillips had hired help in the house; she could have used a servant or two, for she bore her husband twenty-one children. To be sure, she had an early start; she was sixteen when she married.

The women of the house were expected to see that the kitchen was kosher and of course to use the mikveh, the ritual bath, periodically. The truly observant among the men were most insistent that women not omit these ceremonial ablutions. Had not God Himself enjoined this monthly cleansing in the Bible? We Jews live in a free country; let us prove to our Father that we are grateful so that He may speedily send the Redeemer to Zion and restore us all to the Promised Land. Violate this divine injunction and God will punish us severely!

It is not known how frequently the women visited the synagogue, but there was no danger in the eighteenth and early nineteenth centuries that the sanctuary would be "feminized." Attending worship services was a man's job. Women of course went occasionally, especially on the holidays. They mounted the galleries and, behind their latticed barriers, looked down on the men. The girls were particularly eager to preempt the front seats so that they could survey the males down below. There does not seem to be any definitive evidence that in pre-Revolutionary days the girls attended the congregational parochial school; there is no question that they were admitted in post-Revolutionary decades. In all probability, however, women at all times were taught to read the Hebrew prayers; rebbes, teachers, were always available. Private schools run by Gentiles abounded and the girls were trained in the three R's. They were expected to write a good letter, although only too often the spelling left something to be desired. A young lady would have to be knowledgeable if she was to help her father or her future husband in the shop. Jewish women, members of an extended middle class, were nearly always literate.

Jacob Mordecai may very well have been unusual in the stress he laid upon education for his motherless daughters. Two of his little ones, sent on to Richmond to stay with relatives, received encouraging letters from their father. Undoubtedly he was proud of his pompous, florid lucubrations, fit more for mature adults than children of seven and nine. Stress was laid on constant reading, good manners, and courtesy to all, even servants, and that, in Richmond, meant enslaved Blacks. Mordecai promised his two little girls that he would love them if they learned to read and write well. This concept of pedagogy would win no praise today, but it worked in the 1790's. His girls, and his boys, too, were all exceptionally well-educated, and when he later opened a successful girls' school in Warrenton, North Carolina, he recruited his teaching staff from his own family. One of his daughters—Rachel—attained a measure of intellectual stature.

It is no exaggeration to maintain that in each generation, every town of size knew at least one or two women of culture. Zipporah Nunez Machado (d. 1799), a Marrano, had been baptized in Portugal as a Catholic. Here in North America she married a "rabbi." Her contemporaries agreed that Zipporah was an unusual woman, charming, and cultured, a master of six languages. Her charity was "unbiased by national or sectarian prejudices." She was the mother-in-law of a Revolutionary War militiaman, the great-grandmother of a "commodore" in the United States Navy and of a Grand Sachem of Tammany, all Jews. Grace Seixas Nathan, an older contemporary of Rachel Mordecai, was a sensitive, well-read person who wrote poetry, some of it reasonably good. Her descendants were worthy of her; among them were the communal workers Maud Nathan and Annie Nathan Meyer, and the accomplished poet Robert Nathan. Grace's brother Gershom Seixas, the Revolutionary War rabbi, had a daughter Sally, who was probably a cut above the average. Her letters to her father have not been preserved; his to her are fortunately still extant. He was constantly writing to his beloved Sally, preening his rabbinical feathers in whimsical and ironic notes. There is every reason to believe that she encouraged this father-daughter correspondence, if only by making clucking sounds of sympathy.

By the first quarter of the nineteenth century, the Seixas and the Mordecai women could boast that they were Americans of the third and fourth generation. But by the 1790's there were others—post-Revolution newcomers from Central Europe—who had little in common with the natives. Rebecca Alexander Samuel was one of the new arrivals. She was no more typical than was Grace Seixas or Rachel Mordecai. Rebecca, wife of a highly skilled watch and clockmaker, dwelt in Petersburg, Virginia, where she made desperate efforts to live as an observant Jewess. She kept the Sabbath and all the holidays, even when Jews about her, fellow-immigrants, barely paid lip service to the most sacred Jewish traditions. She taught her little three-year-old girl to recite the Hebrew prayers and, finally convinced that there was no chance of religious survival for her and the family in that small Virginia town, kept after her husband to move to a Jewish community of size. Somehow or other, the spirit of America had made its impress upon her; she gloated over the fact that there were no rabbis in America who could order Jews about, religiously. This was a free country.

From the vantage point of the 1980's, it is not easy to determine how happy Jewish women were in the days of the early American republic. There is no available evidence that individual Jewesses of this period sought autonomy. Most of them seem to have enjoyed a relatively full life, comfortably enveloped in the security of the Jewish community. But it is also true that many were lonely. Life could be hard for an unmarried sister or a wife when the menfolk left for months or even years on business trips to Canada, the Caribbean, or Europe. Some of the men left never to return; America was a frontier with an ample share of rascals. It was difficult for spinsters or widows to make lives for themselves in a straitlaced age where there were relatively few opportunities for women in the world beyond the confines of the house. Books were hard to come by; candles for reading were expensive; letters were the only medium of communication, and postage was costly. Some girls, eager to have a husband, married out and were lost to the group; Gentile women, anxiously concerned for their future, married Jews. Conversion to Judaism under English rule had been frowned upon by the apprehensive Jewish community; in republican America it was more frequent. Were these neophytes accepted? In some instances they were completely, becoming an intimate part of the Jewish community. On the whole, early American Jews were clannish; they feared intermarriage, for they were determined to survive as a socioreligious entity. Let it be constantly borne in mind that if they looked askance at their Gentile neighbors, it was because even in free America they were exposed to political and social disabilities; in Europe, whence they had come, they were still subject to physical abuse and degrading legislative enactments.

There seems to be very little evidence that the Jewish women of those days felt sorry for themselves; most managed to fashion an adequate social life in those pre-radio and pre-television days. David Franks's teen-aged daughter, Rebecca, had a wonderful time; she was the belle of the British officers' corps when they occupied Philadelphia during the Revolutionary War. She was lively, clever, intelligent. Her mother, a Christian, had been born to a highly respected family. Her sister had married a Pennsylvania Hamilton; Rebecca's father was a wealthy, politically powerful entrepreneur whose London uncles had interests that reached as far east as India. Rebecca had been reared as a Christian, and there is no indication that she had ever manifested any interest in Jews or Judaism, although she was completely devoted to her Jewish father. She was born after Grandma Abigail had died; her father never converted out, though it is equally true that after his intermarriage he was never a member of Congregation Mikveh Israel. Some of Rebecca's contemporaries were aware that she had a Jewish father; in America's Christian world a Jew has often been defined as any person concerning whom there is the slightest reminiscence of Jewish origin.

In North Carolina's Warrenton, in pre-railroad days, the

Mordecai children, girls and boys alike, seem to have had no difficulty entering fully into the social life of the town. They were invited to weddings, went to the races, and attended the balls that were held in the local tavern. The even tenor of the year's events was interrupted by the celebration of the Jewish holidays; the observant father saw to that, and relatives in Richmond alerted them to the coming of Passover and the Days of Awe. Passover was hard on the girls, for they had to abstain from eating bread, which was not denied the Gentile children in attendance at the Mordecai academy. In the larger cities, where the Jewish congregations were found, there were many more opportunities for a social life. There were always parties, Jewish marriages, services in the synagogue, and exchanges of visits.

The big social event in the life of a girl was marriage. In those days there was no future for a young woman except in a home of her own with a husband and children. What other career was open to her? Divorces were virtually unknown in the Jewish community. The Jewish women who married out were nearly always lost to Judaism. Shinah Simon, an aunt of the Gratz girls, married a New York State Christian physician, Dr. Nicholas Schuyler, and converted to Christianity. It was a very happy marriage and was accepted by her Jewish kin except for a sister of Shinah who refused to make peace with the apostate. Shinah never ceased to look upon herself as a Jewess; she loved her Jewish family. Marital prospects for Jewesses were sometimes dimmed by the desire of young Jewish eligibles to marry Christians. The percentage of out-marriages was by no means small, but in a number of instances, intermarriage did not involve defection from the Jewish community. The Jewish partner went to the synagogue, while the Christian wife probably continued to attend her own church. In such marriages the children were usually reared as Christians. Did the Jewish men prefer exogamy because the Christians were less demanding than Jews? This is conceivable, but there is no evidence to provide an answer.

Before a girl could marry, she had to secure permission from the congregational authorities if she wished to use the services of the local religious factotum. The synagogue fathers had no desire to be arbitrary, but they were set against intermarriage; they wanted to be sure that the bride and groom were ready to conform to the demands of rabbinic law. It is likely the young couple came to an understanding on their own, but the formal and final arrangements for a public engagement were made through the parents. This was protocol. Thus Benjamin Seixas allowed his father, Isaac, to negotiate with Hayman Levy, merchant and fur entrepreneur, for the hand of Zipporah Levy. This was during the Revolution, when both families were in exile in Connecticut. Later, Benjamin became a founder of what was to become the New York Stock Exchange. He was a busy man, but he found time to give Zipporah twenty-one children, seventeen of whom survived.

When Richea Gratz was engaged to Samuel Hays, her older brother Simon wrote her a formal note telling her how to conduct herself now that she was getting ready to enter the married state. Richea was one of American Jewry's first "college" students, for she had gone to Franklin College. Actually, it was an academy at best, a combination elementary and high school. Simon, or Simmi as he was known, wrote Richea: Take our mother as your exemplar; please your husband and observe God's commandments. In giving this sage advice, he was of course speaking out of the fullness of his wisdom and experience. He was all of twenty; she was nineteen. This letter, too, was social protocol; it was the style of the day. It does not necessarily follow that Simmi practiced what he preached. Indeed, he married out of the faith—secretly, it would seem—and his wife, Mary Smith, raised a Christian family. One of her eight children embraced Judaism. The Gratzes seem to have ignored Mary; obviously she was neither socially nor culturally acceptable. Ben, a younger brother, also married a Gentile, but the family accepted her; she came of a "good" family. By the middle 1830's, the code prescribing deference to parents in the marriage preliminaries had been somewhat relaxed. Captain Alfred Mordecai asked Samuel Hays for the hand of his daughter, Sarah Ann, but informed him that she had already accepted him. Hays assented, incidentally telling him what a fine girl Sarah was and adding that there would be no dowry. On that same day, the captain wrote his own father, Jacob Mordecai, craving his permission. Alfred knew that the father would be pleased; the Hays family was a good one and Jewish!

In those days all weddings were traditional in mode. The young couple were married under a huppah, a nuptial canopy. Dr. Benjamin Rush has described in detail the marriage ceremony of

Michael Levy and Rachel Phillips. The canopy was of white and red silk; its four posts were held aloft by four young men wearing white gloves; the symbolic glass was shattered in a large pewter dish. When the wedding cake was cut, Dr. Rush was given a piece to take home to his wife; Mrs. Rush and Mrs. Jonas Phillips, the bride's mother, were old friends. They had met in New York, where Mrs. Phillips's father, David Mendez Machado, had served as the hazzan of Congregation Shearith Israel. Rush enjoyed the wedding—and closed his long letter with the hope that the Jews would ultimately come to Jesus.

Early-nineteenth-century American Jewry had its quota of spinsters. There were a substantial number of unmarried German Jews coming in, but these immigrants were not eligible. If Richea Gratz's younger sister—the pious Rebecca—never married, it was not because she had fallen in love with a Gentile whom she would not wed. Her love affair with a Gentile is likely to be a myth. The gap between the native socially elite women and the émigré German men was virtually unbridgeable. Of course, there were exceptions. Sarah Seixas, a daughter of the respected Gershom, married Israel B. Kursheedt, a German. This was a marriage of which her father could approve, for Kursheedt was one of America's most learned students of Hebraic lore. The rabbi was proud of his son-in-law.

It is true that the women were barely visible in communal and religious life throughout this period. They were indeed second-class citizens, never counted for a religious quorum and never assigned roles in synagogal administration. Yet, there is no evidence that this lack of recognition disturbed them in the least, for it had always been the Jewish way of life. There is no need to shed a tear for them; they did not consider themselves oppressed. In the long years from 1654 to 1819, the continent's Jewish women fed no armies and built no ships; they were not doers, but there is every reason to believe that their husbands loved them and respected them. The Reverend Mr. Seixas was a trustee of Columbia College and consorted with the greats of his time—but he walked softly around Ma, his wife. Except for his attendance at services and his Hebrew classes, he stayed at home, under foot all the time. Ma probably thought, but certainly never said, that he was a nuisance. Still, he had his uses; he did the shopping and helped shell peas while teaching a bar mitzvah lad.

·3·

Autoemancipation: The Women Build Local Associations of Their Own 1819—1892

Working Women

T HE aristocratic Seixas was as much an Ashkenazi as he was a Sephardi. His mother and his wife were not of Iberian stock. Germans and "Litvaks" (Lithuanians) had settled in New York as early as the seventeenth century. German Jews, and, of course, their women, predominated by 1840. What did these new immigrants, particularly the women, do for a living? Were they affected by the new industrialism that had begun to make itself visible by the 1790's? There is no known evidence that any Jewish women labored in the new cotton or woolen mills. Working in a factory was beneath the dignity of a Jewish girl or wife. Native American-born Jewesses in "reduced circumstances" preferred to suffer the pangs of poverty rather than struggle for a livelihood in a mill. If women of the older stocks did have to work—and of course some of them did—they kept boardinghouses or eked out an existence as seamstresses. As far back as the third quarter of the eighteenth century, there were one or two Jewesses who worked at home in the put-out clothing industry, laboriously sewing garments with materials supplied by the Newport protocapitalistic entrepreneur Aaron Lopez.

It took decades before a number of wives of the post-Revolutionary Central European newcomers rose to affluence

25

through their husbands. Even in the distant Mother Lode of California, women lent a hand to their husbands, especially when they were bankrupt. These valorous helpmates sold liquor, tobacco, groceries, and drygoods. By the end of the nineteenth century a substantial upper-middle class of Central European Jews had taken shape. Some, it has been pointed out, had acquired wealth as dealers in liquor, meat, jewelry, tobacco, leather, and banking. The small drygoods shops had become large emporia, department stores. The garment industry was for many entrepreneurs a source of opulence. The industry included everything from caps to underwear, cloaks, and artificial flowers. These are the families that flocked to the fashionable watering places only to be rejected by the nouveaux riches Gentile snobs and to be lampooned by envious Judeophobes. This was the fate of the Seligmans, bankers, when they arrived at the Grand Union Hotel in Saratoga in the summer of 1877 and were refused rooms by the management.

One person who certainly stayed away from the fashionable resorts was Anna Rich Marks (1847–1912). Here was a woman who, it would seem, had no social ambitions, no desire to consort with the Christian elite. Anna was a Polish Jewess who left her native land when she was little more than a child and settled in London. By the time she was fifteen, she had married M. Wolff Marks, or, as he called himself in Hebrew-Yiddish, Zeev Wolf. The Markses left for New York, and after a stay there moved on to Utah Territory. When Anna's wagons loaded with goods were barred by a tollgate on the road to Eureka, she called her bodyguards, and with drawn guns moved on through. In Eureka, when her rights to a site were disputed, she again pulled her guns and held her ground. Utah tradition maintains that she was a master of profanity and had no hesitation in using her extensive vocabulary. When the Denver & Rio Grande Railroad tried to cross her land, she and her men held them off at gunpoint until they met her price. Mr. Wolff Marks? This quiet, law-abiding gentleman always gave a stick of candy to the children who came into the store. Anna speculated in real estate, owned mines, and put her surplus cash into diamonds. She became wealthy. Here was a woman in the best traditions of the Wild West, where men were men and women learned to stand on their own two feet.

Down in Atlanta, Georgia, on the eve of the Civil War, Mrs. A. Isaacs was the only Jewess in business. She sold ladies' hats, corsets, cosmetics, fancy goods, and "T. A. Wright's Celebrated Hair Tonic, an infallible preventive for the loss of hair and a certain restorative . . . in case of baldness." Perhaps Sophie Heller is typical of the "German" Jewish woman who rose to riches the hard way. Sophie, a native of Hapsburg Bohemia, was brought to Milwaukee by her parents. She left school at thirteen but did not fail to take swimming lessons and to go to dancing school. (The Milwaukee Germans were turners, gymnasts.) Sophie clerked in a store for a brother and fell in love with an attractive teen-aged immigrant who peddled for a living. Married at about seventeen, she set up house on the $3 a week her husband gave her. She was lonely at times when he was absent, but could always play with the cat and its litter of kittens. She and her husband finally settled in Cincinnati, where they opened a variety store; it does not appear to have been a successful venture. In the 1870's, the family finally turned to the manufacture of sporting goods; Sophie helped by sewing basketballs. She struggled, raised a family, lost children, but by 1885 she and her husband were well-to-do. The business in which she labored long hours finally became a nationally known sporting goods corporation, MacGregor—Goldsmith, employing close to one thousand workers. Sophie was Mrs. Philip Goldsmith. In her memoirs, a charming autobiography, she always referred to her husband as Mr. Goldsmith.

The Goldsmiths were manufacturers, but industry as such was not the forte of the native-born or the mid-nineteenth-century immigrants. Most were petty tradesmen, reaching out to grab the next rung on the way up. Many of these petty bourgeois never made it; they were destined to remain lower-middle-class, at best middle-class shopkeepers. Thus Sophie Heller Goldsmith was not typical of the German Jewesses who were brought over by parents, by a brother who had gone on ahead, by a kinsman, or by an Old Country sweetheart. Over here, the American Jewish fraeulein or hausfrau was supported by her parents or her husband. Like the Jewish women of the eighteenth century, she kept house, and on occasion helped in the shop. There were a number of middle-class spinsters of eighteenth-century American stock who did not disdain to run little shops of their own; there was nothing wrong in making an honest dollar even when one had a few slaves or prosperous brothers. The word "merchant," however, implying dignity, integrity, and substance, was applied only to men.

The Middle-Class Jewess and the Rise of Professionals

After the Civil War, the opportunities for women to make a living increased perceptibly. These were the decades that witnessed the expansion of industry and the rise of numerous commercial establishments. Coeducational colleges made it possible for women to study and advance themselves. Office work for females was no longer deemed ungenteel. Now for the first time, a substantial number of women began to work outside their homes. All this was bound to influence the American Jewess. Teaching in private Jewish academies and in Sabbath and Sunday schools was nothing new in antebellum America; in the second half of the century, more and more women turned to teaching in public elementary and high schools.

Julia Richman (1855—1912) is an illustration—not a typical one, to be sure—of a woman who made a career for herself in the field of education. She had studied at Normal, now Hunter College, and at New York University. She rose relatively rapidly in the city's public school system to become a principal and finally a district superintendent. It is probable that she was the first woman in the city to occupy a post that high. Her biographers are of the opinion that she was the founder of the city's first "parent-teachers association." She is also credited with having introduced classes for retarded children, periodic eye examinations for the youngsters, outdoor homes for consumptives, and employment agencies for the boys and girls who had to leave school. Julia Richman was the first president of the Young Women's Hebrew Association in New York City. There is no question that she was an educator of distinction, a woman who contributed much to the welfare of the children in her charge. It is somewhat surprising that she did not always sense the character and tone of the East European immigrants whose children she sought to educate, to Americanize. Julia Richman and the East European mothers were at times worlds apart, but, then, what did a college-trained woman of German Jewish origin have in common with an uneducated East European Jewess who had only recently come from a backward if not grubby Russian village?

Though it would seem that some of the East Siders disliked her, Miss Richman was nationally known and highly respected in Jewish circles. A grateful New York memorialized her by establishing the Julia Richman High School. At times, the Jewish teachers on the Lower East Side would have their hands full with the mothers of their pupils. On one occasion the mamas smashed the windows of a school when it was reported that the teachers were killing the children. What was this all about? Some of the youngsters were being vaccinated; a few were having their tonsils removed. The rioting was so serious that not only the police but the reserves had to be called out. They hastened the departure of the frantic mothers by paddling them soundly; the mamas finally retreated, taking their precious offspring with them.

By the middle decades of the century, Jewish girls who cultivated gentility found it imperative to play the piano. One woman, an Austrian whose parents brought her to Chicago as a child, became the country's most notable concert pianist. This was Fannie Bloomfield Zeisler (1863—1927). Her cousin was the virtuoso Moritz Rosenthal; her brother Maurice Bloomfield, the Johns Hopkins orientalist, gave Fannie her first piano lessons. Trained by Chicago's Carl Wolfsohn, she started giving recitals when but ten and concerts at fourteen. After studying abroad, she appeared in concerts both here and in Europe in the 1880's and 1890's. Hers was a rather multifaceted personality; she was something of a skilled craftsman who did her own carpentry. Her home became a salon for the Christian and Jewish elite. Fannie was naive enough to believe that in bringing Jews and Gentiles together through common cultural interests, she would dissipate anti-Semitism. She evidenced no interest in Judaism, gave concerts on Friday and Saturday, observed Christmas as a day of gift-giving, and was buried by Horace J. Bridges of the Chicago Ethical Society. Yet, many of the family papers are deposited in the American Jewish Archives.

Fannie Bloomfield Zeisler was a woman of culture and refinement; her family and her husband, European in background and spirit, were members of an upper-middle-class elite. There were a number of Chicago women who cultivated the arts; some of them were destined to become national figures in the decades which straddled the nineteenth and twentieth centuries. Chicago of the 1880's and 1890's was no longer the crude boom town of the 1840's when its first congregation was organized. Yet it should not be forgotten that women like Fannie Zeisler and Julia Richman in no sense typified the American Jewesses of the 1880's. Though the state and city colleges of the country were more open to women, very few girls of old-line families and Central European immigrants took advantage of the new institutions of higher learning. The Germans who had been coming for decades were not affluent as a class, though they were not at all poor. What is more to the point, many were thrifty to a fault. They sent their girls to the elementary school, even to high school, but only rarely to college. Those with substantial means patronized the private Jewish academies—day or boarding schools—in the larger towns. In all probability, the young ladies bypassed the available commercial courses and opted for the "classical" disciplines: the three R's, music, sewing, French. Hebrew was also taught, and some of them learned to read the prayers by rote.

Even before the Civil War, there were numerous families in Charleston, Baltimore, Philadelphia, and New York who worshiped at the altar of the fine arts. As early as the first quarter of the century there was a New York Sephardic immigrant Jewess who was at home in both French and Latin. The Benjamin I. Cohens of Baltimore, lottery promoters and bankers, may possibly be typical of this elite group. When they sent a teenage daughter to school in 1840, it was to a Gentile institution, although the Jewish academy of the Misses Pallache had opened that year. (The Pallache school, however, did not take children over ten years of age.) Isaac Leeser once complained that, given a choice between a Gentile school and a Jewish institution, the would-be Jewish gentry would always favor the Christian institution. The Cohens say nothing about religious observance in a letter to their daughter at school; its stress was upon courtesy, respect for older people, the importance of soft speech and personal cleanliness. A generation earlier, in the prospectus for his Warrenton girls' academy, Jacob Mordecai had informed his clients, Christians for the most part, that he would insist on neatness of person and propriety in manners. Every girl in the Mordecai school had to repair daily to an old Black woman who carefully finecombed her hair. Lice were a problem.

The Cohen women moved in the highest social circles. In 1837, the Benjamin Cohens gave a fancy dress and masquerade ball, an affair so elegant that no local Jews were invited, not even the Ettings, an old colonial family. The flowers were from the Cohens' own greenhouses; the servants were in livery. It was attended by the cream of Baltimore society. Benjamin Cohen was a founder of the Baltimore Stock Exchange, a botanist, and a violinist. The Cohens were not assimilationists; they were Orthodox Jews, Sephardic in rite, who kept themselves aloof from the incoming Ashkenazim who had established Congregation Nidhe Israel.

The Civil War, bitterly fought for four years with over 600,000 casualties, was bound to affect the Jewish women of this country. The wives and daughters in the North were Unionists; they evidenced no trace of Confederate sentiment, though their husbands, who did business with the South, were unhappy when the war erupted. None of these native Jewesses are known to have been abolitionists. The Southern Jewesses were fanatically, almost hysterically, passionate in their sympathies for the new regime. Were they trying to prove that they were more ardent than their neighbors? Why? Eleanor Cohen of Charleston, emotional, romantic, was euphoric in her devotion to the cause. She viewed the Yankees as tyrants, and when Lincoln was assassinated she wrote in her diary: "God grant so may all our foes perish." Philip Phillips, a former Alabama congressman, was a political moderate; his wife Eugenia was a fire-eater. She was expelled from wartime Washington because of her views; only her husband's influence saved her from jail. In New Orleans, she was imprisoned on an island in the Gulf by General Ben F. Butler. Eugenia was an anti-Yankee political activist who took no pains to conceal her love for the South and her contempt for the North.

Eugenia's sister, Phoebe Pember, was appointed matron of one of the largest army hospitals in Richmond. Like Eugenia, she was a well-educated, cultured woman who moved in the best circles of the South. She had married out, but her father had put his stamp upon her. He was one of the best-educated Jews of the prewar South, a devoted and ardent adherent of the faith of his ancestors. Phoebe was not an observant Jewess, but she had little sympathy for the Christianity of her friends; Judaism, she believed, was superior.

Like Eugenia Phillips, Jewish girls in Natchez were belligerently anti-Unionist. This intransigence created a problem for them. The town was occupied by Northern troops long before Lee surrendered; anti-North as they were, the girls could not, did not, ignore the Jewish Yankees. The young Natchez rebels induced their Jewish Yankee soldier friends to secure passes through the lines and then used them to smuggle supplies to Confederates. Their voluminous hoopskirts made detection virtually impossible. One of these Natchez belles later married one of the Northern soldiers. It was a good marriage. The mother of the bride was respected and beloved in Natchez because she had nursed townspeople through yellow fever epidemics; the Christians thought it not incongruous to appoint this Jewess as a director of the local Protestant ophanage. On Passover, at the festal meal, thirty-five people gathered around the table to enjoy her hospitality. She used to say that a home should be "as large as its mistress' heart."

Jewish Women as Professionals

Before the 1880's and 1890's, there were very few Jewish women who made a living professionally in the arts and sciences. The Female (Women's) Medical College of Pennsylvania, the first of its kind in the United States, was established in 1851; seven years later Mary Anna Elson received her degree at this institution—only nine years after Elizabeth Blackwell had become the first professionally trained woman in the United States to practice medicine. Josephine Walter, the first woman, so it is said, to serve a formal internship in an American hospital, was in charge of the children's division of

Mount Sinai in New York. This was in 1885. Sallie Strasburg of Cincinnati was one of the city's best-known dentists and an author of studies on oral surgery.

Not many women found it possible to become physicians and to survive professionally; it was much easier to make a living as an actress. They succeeded because they were women; they were needed to play women's parts. The most famous among them was Adah Isaacs Menken (d. 1868). Menken may not have been a Jewess by birth, although she maintained that she was; there is no question of her complete devotion to Judaism, though she was in no sense observant. She had an international reputation, though this may have been due not to her histrionic ability but to the fact that she appeared in flesh-colored tights when she played the role of Mazeppa. She had a checkered career, for she was married several times and allowed herself a great deal of sexual freedom. As she traveled about, she made many friends among the literati, including Mark Twain, Swinburne, Dickens and the elder Dumas.

A woman who enjoyed a finer histrionic reputation was Rose Eytinge (d. 1911), of Philadelphia: she was an internationally recognized star. She had played in Washington before Lincoln; in London she was known and admired by the leaders in society and literature. She was also a writer, a drama teacher, and the author of an autobiography. In this work, *The Memories of Rose Eytinge*, she was careful to omit any reference to her Jewishness. If Judaism for her was not a badge of shame, it was certainly not a patent of nobility. (Like other Jewish actresses of a later generation, she was primarily concerned with her own career. Professionals of this type rarely emphasize or even mention their ethnic or religious origins.) Eytinge was very happy as an unhyphenated American. Her travels in Moslem lands led her to declare that "in no other country is woman so respected, so sheltered and protected as in America."

The American Jewess in Literature

Rose Eytinge was quite typical of American women who had already begun to turn to the pursuit of literature in the decades before the Civil War. It has already been suggested that in every town there were always one or two Jewish women who were not only interested in general literature but evidenced some skill in writing. These antebellum literati were members of the everpresent middle class. They had some leisure, read widely, and in the circle of the home discussed the best books of the day. These women who wrote had very little formal education; they were largely self-taught. Ten years after the soldiers of the Civil War had laid down their arms, Isaac M. Wise made the bald statement that no American Jewish woman had made any contribution to the field of literature. Wise's problem was that in literary matters he faced eastward, to Europe. He was certainly unfair to his own people here. American Jewry in 1875 did not even number 250,000 persons; a very substantial percentage were immigrants, many, recent arrivals. What did he expect of the women? Yet, in this small group there were women of literary taste, people with ability. Before 1890, several of them were writing short stories, novels, essays, and children's tales. Their contributions were beginning to appear in the country's best magazines. Their serialized novels were printed in the English and German periodicals which Jews were now publishing for their own people. Fiction was a field to which Jewish women very readily turned.

The German Jewish press of this country had a number of talented female writers who have long been forgotten. The poems of Minna Cohen Kleeberg (1841—1878) are no longer read, though she was a very gifted writer. She had received an excellent education in her native Germany, in English, French, and of course German literature. In 1865, she wrote a widely acclaimed poem reproaching the Prussian government for its oppressive taxation of the poor. Before coming here, after the Civil War, she was well-known in Germany as a writer of some distinction.

Minna was very much the feminist. Even as a child she resented that she could not become bat mitzvah; she was unhappy that women were denied the opportunity for a higher Jewish education. Scoffing at the daily prayer, "Thank God I was not created a woman," she answered, "Thank God I was not created a man!"

Aroused by Longfellow's final line in "The Jewish Cemetery at Newport"—"And the dead nations never rise again"—she answered proudly:

> America is a new Zion
> We are not dead!
> By God, we are alive!

Some of her hymns were published by Wise in his hymnal, which appeared in 1868; she is the only woman whose poems he included. Minna was an ardent American patriot who proudly proclaimed to the world that her love for Germany was pure and holy. The ambivalence of devotion to democratic America and to conservative Germany gave her no problems. She was at the same time a religious universalist who objected to Jewish parochial schools, Jewish newspapers, and Jewish clubs. The three pillars of American Judaism, she said, are the Reform temple, the religious school, and the home. The Jew must be a citizen among citizens.

Wise's *Deborah* and *The Echo of the Order*, the journal of the female lodge, the United Order of True Sisters, frequently published German writings of American Jewesses. These women, however, were not American-trained; they had come here as immigrants. No American Jewish writer of that day, woman or man, made a living as a litterateur.

The interest which American Jewesses had manifested in poetry since the early nineteenth century never abated. Penina Moïse was the first to publish; a volume of her poems appeared in 1833. Her generation had tremendous admiration for her and tended to make too much of her poetic gifts. She was a lovely person, suffering poverty most of her life, striving to maintain herself by conducting a small private school for girls. In her old age she was totally blind. Many of her poems became hymns; her piety was fervent, her devotion to her people ardent. She wrote of the Damascus Jews who were persecuted because of a false accusation, and invited the oppressed Jews of Europe to make America their home. Some of her occasional poems, not yet published, are more appealing than the florid and pompous stanzas which are in print. Judged by twentieth-century standards and canons of taste, she was not a poetess of note, but her Charleston contemporaries applauded her writings; they wished to shine in her reflected glory, to be accepted by Gentiles of learning and refinement, and to be deemed an integral part of the well-mannered intelligentsia.

The beau ideal of South Carolina Jewry was the litterateur Isaac Harby, whose tradition was carried on by the women of the clan. Harby's daughter, Octavia Harby Moses (1823—1904), sent five sons into the Confederate Army. One was only fourteen when he volunteered; another was shot down—murdered after he had surrendered. No wonder Octavia was so fiercely unreconciled to the fall of the Confederacy! Her poems, collected after her death, were published by her children and grandchildren. A granddaughter of Harby, Caroline Cohen Joachimsen, wrote romances for Jewish journals and poetry for the newspapers and the better magazines. Caroline's sister Lee (Leah) Cohen Harby (1849—1918) lived for a time in Texas, where she wrote verse and fiction for Southern and Northern newspapers. One of her poems was set to music and used as an official flag song in some of the public schools and colleges of Texas. She made her presence felt wherever she lived—in Charleston, Galveston, and New York City. In Charleston, she was an officer of the Daughters of the Confederacy; in New York she was active in the first non-Jewish women's club established in that city. She was a writer, historian, and clubwoman.

Fully aware of the feminist ferment of the late nineteenth century, Lee warned the girls of her day that it was not enough to be able to keep house and sew; a well-educated girl, a good conversationalist, always had the advantage in the quest for a husband. Anticipating the New Jewess who was to make her appearance at the turn of the century, she declared that the modern woman is not satisfied to be a creature suspended in limbo between man and the angels. The progressive woman is ready to stand on her own two feet. She is a responsible human being who wants to be independent; she has the courage to fight for her principles—all this at least two generations before the appearance of Betty Friedan's *The Feminine Mystique*. These postbellum Harby women were the last outcropping of a secular antebellum culture which had once lifted

Charleston Jewry above all other Jewish communities in the country. With the possible exception of Isaac Harby, nineteenth-century Charleston produced no outstanding Jewish litterateurs—either women or men—but they did cultivate the arts. The Charleston Jewish cultural diaspora reached as far north as New York and as far west as San Francisco.

Adah Isaacs Menken, the actress, was also a poet. Taste in poetry is of course a highly subjective matter, but some critics consider her to have been one of the most sensitive Jewish women writers in America. Her verse in *Infelicia* (1868) is often powerful, reflecting the influence of Walt Whitman. A contemporary of Menken and Moïse, whose poetry was very much admired, was Rebekah Gumpert Hyneman (1812—1875) of Philadelphia. Rebekah was a child of an intermarriage—her mother was a Christian—but she herself chose Judaism and was devoted to her new faith. When her husband disappeared—he may have been murdered—she was left bereft. The following verses may reflect her mood:

> Like some lone bird whose wailing note
>   Tells of its grief—o'er wood and plain;
> Whose melancholy warblings float
>   O'er scenes of sorrow, care and pain—
>   Even such am I.
>
> Or like a flower all crushed and pale,
>   Torn by the wind, its bed upriven,
> Its leaflets scattered to the gale,
>   Careering wild by tempest driven,
>   Even such am I.
>
> No mate to list that bird's sad lay,
>   No hand to raise that drooping flower;
> The song must float unheard away,
>   The bud still bear the whirlwind's power.
>   And helpless lie!

Her brother-in-law, Leon Hyneman, was a vigorous proponent of equality for women in every sphere of life. Rebekah was no feminist—quite the contrary as the following verse proves. It carries the misleading title, "Women's Rights."

She is a flower that blossoms best unseen,
　　Sheltered within the precincts of her home;
There should no dark'ning storm-cloud intervene,
　　There the loud-strife of worldlings never come.
Let her not scorn to act a woman's part
　　Nor strive to cope with manhood in its might,
But lay this maxim closely to her heart—
　　That that which God ordains is surely right.

Another Philadelphian who was respected and admired for her literary gifts was Nina Morais (1855—1918), the daughter of the rabbi of Congregation Mikveh Israel. Somehow, between keeping house, looking after a half-dozen younger sisters, and teaching Sunday school, she found time to write and study. Her father made certain that she received a good education, which meant that she went through a "normal school." Like most of her cultured contemporaries, however, she was self-educated, reading widely. Nina was also a poet. The following sonnet was written in 1908 for the Shelley-Keats Memorial:

Among the cypresses young Shelley lies,
　　Rests Adonais in his violet bed;
　　Their frail dust mingles with the heroic dead—
Scipio's and Caesar's. Joy! In the radiant skies,
Hid in the quivering dawn, the skylark flies;
　　From out the sun its silver notes are shed.
　　But all the pale stars tremble overhead
When from the dark the nightingale replies.

Roma of Ruins, Roma of antique day,
　　Imperious Mistress of the historic page,
Gaze on thy treasures of the Appian Way,
　　Exult in relics of thy golden age:
Yet look upon these strangers' graves and say,
　　What more august in thy proud heritage?

Italian-born Sabato Morais saw to it that she was at home in Italian literature. She wrote on pedagogy, on women's rights, on anti-Semitism for both the Jewish and non-Jewish press. She was an outspoken feminist. The *North American Review* published an essay of hers on "The Limitations of Sex." By the 1880's, the national periodicals had already begun to exploit the "Jewish Question"; it was then that this young woman was called upon to speak for her people and the Jewish women of her generation. In later years she married and moved to Minneapolis, where she became one of the founders of the local women's club and lectured on Ibsen. Her interest in Ibsen's women was inevitable at a time when thoughtful Jewesses were foreshadowing an awakened female consciousness. Like other Jewish women of her day, she came to literature through her training as an elocutionist, a professional field that was cultivated by women, particularly Jewesses, at the turn of the century.

American Jewry has inordinate reverence for Emma Lazarus (1849—1887). There are many reasons for this: She came from an old "Sephardic" family that reached back to the eighteenth century; she died young of cancer; she was concerned about the Russian refugees who sought asylum on these shores. Emma was also sympathetic to the new Jewish Palestinian-centered nationalism, and, most important of all, she was the author of "The New Colossus," one of the best-known sonnets in American literature. American Jews are constantly reaching out for heroes and heroines; they made her their very own. Zionism and the rise to power of the East European Jews in the United States were to insure her immortality. She began publishing poetry as a teenager; she desperately wanted to be recognized as a writer of quality. Despite the fact that Emma Lazarus wrote prose and poetry, basked in the encouragement of Emerson, translated Heine, and published apologias for her people in the best magazines of the day, she nonetheless has remained a minor luminary in the history of American literature. She was not an ardent Jew till the pogroms stirred her to return passionately to her people, though she had already written on Jewish themes before the mass killings in Russia. The pogroms served to heighten her ethnicity. She occupies an important place in the history of American Jewry, if only because of a fourteen-line poem now inscribed in bronze on a tablet adorning the base of the Statue of Liberty. This one sonnet made her justifiably famous; few Americans have not quoted

Give me your tired, your poor,
Your huddled masses yearning to breathe free,
The wretched refuse of your teeming shore.
Send these the homeless, tempest tost to me.
I lift my lamp beside the Golden Door.

When Emma Lazarus died in 1887, more and more women, housewives if you will, were reading books, good and bad; more and more were evincing an interest in literature. The Jewish population in this country was increasing rapidly. Schools were better, parents were beginning to raise their cultural sights; with affluence came leisure and greater opportunities for reading. The general press was improving; Jewish weeklies, in both English and German, were available in the larger towns or through the mails. It would seem that Jewish women's literary societies first made their appearance by the 1870's. Admitted as guests and members of the Young Men's Hebrew Associations of an earlier decade, women had already been given an opportunity to listen, to think, and at times to stand up and talk. Congregational cultural associations, which included both men and women, now appeared in the 1880's. Books were discussed, lectures given, dramas produced. The Pioneers of Saint Louis, established in 1878, was a small women's society of thirty members or less, where the ladies enjoyed cake and coffee, listened to debates, good music, declamations, and even original essays. They discussed economics, pedagogy, literature, and bragged that they had devoted one year each to Browning and Tennyson and two years to Emerson. Women's literary clubs of various genres were established in Detroit and San Francisco in the 1890's, in New York City and North Carolina in the early 1920's. The North Carolina Association of Jewish Women was a statewide organization whose goals were no less than a religiocultural renaissance. These Jewesses aided synagogues, set up traveling libraries, pleaded for Sabbath observance, and established religious schools. The social element in all societies of this type was always important. It is difficult to determine the quality of the intellectual fare; not many documents of these ephemeral organizations have survived.

The Intellectuals

Were any of these nineteenth-century women intellectuals? Certainly Emma Lazarus was, to a degree; Nina Morais Cohen was much more a creative, reflective thinker. A generation earlier, Rachel Mordecai Lazarus (1788—1838) could have easily documented herself as one of the most brilliant Jewesses of the pre—Civil War decades, though she would have been the first to deny that she possessed a first-rate mind. Her letters to Maria Edgeworth, in MacDonald's *The Education of the Heart*, attest to her intellectual powers. For many years, 1815—1838, this daughter of the Jewish apologist and educator Jacob Mordecai carried on correspondence with the Anglo-Irish novelist and educator Maria Edgeworth. For years the young Rachel had worked closely with her father in his Warrenton girls' academy; much of its success may well be ascribed to her. In 1821, she married Aaron Lazarus, a member of a notable Charleston family. He was then living in Wilmington, North Carolina, a town of about two thousand inhabitants. Rachel's correspondence with Miss Edgeworth was initiated in Warrenton, but most of the letters were later dispatched from Wilmington. The question of slavery arose, and although Rachel was no friend of that peculiar institution, she was quick to point out to her correspondent that the sufferings of the peasants in Ireland were incomparably worse than those of the American slaves.

Rachel never met Rebecca Gratz, whom she admired; the Philadelphia Jewess had become a legend even in her own time. It would have been difficult for the Wilmington woman to believe that she surpassed the Philadelphia notable in intellectual and cultural matters. Rachel was more thoughtful, more critical. There is no question that she was an exceptional person.

Rebecca Gratz

Rebecca Gratz enjoyed a national reputation among Jews and possibly even among the Gentiles. She came from a well-to-do family; her brothers were active in a number of Philadelphia's best-known cultural institutions. The Gratz house, over which this dignified spinster presided, was strictly kosher; she herself was not only observant but devout. She was convinced of the superiority of Judaism. This Jewess moved in the best social circles of the city; there is ample evidence that she was welcome wherever she went, but in no sense was she a social climber. Some of America's best-known writers were her friends. Though brother Ben's wives were Christian—he had married twice—and Rebecca was close to them, she made it quite clear that she was opposed to intermarriage. Intermarriage was no problem for her personally; faith would triumph over human affection.

Primarily a volunteer social worker, Rebecca was, in a way, a prototype for those competent upper-middle-class women who were to adorn the American Jewish community in the last decades of the century before they were ultimately politely pushed aside by male professionals. Many remembered her for her charm, dignity, and bearing. Her letters prove that she was not without an introspective sense. She was always a lady, conscious of the amenities, yet in no sense does she seem to have been pompous or unrealistic.

Rebecca Gratz was no radical like her contemporary, Frances Wright. The latter's feminism would have repelled her; Wright's sexual practices would have shocked her. She was not at all comparable to a Sarah Margaret Fuller, an Elizabeth Cady Stanton, a Lucretia Mott, a Harriet Beecher Stowe, a Lydia Maria Child, or a Jew like Ernestine Rose. But statistics must always be borne in mind; in 1860 there were over 31,000,000 persons in the United States; there were, it is estimated, about 150,000 Jews. Does one have a right to expect female leadership of national stature in a relatively small and, in the main, immigrant Jewish community? Academically, she was not on a par with that remarkable group of Jewesses in Germany and Austria who had established their salons in Berlin and Vienna in the early nineteenth century. Women like Henriette Herz, the two Mendelssohn sisters, and Rahel Levin read the finest literature, had philosophical training, and in some instances—as with Henriette Herz—had an excellent working knowledge of half a dozen languages, including Greek and Latin. Men like the brothers

Humboldt, Schleiermacher, and even Schiller flocked to their homes. Mirabeau visited them; Von Gentz and Ranke, Heine and Boerne, the people who were to influence generations, passed through their doors. These women stimulated thought; they encouraged important men to think and to write; they did much to create an independent native culture in Germany; they helped "discover" Goethe; they were among the vanguard of those who shook off the shackles of a trammeling feudal provincialism.

They helped others to achieve freedom, but could not free themselves. They were the slaves of the same medieval prejudices from which they emancipated others. Practically all of them—with rare exceptions—became converts to Christianity. Rebecca Gratz was a proud Jewess. For her, Judaism was a great religion to be possessed and cherished, but not to be flaunted ostentatiously. She had been born under happier circumstances than her sisters across the seas. She had grown up under a free and liberal system. Her father was a respected "gentleman." She honestly deemed no one her social superior. She was emotionally stable, untouched by a sycophantic desire to assimilate herself to a new culture by escaping her own. She never became a distinguished woman because the greatness of achievement was not in her. The challenge was always present. While it is true that the challenge of Jewish disabilities and contemptuous social prejudice was not flung in her face, there was a very real opportunity for struggle on a national scale as a "reformer," fighting against slavery, drink, debtors' prisons, and for women's rights. Apparently she never saw these opportunities: her spirit was humanitarian and generous, but parochial. She had no great mission in life, no overwhelming enthusiasms. Still, in retrospect, Rebecca Gratz can be said to have been the most eminent American Jewess of antebellum America.

Jewesses and Social Reform

Rebecca Gratz did possess a social conscience, though it found rare expression in the hundreds of letters which she wrote. There are exceptions, however. In 1844, Philadelphia was the scene of riots; the nativists and the Irish newcomers were engaged in civil war. Catholic churches were burnt, and well over a hundred people were killed or wounded. Then it was that Rebecca wrote to brother Ben in Lexington bitterly indicting the spirit that made such iniquities possible.

> The whole spirit of religion is to make men merciful, humble and just. . . . Unless the strong arm of power is raised to sustain the provisions of the Constitution of the United States, securing to every citizen the privilege of worshiping God according to his own conscience, America will be no longer the happy asylum of the oppressed and the secure dwelling place of religion.

In 1847 she excoriated her country in no uncertain terms for attacking Mexico. As a Northerner, she had no interest in furthering the slave power in the Southwest; though not an abolitionist, she had no sympathy for chattel slavery. Commenting on the Mexican War, she wrote:

> I feel so much more sorrow and disgust than heroism in this war; . . . to invade a country and slaughter its inhabitants . . . is altogether against my principles.

Most American Jewesses and their menfolk were almost completely untouched by the social reform movement which had begun to manifest itself in the 1830's after the coming of the Scottish libertarian, Frances Wright. As late as 1906, when Lewis N. Dembitz, Brandeis's uncle, wrote the article on "Woman, Rights of" for the *Jewish Encyclopedia*, he limited himself to the talmudic period, which had come to an end sometime in the sixth century. As a committed traditionalist, he believed that the halakah, the rabbinical Law, with respect to women, had been fixed at that time. There was nothing further to be said, at least nothing of an authoritative nature.

What was this social reform? It was—it still is—a humanitarian movement to improve society for men, women, and children to the end that all will be afforded equality of opportunity. Over the years this has meant the abolition of slavery, equal rights for Negroes, eradication of the liquor traffic, international peace, arbitration of disputes between nations, prison reform, better working conditions for labor, and encouragement of trade unions. It has spawned a more equitable distribution of wealth, birth control, the suffrage movement, rights for women, ordination of females, elimination of child labor, and better schools.

Most of these issues were beyond the ken of nineteenth-century Jews, for these were sensitive areas; the timid Jewish newcomers—largely immigrants—had no desire to embroil themselves in controversy. Why invite prejudice? They had enough problems of their own just making a living; each generation here had to provide for the needs of a succeeding wave of immigrants, many of whom arrived impoverished. Charity began at home. Temperance? Jews don't drink; that's the Gentile's headache. Prison reform? Jews stay out of jail; Jewish poor were not driven by hunger and poverty to commit crimes, for Jews took care of their own. Education? Schools? Most Jews were able to educate their girls; as it was, the goals of the parents were modest. The passion for higher education for children would not become prevalent until after the turn of the century, when the descendants of East European stock, handicapped as Jews, would have to compete with Christians. Labor unions? The Central Europeans—shopkeepers and craftsmen, bourgeois to the core—were not proletarian in their sympathies. They saw themselves as businessmen on the way up the economic and social ladder. To be sure, the East European workers in America's urban ghettos wanted shorter hours and better pay, but they did not flock to the labor unions until almost thirty years after their arrival. The frail unions they first established represented but a minuscule fraction of the actual laboring force. Women's suffrage, women's rights? As a group, Jewesses paid no attention to this agitation in the late nineteenth century, though individuals among them were fully aware of what was at stake. Jewish women of that generation, no matter what their European provenance, did not look upon themselves as an abused, oppressed group. A host of other interests were of more immediate concern to them.

There was one exception to the statement above that American Jewesses were indifferent to the struggle for women's rights. The exception, a truly notable one, was Ernestine Louise Siismondi Potowski Rose (1810—1892), the daughter of a Polish rabbi. Ernestine had fled her home at an early age and came to this country in the 1830's with her husband, William E. Rose, a Gentile. By the time she landed she was already a utopian socialist, a prohibitionist, an anti-religionist, and an abolitionist. For a generation she was in the vanguard of those who championed equitable laws for women in marriage, divorce, and the holding of property. She pleaded for improved educational facilities and political equality for all, both men and women. In short, she wanted a woman to enjoy the same privileges and immunities as a man. By the 1850's, Ernestine Rose was widely recognized as a national leader in the struggle to emancipate women. It was her belief that once women were given opportunities, they would respond by improving and furthering society. Without liberty, she said, women cannot be happy. No woman should be the servile tool of a man. Eve civilized Adam by making him partake of the fruit which brought wisdom and understanding.

Does Ernestine Rose deserve a place in the story of the American Jewess? She seems to have had no interest in Jews except as fellow human beings; she defended them ably when they were attacked by a prejudiced commentator. At best, her relationship to the American Jewess is a tangential one. By furthering the status of all women—and she did—she furthered the status of the American of Jewish descent. She was not a women's liberationist; she was preeminently an egalitarian. She did not set out to separate or to "liberate" women from men; her hope was that women would enjoy the same rights as men, and work closely with them on a common plane.

Jewish Social Work and Welfare Societies

American Jewish women did have something in common with Ernestine Rose. She wanted to help all women; since 1820, the more conventional Jewesses had wished to help the Jewish poor, especially women. It would seem that the idea of a society for Jewish women was born in the mind of Rebecca Gratz. It was a new departure in American Jewish history. This Philadelphia organization called itself the Female Hebrew Benevolent Society; the name is reminiscent of the male Charleston Hebrew Benevolent Society, then and still today the oldest extant Jewish charity in the United States. Why did they turn to Charleston? That city then sheltered America's largest and most advanced Jewish community.

The year 1819 is an important date. From that time on, the Jewish women of this country turned to organized social welfare; charity became their métier. Were they influenced by somewhat similar Jewish female philanthropies in Europe? Not necessarily, for the Central and East European women's societies of that time were primarily sick-care, death, and burial fellowships. Such formal organizations were not to be established here for nearly another generation. The definitive influence on the Philadelphia Jewish women was a well-known local general society that had come into being in the very first years of the new century. This was the Female Association for the Relief of Women in Reduced Circumstances, an enterprise in which Rebecca and other Jewesses were active.

Why a Jewish women's organization? Was there an unconscious desire on their part to document themselves, to do something for women as women? Was this innovation of theirs an avowal of feminine consciousness, of collective "sisterhood"? Probably. This much at least is clear: they wanted to function on their own in a man's world; they wanted to be by and for themselves. Without fanfare, these women now staked out an area for themselves voluntarily. They liked it; it was an opportunity to be creative. The men gladly ceded a patch of the charity field to them. The husbands were absorbed in making a living, there was a job to be done, the women wanted to do it; let them do it. It was as simple as that.

Why then in 1819? Why a *Jewish* society? America then was in the throes of a depression that would last about six years. Jews needed help, and only Jews understood their own, so they believed. The new society hoped to further "morality and piety," whatever was meant by these terms. More specifically, it set out to help widows and orphans. They announced that they would educate brilliant children and thus give them a chance to make careers for themselves in free America. The latter hope was only a pious wish; their chief job was relief. They investigated their clients; they ignored the improvident and helped only those of good moral character who were in reduced circumstances. It was definitely a middle-class organization. Actually, the society helped very few, probably not more than one or two families, during the first year. One is almost tempted to suggest that the subconscious motivation to organize was the desire for "sisterhood" rather than the need to respond to a cry for relief. For Jews, there were as yet no pressing problems of urban poverty. They may have established a registry for unemployed seamstresses; they did attend the sick, but in a period of deep economic recession they spent but 10 percent of their resources. Like other Jewish organizations, the women were intent upon piling up a surplus. They had access to public infirmaries and recourse to physicians who volunteered services. Donations were solicited from both Jews and Gentiles; the largest gift the first year came from the estate of a Christian.

The 1819 society was the first of hundreds of women's organizations that were to be established in this country. With this new genre of philanthropy came a new woman: the Jewish social worker. This new woman was exemplified by Rebecca Gratz, who, in later years, was to establish the first Sunday school and help found fuel and sewing societies and an orphanage. By the early 1890's, there was no Jewish community of size without a woman's organization. All were committed to good works, but no two were exactly alike. Some were intent on mutual-aid; others offered relief to the distressed. Some were affiliated with congregations, others were autonomous. Some limited their benefactions to local petitioners, others were willing to aid suffering Jews, and Gentiles as well, in distant communities. Local societies frequently came to the assistance of regional orphan asylums; only the larger metropolises could support such institutions without the help of outside communities.

By the 1840's, female burial societies—modeled on those in Europe—were established in this country; earlier attempts to organize them here had failed. These new women's groups not only nursed the sick, attended the dying, and buried the dead, but often aided the impoverished. Some of the women's societies carried clients on their rolls for years. The nature of the benefits varied; some provided medical care, medicaments, and a cash grant on the death of a husband. In short, a number of these burial societies were also mutual-aid in nature.

As early as the 1840's, a group of women from New York's Temple Emanu-El started a German-speaking mutual-aid lodge of their own. They called themselves the Unabhaengiger Orden Treuer Schwestern (the Independent Order of True Sisters). Like B'nai B'rith, on whom they seem to have patterned themselves, they also chartered English-speaking branches but did not discontinue the use of German till the turn of the century. During the Civil War, many Jewish women's societies stressed the needs of the men in the armed forces and their families left behind. Special associations were set up both in the North and the South to cope with the social problems that followed in the wake of war. Lint and bandages were forwarded to the troops at the front; garments were sewn for the impoverished families of the troops; the sick and the wounded in the hospitals were visited and given food, delicacies, soap, stationery.

Not infrequently, the new women's societies were faced with a problem: the ladies did not know how to conduct meetings. The problem was solved by electing or appointing a male president or secretary. This procedure was also employed in a later generation when the East European immigrant women established their mutual-aid hometown societies. Similarly, in 1848, when the Seneca Falls Conference issued its Women's "Declaration of Independence" and created the country's first women's movement, Lucretia Mott had to turn to her husband to act as chairman.

Ostensibly, if not actually, most Jewish female societies were in origin philanthropically oriented. Though mid-nineteenth-century Jewesses very rarely established purely social organizations, sociability was nonetheless borne in mind. Euchre and whist, coffee and conversation, limited membership, characterized some of them. Only a few societies admitted that they met solely for the purpose of exchanging pleasantries. The As You Like It Association of Lexington, Kentucky (1901), is a case in point. The matrons and young ladies in town who were invited to join and assemble one afternoon a week for tea and cookies, paid dues of 10 cents every time they met, and assiduously devoted their afternoons to chitchat and gossip. On one occasion they did give $2 to a poor family, but that was only after a protracted discussion. "As You Like It" was a completely friendly, completely innocuous group. Men had unabashedly founded social clubs since the late 1840's where they could eat, drink, and play cards. Women were not admitted as members, although they were frequently invited as guests; they were always welcome at the balls, musicales, and dramatic presentations.

The programs of the benevolent societies had much in common; the newcomers met and debated the specific case on the tapis, or discussed the needs of the local congregation. Fund-raising consumed a great deal of their time and efforts. In the large cities there were elaborate masquerade balls, especially on the Purim holiday; thousands of dollars were contributed. Strawberry and ice cream festivals might well be an important event in the women's society in Trinidad or Leadville, Colorado, in the Hebrew Ladies' Aid, in the Frauen Verein, in the Female Hebrew Benevolent Society, in the German Ladies' Relief Society. Why German Ladies? The German women—the Hungarians, too—set up their own social-welfare groups, independent of the associations established by the natives. Social and ethnic disparities encouraged particularism.

For the individual Jewess, social work might well be a way of life; she fulfilled herself. Frances Wisebart Jacobs (1843—1892) is representative. There were many others who would have served equally well to document this statement. Frances Wisebart was a native Kentuckian who had married a Denver pioneer, Abraham Jacobs, in the early 1860's. During the 1870's, she first devoted herself to Denver's Hebrew Ladies' Benevolent Society, and before long, moved into the field of citywide philanthropy. She helped found the first welfare federation, the Charity Organization Society, in the late 1880's. In a way, this federation of over twenty welfare agencies was a forerunner of the Community Chest. For several years Mrs. Jacobs had served as secretary of this, the town's outstanding eleemosynary institution, and was hailed throughout Colorado as the Queen of the Charities. The Woman's Christian Temperance Union elected her as an honorary member. A Christian clergyman said of her: "She never forgot a man's divine pedigree. The meanest wretch with whom she dealt bore for her some stamp of heavenly birth." Shocked at the neglect of the hundreds of penniless tuberculous men and women who came to Denver only to starve and die in the streets, parks, and alleys of the town, she roused the community to make provision for these impoverished invalids. The sanatorium that was finally built after her death was called the Frances Jacobs Hospital. Later its name was changed to the National Jewish Hospital for Consumptives. Today in the state capitol at Denver there are sixteen stained-glass windows in the dome dedicated to Colorado's pioneers. Only one of those memorializes a woman: that woman is Frances Jacobs.

Throughout the years 1819 to 1892, women played an important part in the philanthropic life of the Jewish communities, despite the fact that their husbands, who excluded them from many male organizations, tended to put women in second place. When the men established lodges, the women's divisions were merely "auxiliaries." Yet they were fund-raisers for almost every occasion, and also prime supporters of the synagogues. They were the wheelhorses; they pulled more than their share of the load. But they were no shrinking violets; constantly they created societies of their own dedicated to specific tasks, most of which were philanthropic in nature. The welfare associations they established were geared to bring relief to old and young, families and orphans; they sewed garments, supplied fuel, and supported schools. Only a few women in each society were activists, doing the social work; most members merely paid dues. How many women belonged to these auxiliaries, to these charities? The smaller the town, the larger the proportion of members in the Women's Aid, the Ladies' Aid. The actual percentage of women in the metropolitan centers who belonged to these associations was very small, but for those who wanted to do something outside the home the society was important. By the last quarter of the nineteenth century, American Jewish women were coming into their own through the separate groups they were establishing. This pleased them very much; they enjoyed being themselves.

The Sunday Schools

Rebecca Gratz's Sunday school was certainly a religious and educational institution, but it is very probable that it was equally "philanthropic" in intent. Though children of the native families attended, there is reason to believe that the primary goal was to provide religiously, culturally, and morally for the children of the recently arrived Central European Jewish immigrants. While it is true that the newcomers were not an impoverished group, it is equally true that as immigrant artisans and petty tradesmen, they were in straitened circumstances. The number of Jews in the country was increasing steadily. By 1840, the Jewish community was at least six times the size it had been in 1776. The children of the newcomers had to be kept off the streets on Sunday; they had to be Americanized if the fair name of the old settlers was not to be tarnished. The Philadelphia Christians set out to solve their problem of unruly youths roaming the streets on the Lord's Day by establishing a Sunday School Society in 1791; in 1817, several Christian denominations in town came together in the American Sunday School Union. Twenty-one years later, Rebecca Gratz began her venture; like the Christian prototype, it was Jewishly "non-denominational." The Sephardic progenitors were dealing primarily with Ashkenazic children. Thus it was that the new project came into being in 1838 in the midst of a devastating national business depression. In a philanthropic, humanitarian sense, the school was a benevolent act of the elite on behalf of the "masses." One is almost prompted to suggest that what now emerged were the first faint intimations of the later settlement house. In some schools clothing was provided for the poor children. The hope was nurtured that the survival of the next generation of Jews would be guaranteed through religious indoctrination. Morality was stressed; not only the mind but the soul was to be nurtured.

Since the only model on hand—one to which they almost slavishly conformed—was Protestant, the curriculum, too, bore the stamp of that church, though Rebecca was anything but an admirer of the Sunday School Union's theology. The English Bible which they used, the only one printed for many years, was the 1611 King James version; Watts's hymns were sung; English prayers were taught. At first, some of the textbooks used were Christian; where the word "Jesus" or "Christ" occurred it was covered over. The only Jewish manuals available in English were older theological works published in London or Jamaica. A year after the first school opened, Isaac

Leeser prepared an original catechism for the use of the youngsters; his disciples prepared additional ones. From the very first moment, the Sunday school movement was a great success. Schools were opened in Richmond, Charleston, Savannah, Baltimore, New York; in postbellum days, after the decline of the Jewish all-day (parochial) schools, Sunday schools were to be found in most of the country's towns and cities. The movement was so successful that a national federation was put together in the 1880's; this was the Hebrew Sabbath School Union.

Why were the Sunday schools successful? They were held on Sunday, the instruction was in English, and the teachers were women, preponderantly natives, "Americans," who could appeal to children whose prime loyalties were to the American civic ideals in which they were already being indoctrinated in the secular schools. Apparently the youngsters also liked the public school type of competitive exams which had been adopted by the Jews in the new educational institution. They had a chance to "show off." They enjoyed the prizes, the gifts of oranges and pretzels. By the 1890's, this type of school, which then included thousands of children of East European stock, had become America's most important Jewish acculturational agency. It was a creation of women, and women alone, primarily Sephardim.

Judaism and the American Jewess

Rebecca Gratz was in no sense unusual in her devotion to Jewish tradition and in her determination to foster it. The typical nineteenth-century young Jewess was loyal to her faith; she would not intermarry, and summarily rejected apostasy. Yet, there were tremendous pressures on her to intermarry if she lived in a small town where there were no suitable Jewish mates. Intermarriage was the only recourse left to girls who were determined to have a home of their own. In a way, Jacob Mordecai's family is a classical example of what happened to the children of an observant Jew who were reared in a village. Of his seven daughters, four remained unmarried, two married Jews, one married a Christian. Of his six sons, one remained unmarried, one married a Jewess, four married Christians. But, and this merits mention, the children who entered the married state did so after they left the parental home in Warrenton. Filial reverence and the Christian indoctrination to which they had been exposed were both not to be gainsaid.

Nominally at least, most American Jewesses were Orthodox; some were very observant. Immigrant women, married back home in the German and Austrian lands, often continued to wear the prescribed wig. Some of them would not even comb it out on the Sabbath; that was forbidden work. They would not light a fire on this holy day; they would not carry even a handkerchief on Saturday. All the holidays were observed; no bread was eaten on Passover. Poor little Maud Nathan; she liked matzo, but if Good Friday fell on Passover she missed her hot cross buns. Still, Orthodox or not, Christmas was celebrated in one form or another by many of the observant Sephardim. During the High Holydays, almost all women and men flocked to the synagogues.

In the third quarter of the century, many families still kept kosher, at least at home; by the 1880's, kashrut was observed in the breach at most Jewish public gatherings and in some households. When the pious mother or mother-in-law made an unexpected call at home, the oysters on the table were snatched up and put on the floor, providing an unscheduled feast for the dog. One young Jewess who was being educated in a Catholic girls' school was not expected to cross-stitch a Virgin Mary; this created no problem: the good sisters gave her a Moses in the bulrushes. Little Delia, a young daughter of one of the Cincinnati Cohen families, went out "begging" on Purim all dressed up in papa's best pair of trousers. When he discovered it, he thrashed her so soundly that she remembered the beating as long as she lived.

There is very little evidence that women attended the daily Orthodox services. Actually, it would appear that daily services were rarely held in the smaller towns of the hinterland. In the cities, women did come on the Sabbath, particularly if they worshiped in the Reform temples where the sermons and much of the liturgy were in English or German. It is difficult, very difficult, to determine if women refrained from attending the synagogue because they had so little to say, because their role in the ritual was almost nonexistent. The preeminence of men in the synagogue and the Christian church is a tradition that goes back to the Old and New Testaments. Genesis 1:3 makes this unequivocally clear; God said to the first woman: "He [man] shall rule over thee." Saint Paul was more explicit in I Corinthians 14:34: "Let your women keep silence in the churches, for it is not permitted unto them to speak, but they are commanded to be under obedience as also sayeth the [Jewish] Law."

Today, some writers believe that the nineteenth-century Christian woman exemplified the cult of "true womanhood" in piety, purity, devotion to the home, and submission to male authority. Jewish women also believed in homemaking, purity, and piety; in these ideals they were in agreement with their Christian neighbors. Submission? This is something that is very hard to document. There is very little evidence that in the give-and-take of married life the Jewish wife said yea to his yea and nay to his nay. Many men were but the lengthened shadows of their wives. Indeed, like the Gentiles about him, the Jew of native stock put his wife on a pedestal. This Christian ideal of chivalry, this concept of the feminine mystique, had almost become part of America's civil religion. Jews adopted it and, at least in public, made fervent avowals of its reality.

In an 1842 address, the Charlestonian Nathaniel Levin said that although men are superior to women in reasoning and knowledge, women are the ones who are primarily responsible for progress in civilization. In this country they enjoy equality with men; they have more influence than men. And, he implies, in their own way they achieve more. In good works, it is they who point the way like an angel of light. Mellowed by food and alcohol, a romantic of the 1840's saluted the gentler sex: "Woman! What can *man* say of her when God deemed Paradise unfinished until she smiled amidst its bowers." Isaac M. Wise never ceased to praise women, especially when he rose at a banquet with a glass of wine in his hand to respond to a toast to the ladies: they are the patrons of art and music; it is the woman who creates great states and empires; women are the guiding stars of the universe. Women, he insisted, are intelligent, morally sensitive, possessed of a capacity for leadership.

There is reason to believe that in religious matters nineteenth-century Jewesses stressed the ethical rather than the ritual and the ceremonial. Their moral and pietistic precepts are reflected in various documents. Writing to a younger brother about to depart for England, his older sister advises him: Fear God, honor your superiors and parents, keep the Law, tell the truth, and let virtue be your guide. The ethical injunctions Deborah Moses laid down in her will are very moving. This daughter of Philadelphia's rabbi, Jacob R. Cohen, instructed her family to avoid all pomp and parade. She asked for a simple funeral, just a wooden headboard, no footpost, no inscription. Why arrogantly perpetuate an ephemeral name? "Mourn not beyond the hour sanctified by nature and pure grief. The tears which spring from the heart are the only dews the grave should be moistened with; the dead receive sufficient honor in being called to face their God."

Reform Judaism and the American Jewess

As far back as 1837, the young German Abraham Geiger, destined to become the spiritual father of Reform Judaism, called attention to the religious disabilities to which Jewesses were subject. Sympathetic to their plight, he expressed the hope that there be no distinction in the marriage ceremony between the bride and the groom, no demarcation between men and women in the religious services; they were both equal. In the 1840's, when Germany's rabbis met in a series of conferences, they took cognizance of the secondary religious position of women, but accomplished nothing. The Augsburg Synod of 1871 did pass a number of resolutions enhancing and elevating their status, but by that time its well-meant decisions had already been anticipated in this country, at least by liberal coreligionists.

The Jews in Germany had introduced confirmation for girls no later than 1818; by 1830 the short-lived Reformed Society of Israelites in Charleston had already emphasized the religious equality of women in the ceremonies of child-naming, marriage, and burial. These innovations reflect Protestant liturgical influences. These Reformers had also introduced confirmation, but limited it to boys. By the 1840's, confirmation for boys and girls had been introduced into New York Orthodox and Reform synagogues. That same decade, Rabbi Max Lilienthal of New York, still traditional, admitted women to his choir. His Albany colleague, Isaac M. Wise, went a step farther; he not only trained women to sing in his choir, but also introduced the family pew in his secessionist, Reformist sanctuary. To be sure, Shearith Israel of New York, hewing to the line, retained a women's gallery in the new Mill Street Synagogue, but the latticework was gone; women could now look down upon the men and men could look up at the women. In the 1850's, David Einhorn of Baltimore and Julius Eckman of San Francisco pleaded eloquently that women be granted more religious rights. They were undoubtedly influenced by the early Reformers in Germany and the growing feminist agitation in the United States.

The American liberal rabbis were among the first to break with Orthodoxy. This was in 1869, when they met in Philadelphia and in formal resolutions rejected the disabling biblical and talmudic laws of divorce, marriage, and remarriage. This was a radical move. In all these matters, so the rabbis declared, the decisions of the civil courts and the state statutes were binding. The assembled spiritual leaders raised the status of the bride by introducing the double-ring ceremony. Actually, it is very probable that here in the United States, most liberal congregations disregarded the need for an all-male quorum when they conducted services. One suspects that by 1869, when the rabbis met, many if not most American Jewish laymen were long wont to disregard those very prohibitions which the liberal rabbis so solemnly abrogated. These spiritual leaders were probably merely confirming what was established practice, at least in their own congregations.

Even before the Reformers met in Philadelphia, there was talk of rights for women in the American synagogue. It is difficult to determine whether the women were pushing, or whether liberals like Isaac Mayer Wise were leading them and encouraging them to seek religious equality in this basic institution. Let it not be forgotten that women were needed in the synagogue because the attendance of the men always left something to be desired. For them, the shop, business, took precedence. Ever since his Albany rabbinate, Wise had been an avant-garde rabbi in his relations with women. When in the late 1850's he pleaded the cause of the fair sex, he was not necessarily a feminist. He spoke as an American who was fully aware of the status of women in the Protestant churches. He wanted the widows, wives, spinsters, and daughters in his congregation to enjoy the same privileges which the Protestants accorded their female members. He did not fail to remind his people that if women sang in the choirs, sat in pews with their families, and were confirmed with males, it was due to him and the Reformers. He had consistently advocated votes and offices for women in the synagogues. Like Moritz Loth, the lay founder of the Union of American Hebrew Congregations, he too recommended that a college for Jewish women be established. Synagogue prerogatives accorded women were not concessions, but rights due them.

Actually very little progress was made in including women in synagogal administration. As early as the Pittsburgh Rabbinical Conference (1885), Kaufmann Kohler came out unequivocally for absolute equality for women in all aspects of religious and synagogal life. When the Platform was formulated, women were ignored. Wise was probably sincere in his agitation on behalf of women, but he could not move without the men; he was not a free agent. In his lifetime no woman in his temple was elected to an important honorary post. Jewish men were loath to make any concession when it came to controlling the apparatus of this important institution. It was to be almost a century before the ladies were to be given equality with the men even among the Reform Jews of this country.

The changes just described characterized only the Reform synagogues. In the 1890's, Reformers were definitely in the minority; most American Jews were nominally Orthodox, adhering in principle to the ancient rabbinic laws which disabled women in the realm of marriage and divorce, segregated them in the sanctuary, and downgraded them in the service. In actual practice, by the time-hallowed American device of bland salutary neglect, they made accommodations as the spirit moved them. This was true even in some East European circles.

Notes on the Jewish Woman

It is not improbable that German Jewish immigrants, coming here with their European preconceptions, saw no reason to ameliorate the status of women in Judaism. These newcomers believed in Law and Order. Many of them, too, had their own notions about the place of women in the home. However, the American girl was anything but submissive; there is no indication that she, roosting comfortably on a pedestal, had any desire to come down. Like Saint Simeon Stylites, she was determined to stay; she enjoyed her perch. Many of these Central European immigrants believed, like a later Hohenzollern, that women's place was in the kirk or in the kitchen with the kids (*Kinder, Kueche, Kirche*). Samuel Maas, one of these new arrivals, German to his fingertips, was soon engaged to his cousin Caroline Hart of Charleston, South Carolina. She was a typical independent American young lady. In one of his love letters he told her in his fractured English that she must listen to him, that he intended to be the boss at all times. But apparently she did not listen to him, for she never married him and lived as a spinster to the ripe old age of eighty-two. If Sam was brokenhearted, he recovered. He married the German-born sister of Jacques Offenbach, the famous composer. Sam's wife did listen to him; she bore him four children. Let this be said in defense of the dictatorial Maas: when he wrote his love letter to Caroline, he was not yet Americanized; though he had been in the country for several years, he still had a lot to learn.

Isaac Leeser, too, was a Central European, but there was little that was Germanic about him. The Richmond of John Marshall, where he had lived, had made him a thorough and complete American. Yet like Sam Maas and most Americans, immigrants or natives, Leeser believed that the man was the head of the house, but, he insisted, husbands must be kind and indulgent and cherish their wives. No married man should be unfaithful even in thought. Wives, in turn, were to yield to the wishes of their spouses, unless the husband presumed to introduce religious innovation into the home. Departures from the Law must be opposed. Jewish women must be well-educated; they were to be educated with men equally. This was his plea in the 1840's, in a day when colleges for females were just being established.

What did men in those days, Jewish men, think of women? If many believed in the innate inferiority of females, they were careful not to voice their opinions. Many did believe that men were superior in reasoned thought, logic, and business sense, but that women were superior in kindliness and the capacity to appreciate the fine arts. Is it probable that gravestone inscriptions can measure the status of women, that the concept of the ideal antebellum wife may be mirrored in epitaphs? Possibly, but there is always the suspicion that even here posthumous reflections may be mere stereotypes. Bereaved husbands tend to be sentimental. Referring to his late wife, James Michael Simpson said that she was

kind, generous, and benevolent; she was a tender and indulgent parent, devoting her entire energies to the happiness of her offspring and endeavoring through an eventful life to instil into their minds and hearts a firm and constant reliance upon divine providence.

For Abigail Rebecca Ancker her consort ordered the following eulogy to be incised:

in the discharge of the important and varied duties of life, she was truly happy; as a Jewess, pure and zealous, as a wife ardent and affectionate, as a parent fond and devoted. She passed from time to eternity with the fullest assurance of a blessed immortality beyond the grave. To her, death has lost its sting, the grave, its victory.

In his travels through the United States in 1859 to 1862, Rumanian-born Israel Joseph Benjamin was more critical of live American women. The education of the Jewish girls here is being neglected, he wrote, for they stop school at fifteen. It's too bad that they are sent to female seminaries where they kneel and recite Christian prayers. After they reach their fifteenth year they start going to balls and dances; they are intent on having a good time. He might also have added they were out looking for husbands. American Jewish girls, he complained, are indulged by their parents. From his description of them, it is obvious that they were the prototypal Jewish American Princesses ("JAPS") of the late twentieth century. Benjamin II, as he called himself, described the American social pantheon in just two words, money, women: the men make it, the women spend it. This was all too simple. He knew better; the German Jews, men and women, were very frugal.

Just about four years before Benjamin II came to the United

States, the immigrant Amelia Ullman came down the gangplank of a Mississippi steamer to join her husband in St. Paul, a Minnesota boomtown. This was three years before the territory was admitted to the Union. St. Paul was on the edge of civilization; the frontier was perilously close; another twenty-two years would pass before Custer would die on the Little Bighorn. When Amelia married Joseph she told him that she brought no dowry but that she would go with him to the end of the world. She did.

In St. Paul she lived on bacon, potatoes, and tea, and slept with bedbugs. The town was not without some cultural life, for the intellectuals gathered together in a reading circle. St. Paul did boast of a bookstore. In the dead of winter Amelia went south on a sleigh to tap the railroad that went into Chicago. Traveling through cold and storm and blizzards for five days and nights, she finally reached Chicago, where she had to wade through mud in the unpaved streets. She was strong-willed and dauntless, an urban frontierswoman. In her memoirs she says very little of her husband. A schlemiel? Hardly. When Joseph died, he headed one of the world's greatest fur and hide empires.

It is clear from Amelia's autobiography that once she made up her mind she did what she wanted to do. She ploughed ahead allowing nothing to deter her. But soft women, too, often reached their goals with a minimum of stir and militancy. The capacity of such a gentle soul to manipulate her husband is documented in the career of Sigmund Shlesinger (1848—1928), a frontier hero and Indian fighter. The Hungarian-born Shlesinger landed in New York City as a boy of sixteen and worked there for a while as a streetcar conductor; nothing he did enabled him to make a living, or satisfied him. A free agent, he struck out for the West and landed at Hays City in western Kansas. The young man worked there as a bartender, porter, amateur baker, and tyro beermaker, using a washtub to concoct his brew. Together with a partner and a total joint capital of $5.00, he opened a cigar store serving such customers as Buffalo Bill, Wild Bill Hickok, and General George A. Custer. Once more he failed at everything to which he set his hand. In desperation, he joined a group of mounted scouts who had been recruited by the government to pursue marauding Indians. On September 17, 1868, the men were ambushed, and entrenched themselves on a sandy island in the Arickaree Fork of the Republican River. There they remained for nine days, besieged for five days by an overwhelming force of Indians. The young soldier kept a diary in which he jotted down the events of the day: "scalpt 3 Indians, killt a coyote & eat him all up." His commanding officer and comrades acknowledged his heroism, his coolness under fire:

When the foe charged on the breastworks
With madness and despair,
And the bravest souls were tested,
The little Jew was there.

But the West was not made for him. He returned East, settled finally in Cleveland, married a Jewish girl, but showed little if any interest in Jews or Judaism. The woman he married took him out of the Christian neighborhood where he lived and moved him into the Jewish quarter. Then she saw to it that he joined the B'nai B'rith. It was not long before he became an active communal worker; together with others he organized the Hungarian Benevolent and Social Union, a free loan society, a Hebrew Relief Society, and the local Jewish federation of charities. Ultimately he achieved recognition as the vice-president of a Reform synagogue. Thanks to his wife, most of his descendants are Jews today; a great-granddaughter is married to the rabbi of Chicago's most prestigious temple. It is obvious that Sigmund Shlesinger was bold enough to stand up to six hundred screaming Cheyennes and Sioux, but not to a gentle woman who was determined to make a Jew out of him.

Sig Shlesinger finally became a successful tobacco merchant; the Ullmans made a fortune; Isaac Gomez, Jr., was a failure. Gomez, a New Yorker, was a member of one of the most distinguished Spanish-Portuguese families to settle in this country. They had come here no later then the first decade of the 1700's. Luis, Isaac's grandfather, was a successful merchant-shipper and one of the pillars of the New York Jewish community. Isaac was never a successful businessman; his prime interest was in English literature. In 1820, he published an anthology in prose and verse. It was not a Jewish book; its importance—beyond any intrinsic merit it might possess—lies in the fact that it was one of the very first literary works compiled by an American Jew. He called it *Selections of a Father for the Use of His Children.* John Adams had a copy, and liked it well enough to write Gomez and tell him that "to me it shall be a manual on my table."

Gomez's greatest virtue—and it is a virtue—was his devotion to his wife. In 1829, at the age of sixty-one, after thirty-eight years of a happy married life, he gave his wife a very special gift. It was a book, a manuscript prayer book which he had copied from a volume of David Levi's English translation of the Sephardic rite. He bound it in leather, marbled its edges, and gave it to his beloved wife with this letter: "I thank God for having created thee for me and me for thee . . .and I trust that you are well convinced that did I posses the riches of Peru my greatest hapiness would be to lay them at your feet." Can any man be said to be a failure if he manifests such affection and such respect for his wife? If Abigail Lopez Gomez elicited such love and devotion from her husband, who can doubt that she was an ornament to her sex and society, and that in her, the feminine mystique was a reflection of divinity itself.

Intimations of the New Woman

By the last quarter of the century, there were intimations of a "new woman" in American Jewry. A few, but only a few, of these women began to evaluate their role in society critically. What prompted them? The people who determined their thinking were all Gentiles, Protestants. For some time, cultured Christian women, some of them feminists, had been debating the status of their sex in their clubs. These were the women who were demanding more consideration for females in law and society. Jewish women of those decades were very much on the periphery of the nascent movement, though individuals among them were well-aware of what the radicals were saying. By the 1870's, Jewesses, in letters to the editors, were telling a new generation of girls that there was a world outside the fence that surrounded their homes. There was not even one Jewish girl at Vassar, volunteered one young lady, to which another, from

Charleston, responded that the young ladies she knew read and studied. There is indeed more to life than the scramble for a husband, she continued. Even New York's Shearith Israel, Orthodox to the core, had inaugurated a series of lectures for its womenfolk.

A handful of affluent, cultured women were engaged in constructive social work, especially in the Jewish ghettos; they brought help, advice, food, clothing, and a degree of Americanization to the women of the Lower East Side. These volunteer social workers wanted to remedy the existing evils in a constructive social sense; they wanted to help their clients resolve their problems, to build better lives for themselves. What moved these women from well-to-do homes to help others? That is not easy to determine. Possibly, they were mindful of the traditional humanitarianism of prophetic and rabbinic Judaism, of the work that their mothers had carried on in an earlier generation. Possibly, unwittingly, these women from affluent homes were eager to discover a better, more meaningful life for themselves. And, of course, there was the constant example of Christian women who were selflessly devoting themselves to others.

By the early 1870's, there were individual Jewesses who were talking about the vote for females; some even dared to speak at rallies for women's rights; a few were finally ready to evince sympathy for a movement that was no longer young. In 1874, the *Jewish Messenger* assured readers that Jewish women were not interested in the franchise or in preaching, unless it was to dress down their husbands! Even Rabbi Liebman Adler, a defender of the rights of women, had warned the ladies of his congregation to stay out of politics; it was too dirty a business for a pure woman. If she did want to effect changes, then let her work through her menfolk. Cornelia was the mother of the Gracchi; she herself did not have to go to the Forum.

The Jewesses who wanted to make something of themselves went to the Forum! These are the postbellum achievers who moved into the realm of literature, teaching, music; some even dared to compete in the marketplace. It was in the decades of the 1870's and 1880's that these purposeful few asserted themselves. It is much more important that in these very years a number of women succeeded in preparing themselves for leadership in the decades yet to come.

These few could not have been trained unless the times were right, unless there were those who were conscious of the need for new attitudes toward aspiring women. Among those who now prepared themselves for future careers were Lillian Wald, Maud Nathan and her sister Annie Nathan Meyer, Rebekah Kohut, Hannah Solomon, Hannah Bachman Einstein, Henrietta Szold. There were others, many others. There were women who were to distinguish themselves in the natural sciences, but who, even today, have not yet found recognition in the standard Jewish histories which men write.

It was not easy for these individuals to move forward in an age when Jews frowned on women who sought careers outside the home. These pioneers faced a triple hazard; they had to cope with an American community which looked askance at both career women and Jews, and they had to fight home, husbands, and a three-thousand-year-old social system. These Jewesses chose to disregard the tradition that would have them remain modestly in the background. Very few of them turned away from Judaism itself, but they did not hesitate to reject a Jewish-Christian life-style which blocked their development. America, after a fashion, offered them a chance to make their way; they took advantage of it.

What happened in the years 1870 to 1900 that made it possible for ambitious young Jewesses to prepare themselves for a career? Most of these young ladies were well-educated. A few had come up the hard way; they were self-taught. German immigrant parents who had attained a degree of affluence permitted their daughters to study. The girls in the wealthier families had been exposed to European culture: to its art, sciences, music, and literature. Here in the United States, they admired and imitated the notable Christian women whose careers were mirrored daily in the press. The humanistic religious thinking of the liberals among the Christian clergy and the rabbis moved them to lives of service. The 1890's would usher in a progressive age that had moral dimensions. Sensitive Jewish women were open to new visions, a new tolerance, new incentives. They were confronted with ethical challenges which some of them had the courage to meet.

A Review, 1819—1892

By 1819, a number of brilliant Jewesses in Europe, entering the world of intellectual emancipation, had become leaders in the salons of Berlin and Vienna. They did not identify with Judaism. Here in the United States, among the five or six thousand Jews of the early 1800's, there were already a few Jewish women reading good books, writing poetry, reaching out tentatively to a challenging new world of thought, emotion, and modernity. They identified with Judaism ardently.

As a group these Jewish female intelligentsia had no interest in women's rights until the last decade of the century at the earliest. Rarely, but only rarely, did a young girl strike out for herself. Josephine Sarah Marcus was such an exception. She ran away from home as a teenager, joined a theatre group, and soon became the consort of Wyatt Earp, the western gunfighter and peace officer who achieved fame and notoriety in Tombstone, Arizona. Josie remained faithful to Earp; she went with him to the arctic reaches of Alaska during the Gold Rush. She accompanied him into his world of gambling and horse racing, worked with him as a prospector in the Mojave Desert, and when he was gathered unto his fathers, saw to it that he was buried in a Jewish cemetery. Though there were times in her youth when she ignored the proprieties, she never publicly flouted them. Outwardly she observed the amenities that characterized a dignified matron.

With very few exceptions, the American Jewesses of the postbellum years were apparently satisfied with their lot in life. They were not rebellious females with a grievance against society. Actually, many were indeed reaching out beyond their homes; they were not really conscious of a self struggling for independence, autonomy, recognition. From the vantage point of the approaching twenty-first century, these women of 1890 were indeed subject to real disabilities, but from all indications they did not consider themselves an oppressed group. They had attained a degree of fulfillment; they were content because they had already carved out a world for themselves. They were living in gynocratic philanthropic enclaves which they had fashioned and in which they ruled supreme. It was a broadly conceived world of social welfare which embraced everything from buying shoes for impoverished youngsters to teaching them the Ten Commandments.

Despite her absorbing interest in the town's Ladies' Hebrew Benevolent Society, the nineteenth-century American Jewess never forgot that her prime concern was the home. It is true that the beauties of the "Jewish home" have been exaggerated by complacent papas, but there is ample evidence that there was within them devotion, sacrifice, kindness and love. The home was the core of Jewish life for women; they were concerned about their husbands, their children. In this respect, there was no change in the history of the American Jewish woman since the arrival of the first family in the seventeenth century. In 1890, the family remained firmly entrenched as Jewry's basic institution. Papa was the nominal lord and master; his chief concern was his store or job. Mama was in the kitchen when she was not with the Ladies' Aid; the daughter was in the parlor putting in her daily stint pounding the piano. In a country that worshiped success, the goal of a typical Jewess was to raise a family, rise to affluence, practice the customary amenities, and, when she had time, read a book, a sentimental romance.

·4·

The Emerging American Jewess, 1893—1919

Education

I T did not require much schooling to read one of Mrs. E.D.E.N. Southworth's novels—this much schooling the women possessed. Indeed, illiteracy among the natives and the Americanized immigrants of German stock was practically nonexistent. By the turn of the century, there were already a respectable number of ambitious women who were set on making careers for themselves because of their training in a secondary or a higher school. Over the decades of the twentieth century, the Jewish girls gradually extended their academic reach, influenced by the spirit of the times, and a desire to advance themselves both culturally and socially. In the earlier decades of the nineteenth century, however, an elementary education was adequate. Then came a finishing school. Later they started going to a high school. In Cleveland, more girls than boys opted for high school; the boys went to work, the girls were preparing to teach. As late as 1915, relatively few Jewesses were enrolled in institutions of higher learning. A statistical study revealed that of the ten thousand Jews in colleges, only one thousand were women. There were almost three times as many Gentile women in attendance as Jewesses. However, the percentage of Jewish women in the Eastern schools was about 5 percent; in the metropolitan areas they were beginning to flock to the colleges, where education was good and often free. Many of these students were the children of East European immigrants. By 1920, an increasing number of bright girls were beginning to matriculate. That year about 2 percent of the girls at Wellesley were Jewish; this at a time when the country's Jewry numbered a little over 3 percent of the total population! But let it be borne in mind, Wellesley was an exclusive school. All in all, by that time the percentage of Jewish women in schools of higher learning was probably as high as that of Gentile women. However, the facts must be viewed in their context. Most girls, natives or newcomers, were looking for a husband, not for an education. Marriage and home was deemed a proper fulfilling career for every young lady.

In the colleges, Gentiles kept Jewish girls at a distance socially. And since the Gentiles set the tone, the imitative Jewesses had no choice but to establish sororities of their own. By 1917, there were five such national associations. This was in no sense a youth movement. These young ladies had no quarrel with established authority. Their sororities did not symbolize rejection of the basic standards established by their parents; the ideals of most girls were essentially bourgeois. It is true that the children of the Central European immigrants wanted no German, more speedy Americanization, and less Hebrew in the liturgy; ultimately they hoped to enter the social world of the rising middle class.

Making a Living

With education came jobs. Schooling stimulated Jewish women to make something of themselves; a few even opted for a career rather than domesticity, though it is probable that they would have sought both if the two could have been reconciled. Women who had grown up in an earlier decade, when young ladies did not go to college, now took courses to improve themselves. One affluent volunteer social worker listened to lectures on sociology, criminology, and scientific philanthropy. A few who were determined on an independent life for themselves pursued graduate work both here and abroad. Now and then a Jewess received an academic appointment—this in an age when scholars like Ludwig Lewisohn, Morris

R. Cohen, and Horace M. Kallen had to fight desperately to secure and retain college jobs.

It was somewhat easier for Jewish women to make their way as divas, virtuosos, and conservatory teachers. Endowed with a glorious voice and an indomitable determination to rise to the top, the Rumanian immigrant Alma Gluck (1884—1938) succeeded in making her debut, though not in a major role, at the Metropolitan Opera House in 1909. Grateful for all that America had made possible for her, she never forgot to fly the flag on the Fourth of July. Artistry seems to have run in the family, for Alma's son, Efrem Zimbalist, Jr., became a noted actor. The Glucks, Alma and her husband, became Christians; so did other Jewesses of her generation. Why? This is difficult to determine. Conviction? Possibly. For some of these converts, Christianity was Americanism. There was no social status in Judaism, in being a Jew; there was in Episcopalianism. It is not improbable that Gluck, a Rumanian emigrant, saw nothing ennobling in the Balkan Jewish religious traditions from which she had emancipated herself. In the new cultural world into which she entered, Judaism meant little if anything to her; it could only be a hindrance. The cultured Berlin salon women were of the same thinking.

The stage had always attracted Jewish women since the days when Adah Isaacs Menken toured the theatres and music halls of America. If one were to judge by "Jewish" names, there were Jewish actresses here long before that. The women who appeared on the stage in New York City in the decades before and after 1900 included some who had already made a career for themselves by using Yiddish as their artistic vehicle. Bertha Kalich starred in the Yiddish theatre before she brought her intensity and emotionality to the English stage; aided by her friend Emma Goldman, Alla Nazimova introduced the traditions of the Moscow Art Theatre. Few theatrical innovators have contributed more to the American theatre than Theresa Helburn (d. 1959), who for many years was the executive director of the Theatre Guild, and, in a later decade, brought George Bernard Shaw, Eugene O'Neill, and the musical *Oklahoma* to its subscribers and clients. She and her coadministrator Lawrence Langner helped produce over two hundred plays.

Fannie Brice (née Borach) was a mimic, comedienne, and torch singer who delighted audiences in the theatre and over the radio for over a generation. This daughter of an East Side saloonkeeper had begun her career at the age of thirteen, when she won an amateur-night contest. She was one of the attractions of "Ziegfeld's Follies." Another one of Ziegfeld's stars was the French-born Anna Held, later to become his wife. According to the solemn assurance of her press agent, this petite comic-opera star bathed daily in gallons of milk.

Enterprising needy women in that generation were no longer compelled to remain at home and endure genteel poverty. Forced to support a large family, the Rosenfield sisters established one of the largest secretarial and translation services in the country. At one time they had six offices and employed forty typists. Rebekah Kohut (1864 [1866?]—1951) was faced with the same problem as the Rosenfield sisters. Widow of the great scholar Alexander Kohut, she was left with a number of stepchildren to support when but thirty years of age. There was an estate, but in a few years that was lost. She girded her loins, and in 1899 opened the Kohut College Preparatory School for Girls, a day and boarding institute where she taught about one hundred girls a year. She maintained high academic standards and attended classes in pedagogy at New York University in order to make her work more effective. The school was very successful, but she gave it up in 1906 because she felt her children needed her. Even before her husband's death, she had evinced an interest in social welfare that was, over the years, to make her one of New York City's outstanding workers in the philanthropic field. She described her struggles and her achievements in several autobiographical volumes; they are well-written, informative, and what is even more important, interesting.

Women turned to nursing and social work. A few became lawyers; some became physicians. Ambitious girls had been going to women's medical schools for almost two generations. Matriculation was easy, for standards were low; actually the curricula of most medical schools before the Abraham Flexner Report of 1910 were so inadequate that many Americans found it advisable to pursue advanced study in Europe. By the end of the 1800's about 10 percent of the students in the eighteen better medical colleges were women. It was not until the early decades of the next century that male physicians succeeded in establishing an unofficial but effective quota for all females, as they did for Jewish applicants. From that time on the number of women graduates was sharply reduced.

Frances Stern achieved distinction in the new field of dietetics and home economics. What she set out to do, not unsuccessfully, was to combine studies in homemaking, diet, and nutrition, compatible with available income, into one harmonious whole. In this effort, she showed herself to be a unique social worker.

By the time World War I had come to an end, a number of American women had won some recognition for their work. In the 1890's, the bacteriologist Lydia Rabinowitsch-Kempner (d. 1935), a native of Lithuania, taught for a time in the Women's Medical College in Philadelphia before returning to Berlin, where she worked closely with Robert Koch. She is said to have been the first woman in Prussia appointed a professor. Martha Wollstein busied herself in the Rockefeller Institute, but although her immediate superiors were Jews, she never received a formal appointment to the staff. Ida Henriette Hyde (née Heidenheimer) served as professor of physiology at the University of Kansas. She had engaged in research in the United States and Europe, but constant obstructions by her instructors made it extremely difficult for her to pursue her studies. Miss Hyde went to Germany to further herself at a time when no woman could matriculate at any German university; she finally received her doctorate at Heidelberg, the first woman ever to receive a degree there. She opened the way for others to follow the path which she had hewn for herself through a jungle of prejudice—one distinguished scholar had vowed that "skirts should never enter his laboratory." In 1896, she was the first of her sex permitted to do research at the Harvard Medical School. She recounted the heartaches she encountered in Europe in an article to which she gave the rather felicitous title: "Before Women Were Human Beings."

Kate Levy, of New York and Chicago, a physician, taught medicine for a time at Northwestern University. Another physician, Love Rosa Hirschmann Gantt, of Spartanburg, South Carolina, fought the ravages of pellagra and worked to establish a public health program in southern Appalachia despite vigorous opposition from the state authorities. South Carolina's governor and his associates were of the opinion that medical inspection of schoolchildren was an invasion of the sacred privacy of the individual. Dr. Gantt was also interested in fighting delinquency among young girls and giving women the right to vote.

Aside from the indifference of the colleges and the hostility of the instructors, a major problem faced by women who wished to do graduate work in the natural and social sciences was the obstacles placed in their path by members of their own family. Jessica Blanche Peixotto (d. 1941) was kept out of college for ten years by her father, who frowned on her desire for further academic study. At college, too, she ran into trouble with the faculty, for she urged the girls to shorten their skirts to the shoe tops. Despite all this, she finally became a full professor of economics and a vice-president of the American Economic Association.

Adhering to the trend established in earlier days, women turned in large numbers to teaching. Florence Eilau Bamberger specialized in pedagogy. Born in 1882, she was the first woman appointed to the faculty of the school of philosophy at Johns Hopkins and finally became a full-time professor. In the 1930's, she was an executive in the College for Teachers; her final assignment there was as director of the entire school of pedagogy. This was no mean achievement; in those days, Johns Hopkins was not eager to give professorial appointments to Jews. Florence Bamberger had begun her career in the public schools as a supervisor; in later years she was visiting professor at a number of American colleges. Like other notables in her field, she was progressive in the views which she expressed in her books and brochures.

The Jewess in Literature

As American-born women entered into the world of education, learning, and literature, they began to make their presence felt in ever increasing numbers. Throughout the early twentieth century, they faithfully continued a literary tradition then over a century old.

As early as the eighteenth century, girls were taught to write a good English letter; their daughters and granddaughters had already turned to poetry by the opening decades of the nineteenth century. In post—Civil War days, these young ladies insinuated themselves into the male literary societies of the new generation of "Young Men." The cultural horizons of these women were further broadened by their visits to the men's clubs, where plays and operettas in both English and German were presented. Trinidad, Colorado, a bustling coal-mining town on the Santa Fe Trail, could boast of its Montefiore Literary Society in 1894, and proudly displayed a lithograph of the famous Anglo-Jewish philanthropist alongside a picture of his Continental counterpart, Baron Maurice de Hirsch. Three people constituted the program committee, the rabbi and two women. Was this the sum total of the Jewish literary and cultural resources of the community? Very likely. In 1905, when the social worker Charles S. Bernheimer compiled his excellent book, *The Russian Jew in the United States*, he chose four women to help him: Henrietta Szold wrote on the elements of the Jewish population in the United States; Minnie F. Low, a social worker, discussed the Chicago Jewish charities; Dr. Kate Levy described the health and sanitation conditions under which the "Russian" Jews of that city lived; and Mrs. Benjamin Davis wrote a chapter on the religious life of the East European Jews in Chicago. She was quick to point out that very little provision was made for the religious education of girls. What she could not know was that the very next year Cleveland girls were to help put out an all-Hebrew magazine in their religious school; Samson Benderly in New York was to train women to be religious-school leaders (1910), and Mordecai M. Kaplan was to introduce the bat mitzvah ceremony (1922). Girls were to be treated as peers of the bar mitzvah boys.

By 1919, it would not have been difficult to compile a bibliography of English books, stories, plays, and novels written by American Jewesses. The record was not unimpressive. Emma Wolf had discussed the problem of intermarriage, and Martha Wolfenstein, a rabbi's daughter, had published some charming nostalgic tales of the German ghettos. Edna Ferber (1887—1968) and Fannie Hurst (1889—1968), two Midwestern natives, were now coming into their own; their names would become household words in decades to follow, and they would find their niche in the history of American popular fiction. Both wrote short stories and novels that were eagerly read. Ferber, the more successful of the two, was awarded a Pulitzer Prize; both wrote books and tales that were made into motion pictures. A proud Jewess with a wry sense of humor, Ferber once wrote:

> The entire output of my particular job depends on me. . . . All the wheels . . . contained in the space between my chin and my topmost hairpin. And my own horror is that some morning I'll wake up and find that space vacant and the works closed down, with a metal sign over the front door reading: "For rent, fine, large, empty head; inquire within."

Hurst married a Russian Jewish musician, much to the dismay of her mother, who looked upon all East European Jews with utter contempt. What a comedown for a nice German Jewish girl from St. Louis, Missouri. A kike! (In another decade, American Jewish suitors of East European parentage would be welcomed in the best homes. Ethnic provenance would mean nothing if the young man was otherwise acceptable and attractive.) Now long forgotten, Martha Morton was one of America's most successful playwrights. Mary Antin, an immigrant from Polotsk, wrote beautifully and touchingly on immigration and her beloved America. She was something of a heroine because of the national recognition she had received for her writing while still a teenager. In 1912, she wrote *The Promised Land* and later *They Who Knock at Our Gates*. Her presentation of the immigrants was a healthy antidote to the pseudoscientific claptrap of the racists and the chauvinism of certain political economists and sociologists. It was Antin who said: "What we get in the steerage is not the refuse but the bone and the sinew of all the nations."

Rosa Sonneschein (1847—1932), a most charming woman, a Hungarian immigrant, had come to this country in 1869 with her brilliant rabbi-husband. She too was brilliant and able. In 1895, her *American Jewess*, a women's paper, made its appearance, but even she, with all her verve and appeal, could not keep it alive. When they did read, the thousands of East European ghetto women turned to Yiddish weeklies and newspapers; there were a very substantial number of English readers among the native-born women, but there was little in Sonneschein's paper to attract them. She pursued a moderately liberal course, expressing sympathy for the new Zionism, pleading for synagogal rights for women, and stressing the beauties of home and marriage for girls. Propagating the race is woman's most important mission. Certainly she could not compete with the *Woman's Home Companion* and the *Ladies' Home Journal*, both more attractive in content, form, and illustration. Ultimately, these two monthlies would enjoy a circulation in the millions, but by 1899 the *American Jewess* had ceased to appear.

Influenced by their fellow-Baltimorean Leo Stein, the Cone sisters, Claribel (1864—1929) and Etta (1870—1949), developed an ardent and intelligent interest in French contemporary painting. Their magnificent joint collections of modern art, textiles, and ceramics ultimately found a home in the Baltimore Museum of Art. In Paris, where she had settled, Leo's sister Gertrude Stein (1874—1946) had begun to make a name for herself. The family had made money in the manufacture of clothing, and saw to it that Gertrude was educated at Radcliffe. Shrewd, highly intelligent, with an avid interest in reading—which once even included the *Congressional Record*—Gertrude became an expatriate, spending most of her life in Paris, where she presided over a salon, collected modern art, encouraged painters of the new schools and developed a distinctly Steinian avant-garde literary oeuvre. Gertrude Stein was convinced that she was "the creative literary mind of the century," and was certainly controversial, always interesting, and not without influence on such American writers as Ernest Hemingway.

Women, Judaism, and the Rabbinate, 1893—1919

Like her mid-nineteenth-century mother, the typical Jewess of the early twentieth century was committed to religion, in principle at least, although by the 1890's a substantial minority among Jewish women were unaffiliated. A minuscule group had no desire even to be identified as Jewish religionists. Ida H. Hyde was an Ethical Culturist; Mrs. Gantt had married a Presbyterian, but remained an ardent devotee of Judaism and served as president of the Ladies'

Auxiliary of Congregation B'nai Israel in Spartanburg. Dr. Kate Levy, the Chicago physician, worked in a local Jewish settlement house and labored for the Jewish community. It is very difficult to generalize about those Jewish women who had long put away their kitchen aprons; no two were alike.

This period might be dubbed the Age of the Emerging Jewess; it might just as well be called the Age of Reaching Out. Slowly, very slowly, women began moving into a taboo area where they had never ventured before, the rabbinate. In earlier years they had thought about it; now they began to talk about it. There had been a female student at the Hebrew Union College when the first classes met in the subterranean vestry rooms of Cincinnati's Mound Street Temple in October 1875. Little Julia Ettlinger, a mere child in the public school, might have been back home, sitting on the kitchen floor juggling jacks instead of juggling Hebrew verbs with thirteen high school lads. For generations, girls continued to enroll in this school and earn the Bachelor of Hebrew degree; one almost finished the rabbinic course, but none was ordained before the 1970's. In 1892, Hebrew Union College Professor Heinrich Zirndorf wrote a book, *Some Jewish Women*, but thought it wise to stop with the talmudic period. That same year, a handful of assembled liberal rabbis recommended equality for women in synagogal administration, but nothing more was done.

Five years later there was a newspaper report, for what it was worth, that a woman was serving as president of the Corsicana, Texas, congregation. The wheels were turning slowly. In 1921, the Hebrew Union College authorities refused to oppose the ordination of women. The problem was a real one; a female student wanted to know where she stood. Soon, the Central Conference of American Rabbis was more or less compelled to address itself to the issue. Professor Jacob Z. Lauterbach, Reform Jewry's authority on "canon law," declared *ex cathedra*, as it were, that the ordination of women was contrary to the spirit of tradition. He was quite right, but he failed to mention what of course all the rabbis knew: that here in the United States, as far back as 1869, Reform Judaism had broken abruptly and decisively with Jewish legal tradition. Then, having done his duty by God and His Law, this very same professor and a group of others proceeded to sign a resolution stating that ordination should not be denied women—but again nothing more was done. The following year, 1923, the Board of the College went on record as definitively opposing the ordination of women. Years later, in 1939, Helen Hadassah Levinthal, the daughter of a Brooklyn Conservative rabbi, successfully completed all the requirements for graduation at New York's liberal seminary, the Jewish Institute of Religion. Rabbi Stephen S. Wise, the president, who stood out on the left on most social and religious questions, could not bring himself to ordain her. Women judges, yes! Women rabbis, no! The times were not ripe.

The push for the ordination of women really began with Ray (Rachel) Frank (1864/5—1948), a Californian; she aspired to rabbinical leadership, though she was never to make an unequivocal declaration of intent. Early in the 1890's, the European Jewish press carried garbled accounts about her. They said she was a graduate of the Hebrew Union College, that she was a preacher in Oakland, California, that she had officiated as a rabbi in Oklahoma. What are the facts? Her background was Orthodox; her father, a former Indian agent, claimed descent from Elijah of Vilna, the eighteenth century's most distinguished talmudic scholar. Ray had received a relatively good secular education and had improved herself by reading wisely. She was a close friend and correspondent of the California journalist and writer Ambrose Bierce. Completely self-taught in Jewish matters, Ray was well-versed in both Jewish history and Judaism, though there is no doubt that her sources were all secondary. She taught school in a Nevada village, worked as a journalist, lectured, wrote short stories, trained as an elocutionist, and preached frequently—and it is said, eloquently. In 1890, this spirited, aggressive woman induced Spokane Jewry to meet for the High Holydays and conducted services for them.

By January 1893, she had visited the Cincinnati rabbinical seminary and had listened to lectures for a few months. What she had in mind is difficult to determine; a local newspaper referred to her as a female messiah! By this time, Ray Frank's reputation was nationwide; the rumors about her continued to circulate. It was said that congregations were ready to engage her; actually, she was never employed as a rabbi, though she was often invited to speak from both Jewish and Christian pulpits. Initially hostile to women's rights, she made her peace with the prospect years later, when the adoption of the twentieth amendment was inevitable. After her marriage to Professor Simon Litman of the University of Illinois, she finally settled in Champaign-Urbana, where she took an interest in the first Hillel Foundation, which had its origin there. Actually, Ray Frank was very much interested in the rabbinate, but she had qualms. She believed that rabbis could enjoy no real freedom in the pulpit as long as they drew a congregational salary. She emphasized this years before Stephen S. Wise established his Free Synagogue. When the Jewish Women's Congress was convened at the Chicago World's Fair in 1893, Ray opened it with a prayer and made one of the principal addresses. In an interesting but equivocal speech, she told her audience—all middle-class females—that woman's place was in the home, that no woman wanted to be like a man. Subconsciously at least, that was for the record. She also told her auditors that women were the intellectual equals of men, that in the area of the practical—she meant synagogal work—they were men's superiors. The ladies had earned the right to be rabbis and congregational presidents. Here she was indeed speaking for herself.

The Sisterhood as Synagogal Auxiliary

Ray Frank unfailingly exploited her personality; her medium was the Judaism to which she was utterly devoted—not that she was exceptional in this respect. During the 1890's, thousands of women played a very active part in congregational life in the sisterhoods, the women's societies attached to synagogues. One of the older San Francisco Jewish congregations had a sisterhood of seven hundred members. It is not easy to determine why so much interest was generated and employed in synagogal work at this time. Was it because the women had more leisure? Were they influenced by the activity of their Christian counterparts in church auxiliaries and civic clubs? Were women, for some reason that defies our analysis, now bent on asserting their female consciousness? It was all but inevitable in the early twentieth century that the astute executive secretary of the Union of American Hebrew Congregations, Rabbi George Zepin, would encourage these auxiliaries to work even more closely with their own congregations and with the national Union. In 1913, they came together in the National Federation of Temple Sisterhoods. A few years later, the women's organizations of the Conservative movement followed suit and established the Women's League of the United Synagogue.

What did these sisterhoods set out to do? In 1915, Mrs. Carrie Simon, one of the founders of the Reform movement's National Federation of Temple Sisterhoods, delivered a programmatic address at a biennial convention of the Union of American Hebrew Congregations. Hers was a cautious, relatively conservative statement; she stressed social service, the synagogue, the religious school, and the home. Although not a feminist, she did remind the Union delegates of their failure to co-opt many women for service on synagogal boards. Were women ready for such responsibilities? She answered that tacit question by lauding the achievements of the many Jewesses who were distinguishing themselves as poets, novelists, essayists, educators, civic and social workers. She did make one particularly constructive suggestion: something had to be done about the intermarried couples. However, instead of haranguing her audience on the evils of marrying Gentiles, Mrs. Simon suggested that it was the job of the synagogue and its sisterhood to bring intermarried couples closer to Judaism. This was a constructive approach which a later generation would employ successfully.

What did the sisterhoods do? What did they *not* do! To a substantial degree, they were the money-raising arm of the synagogue. They held fairs, whist parties, rummage sales; they published cookbooks which brought in thousands of dollars. They solicited funds to outfit the temple; they equipped the kitchen, catered the annual Passover dinner and congregational banquets. When East European refugees began arriving in Atlanta, the women of the Reform congregation opened a soup kitchen in the basement of the temple. It was the "ladies" who paid off the synagogue's mortgage and provided scholarships for Hebrew Union College students. The women, as "promoters of everything good and noble," were expected to help support the "indigent" youngsters. The sisterhoods arranged musicales, organized classes, planned lecture series, and entertained young men and women attending the local university. The funds to maintain the Sabbath schools frequently came from their coffers; the sisterhoods, or their associate societies, would even purchase clothes for an impoverished confirmand. The holiday entertainment to which the children looked forward so eagerly was sponsored by this omnipresent synagogal society. These organizations established junior female auxiliaries and called parent-teacher associations into being. On rare occasions, the sisterhood would even conduct a worship service in the sanctuary.

The men in most Reform and Conservative synagogues were always ready to let their wives do the work, to maintain the house of worship as a going concern. The husbands were only too happy to delegate responsibility; charity was women's work. These women's societies were, in a way, the most important link between the congregation and the home. In a later generation, when Reform sisterhoods moved out into the community at large, they evinced an interest in international peace, but more realistically devoted a great deal of time to the blind. In this work they cooperated closely with the Women's League of the Conservatives. These two religious associations set up a Talking Books Library which prepared hundreds of works for the blind of all religions and races. Because the ladies of the Women's League were generally closer to Jewish tradition, they emphasized Sabbath observance, dietary laws, home ceremonies, and Jewish education for both children and adults. Did the ladies of the sisterhoods in the 1920's believe that they were a brave little band arrayed against the world, united by mystical ties that bound them together as women? The answer is no. Did they enjoy a socioreligious feeling of "community" which strengthened the ties that united them as women and Jews? The answer is yes.

Women's Clubs and National Organizations

It is probable that by 1920, the typical sisterhood was no longer a charity dispenser rendering "personal service." The sisterhood member thought of herself as a religionist whose prime concern was to keep the sygagogue solvent. She was the congregation's "housekeeper." She was certainly no clubwoman oriented to general culture or to society at large, someone given to fretting about the state of the universe. That was not her job. Of course there were Jewesses who wanted to be clubwomen, just like their Christian peers. Gentile women had been asserting themselves ever since the late 1860's; one of the instrumentalities they employed was the club. Through it they set out to build a new way of life, in the hope that their inmost selves, their psyches, would come to flower. They created an endless series of clubs ranging through the arts, the social sciences, and diverse realms of philanthropy. The goals envisaged were civic reform, suffrage for women, abolition of child labor, and control of crime and alcoholism. The clubwomen sought better government and international peace. They were determined to cope with problems exacerbated by the new unrestrained industrialism. This women's movement was no small thing; by 1914, the General Federation of Women's Clubs had over a million members; by 1920, equal suffrage was the law of the land. Women were here not only to be seen, but to be heard.

By 1890, there were already a number of Jewish women displaying the club mentality; they had no clubs, but they wanted civic reform and political rights for themselves. Radical Reform rabbis, like Emil G. Hirsch, of Chicago, were in a quandary. They dared not abandon their liberal stance: women were entitled to equality—but was not a woman's place in the home rather than the voting booth? Hirsch told the women that they really did not want the franchise; most in fact did not, but there were some who did. Writing in a Jewish newspaper, a San Francisco editor assured the ladies that the vote would generate domestic rivalry. Young Belle Fligelman, of Helena, Montana, was of a different opinion; as a suffragist, she went out on street corners and campaigned for women. Mother Fligelman, wife of the owner of the New York Dry Goods Store, was unhappy, and threatened to lock Belle out of the house if she persisted. She persisted, spent the night at the local hotel, and sent the bill to her father. Mother relented. Belle campaigned for Jeannette Rankin, the first woman elected to Congress, and in 1917 accompanied her to Washington as an aide.

There may have been no Jewish clubs, but there were two kinds of Jewish "clubwomen"; the one was a *Jewish* clubwoman—the other was a *clubwoman* who happened to be Jewish. (A clubwoman was a type; it was immaterial whether one belonged to a club or not.) In a number of cases, the ladies were both clubwomen and committed Jewesses. The clubwoman per se was primarily interested in general, civil, humanitarian, and cultural goals; the "Jewish clubwoman" devoted herself primarily to Jews and their problems.

Annie Nathan Meyer, a young scion of a Revolutionary War militiaman, the daughter of a family whose members were pillars of the Spanish and Portuguese Synagogue, had an exemplary career. Although she had no formal college training, she believed that New York's women had a right to a school of their own. In 1889, when only twenty-two years of age, she induced Columbia to establish Barnard College for women. Two years later she edited and wrote the introduction to a book entitled *Woman's Work in America*. Some of the most distinguished women in America contributed chapters. In her introduction, Annie wrote that women were moving forward; they were out doing things, surviving despite the hardships they faced as women. Was she a feminist? Not necessarily, for she was willing to grant the vote to women only if they could qualify educationally.

Jennie (Mrs. Moses L.) Purvin (1873—1958), of Chicago, was an activist in both the general and the Jewish communities. She fought for supervised public recreational facilities in her city and saw to it that the lakeshore would no longer be used as a garbage dump. She is the person who was largely responsible for establishing the city's bathing beaches. (When she was a girl, her parents had not thought it proper for young ladies to learn how to swim!) She led parent-teacher associations and worked closely with the Women's City Club. Purvin helped sponsor open-air concerts, and for two years served as treasurer of the Illinois Federation of Women's Clubs. Civic and humanitarian tasks kept her busy till the early 1930's, when the ravages of the Great Depression induced her to seek employment with Mandel Brothers, one of the city's largest department stores. Then a woman of sixty, she established Mandel's art gallery to further native talent, and ran camp advisory and women's club bureaus. It was through her efforts that a variety of services were made available at Mandel's for the women's associations of the city.

Jennie Purvin was a "good" Jewess; her brother Harvey, a rabbi, was a devoted disciple of Emil G. Hirsch. She was a dedicated civil servant and social worker. When she had time, she wrote short stories and published essays on the social problems of the day. When the young, struggling Zionist movement needed her help, she rallied to its support, serving as vice-president of the prestigious Chicago Committee for Palestine Welfare. This was a group headed by Chicago's female Jewish social leaders. Jennie served as secretary of the Chicago branch of the Jewish Welfare Board, president of the local section of the National Council of Jewish Women, and head of Sinai Congregation's sisterhood; she was a member of the city's Board of Jewish Education and administered a loan fund to help those Hebrew Union College students who attended the University of Chicago during the summers. In 1910, Chicago's eighty Jewish female associations were federated. This was indeed an achievement of note. These women came together and discussed anything and everything—suffrage, education, juvenile delinquents, the blind.

It was something of an achievement when Mrs. William Dick Sporborg was elected president of the Federation of Women's Clubs of the city of New York. Later, in 1926, she was called upon to lead the National Council of Jewish Women. Even more distinguished was the career of Mrs. William Einstein, one of the outstanding Jewish clubwomen in the United States. Hannah Bachman Einstein (1862—1929) was for many years the presiding officer of New York's Temple Emanu-El Sisterhood for Personal Service. Instead of sewing shrouds for the Holy Society, for the Righteous Women, she took courses at both Columbia and the New York School of Philanthropy. A trustee of the United Hebrew Charities, an important figure in Mount Sinai's Nursing School, a board member of the National Jewish Hospital for Consumptives, she was also an honorary president of the city's Federation of Jewish Women's Organizations. As an outstanding volunteer-professional, she was typical of the new breed of Jewess who labored to introduce those types of social legislation which prefigured the New Deal. Determined to keep families together, Mrs. Einstein lobbied vigorously to

secure pensions for dependent mothers. She was opposed to or-
phanages; impoverished women, she felt, should be subsidized so
that they might remain at home and rear their families. She was one
of the very few women treated as an equal by the elite on the board
of the United Hebrew Charities; no mere joiner, Hannah Einstein
was an intrinsic part of the power structure—she was a doer.

There were women of action in every part of the country;
Hannah Einstein in New York, Jennie Purvin in Chicago, Ida Weis
Friend in New Orleans. It was not easy for women, Jews or Gentiles, to press for social change in the South at the turn of the century. Some Council members in New Orleans were concerned about
the Blacks. They were the truly submerged people; they had finally
touched bottom. To be sure, New Orleans was more tolerant than
most Southern cities. Ida Weis was well-educated for a girl of her
time; her parents had sent her to Europe. It was not too difficult for
her to play the role of a communal worker; her father, Julius Weis,
one of the city's most influential citizens and one of the most
distinguished Jews of the South, was acclaimed as a cotton factor,
banker, and philanthropist. Like Jennie Purvin, Ida Friend bridged
the gap between the two disparate worlds of the Gentile and Jewish
clubwoman. She was a Democratic national committeewoman for
Louisiana, a prominent Wilsonian Democrat, president of the New
Orleans Urban League, of the state's Federation of Women's Clubs,
and, finally, head of the National Council of Jewish Women.

For reasons that are not easy to determine, Chicago Jewry produced a number of notable clubwomen in addition to Jennie Purvin.
Among them were Sadie American, Hannah G. Solomon, and
Jeannette (Mrs. Ben) Davis. Mrs. Davis, a Conservative Jewess, was
the daughter of Samuel Hillel Isaacs, a scholarly antebellum Lithua-
nian immigrant, who distinguished himself as an authority on the
Jewish calendar. She went to Normal School, and after receiving her
degree became a teacher. Influenced by her father, no doubt, she remained loyal to the age-old beliefs, and hallowed the Sabbath in a
traditional fashion. It was her contention that Jewesses who revered
their faith would rest, not shop, on the Sabbath and would spend
time reading the Bible. She probably belonged to that group in the
National Council of Jewish Women which reproached Hannah G.

Solomon for not sanctifying the Sabbath in the customary Orthodox manner. Mrs. Davis was an important figure in Chicago's Hebrew Institute, a settlement house—community center patronized by thousands of young folk of East European stock. She was president of Chicago's Conference of Jewish Women's Organizations and vice-president of the Women's League of the United Synagogue. Her career is eloquent testimony that a woman could be faithful to the old ritual and, at the same time, be a modern clubwoman facing the world about her with all its challenges.

Hannah G. Solomon

There can be no question that there was ferment in American Jewish womanhood in the early 1890's, if one is to judge by the sermons and editorials of reproachful rabbis. The men were apprehensive—their male monopolistic world was threatened. The women may not have known what they wanted, but they were reaching out. The growing consciousness of self on the part of cultured American Jewesses eventuated in the National Council of Jewish Women (NCJW). The ladies had set their hearts on being clubwomen; not only in yearning but after the flesh. They wanted their own organizations, for they were only too well aware that as a class, they were not welcome in the non-Jewish women's clubs. Because these Gentile associations were never devoid of a social character, they were very frequently anti-Jewish. The decade of the 1890's was a period of growing Judeophobia, often disguised, to be sure. Thus it was that the NCJW came to birth at the World's Parliament of Religions, which met at the Chicago Columbian Exposition in 1893. The ecumenical spirit was not absent; two Jewesses were invited by the World's Fair Congress Auxiliary to present papers at a general Parliament of Religions. The Jewesses, like their Christian counterparts, also gathered together in a separate denominational congress to listen to papers of sectarian interest. Hannah Greenebaum Solomon (1858—1942), a member of the exclusive Chicago Woman's Club, was asked by the non-Jewish leaders to call together the Jewish Women's Religious Congress. This she did. This was the first national assembly of Jewesses in the United States.

Hannah Greenebaum Solomon was a member of the Chicago Greenebaum clan, people of means and influence, important in the cultural and musical circles of the larger community. Hannah, like Fannie Bloomfield Zeisler, was a fine pianist and studied under Carl Wolfsohn. She came from a family of doers. In 1853, her father, Michael Greenebaum, had led a mob that rescued a fugitive slave from the hands of a United States marshal. Her parents saw to it that she received a good education. In 1904, she served as an interpreter for Susan B. Anthony when both were delegates to the Berlin International Council of Women. Reflecting the environment in which she was reared, this Reform Jewess wanted no Jewish political state, though she did approve of Palestine as a haven of refuge, and praised the achievements of its colonists. In 1905, after resigning as president of the Council, she continued her career as a clubwoman. Among the institutions to which she devoted herself were the Illinois Industrial School for Girls, the state Federation of Women's Clubs, and the Council of Women of the United States. While serving on a local civic committee, Mrs. Solomon inspected a garbage dump while dressed in a trailing gown of white cotton lace, clutching a matching parasol in her white-gloved hand. But she never floated on cloud nine; this diminutive creature—she was under five feet—knew exactly what she was doing.

The National Council of Jewish Women

When Hannah Solomon called the NCJW into being, she no doubt realized that there was no future for the middle-class, culturally-minded American Jewess in the "better" civic and sociocultural clubs. As a committed religionist, she wanted to establish an organization where Jewish women could express themselves without let or hindrance. She set out to get women out of the kitchen; in fact, many women of her class had long emancipated themselves from the kitchen stove. This new emerging Jewish "fellowship" was patterned, in name at least, on the National Council of Women of the United States, an umbrella organization created in 1888 to unite women working for worthy causes, particularly in the area of political privileges. Hannah Solomon had always been a fervent advocate of equal suffrage, but the NCJW itself was not committed to votes for women; neutrality was imperative in this controversial issue since the husbands, it appears, were not interested in securing the vote for their wives.

Hannah Solomon was not the sole founder of the new national society. She had the support of a number of women, among them Sadie American (1862—1944), who did most of the organizing work. Sadie was a brilliant executive, an important figure in the general social-welfare world of Chicago and New York, and probably more influential on Chicago's philanthropic scene than any other Jewess in the city. She had worked in the Maxwell Street Settlement, taught Sunday school for Emil G. Hirsch, and preached in churches and temples. In later years she moved on to New York City, where she was active in at least one hundred civic and philanthropic associations; she may well have been the outstanding American Jewish social-work clubwoman of her day. The new society, the NCJW, owed as much to her as it did to Hannah Solomon. Both women were strong personalities, and it is not strange that on occasion they clashed, despite the fact that Solomon was the "boss." When Hannah was once criticized by some scripturally-oriented Council Jewesses who resented her failure to observe the Sabbath in a traditional manner, she answered: "I consecrate every day."

Fields of Work, Programs, Goals, and Achievements of the NCJW

What did the NCJW set out to do? What were its programs, its goals, its accomplishments? The conservative-leaning Union of American Hebrew Congregations suggested that the ladies in this new organization emphasize Judaism, Jewish history and literature; their ultimate sphere of influence was the home! Influenced by the women's club movement and the political and religious reformism of Emil G. Hirsch, the founding mothers of the new organization inevitably pleaded for social-welfare changes of a broad, nonparochial nature. Their concern for the larger world about them was reflected in the second half of their organization's motto: "Faith and Humanity." Hannah Solomon and Sadie American were well aware of the challenge of the time, yet they could move no faster than their followers. It was not until the second decade of the twentieth century, after Solomon and American had retired, that the Council began to reach out, to work for slum clearance, low-cost housing, better public schools, child labor laws, juvenile courts, mothers' pensions, uniform marriage and divorce laws, civil service reforms, public health measures, legislative remedies for social ills, and international peace. In later twentieth-century decades, the National Council was active in establishing pre-schools for tots, and programs in public schools; they labored to solve the problem of truancy. They were concerned with golden-age clubs, with "meals on wheels" for the impoverished elderly; they welcomed persecuted German Jewish émigrés, and raised large sums to further education in the State of Israel. The Council's caution in moving to the left is reflected in its attitude to the Woman's Christian Temperance Union. The NCJW would not adopt a resolution, recommended by the WCTU, asking it to condemn the Turkish persecution of Armenians. The National Council suspected that the Christians in Turkey were engaged in missionary work; it also feared that any Jewish protest would endanger the lives of that country's Jews. Jews feared and despised missionaries; the apostasy of a Jew could destroy the integrity of a family.

For approximately the first twenty years of its existence, the NCJW limited itself primarily to "Faith"—that is, to Jewish programs, religion, education, and help for suffering and oppressed Jews. In this respect, it was more "religious" than the typical nondenominational women's club. Though the Council was denominationally neutral, it was dominated by acculturation-oriented Reform Jewesses. Its sense of kinship with World Jewry prompted it to come to the aid of the battered Jews of the Russian empire and, in 1912, to organize the International Council of Jewish Women. For the most part, the emphasis in the early days was on the local branches and their programs. Each section was autonomous and set out to do what seemed right in its own eyes. The programs were twofold: self-improvement and study for the members, and social-welfare projects for the immigrants. (Sociability, of course, was also a matter of significance, for these women thought of themselves as an elite group, and in a way they were.) The self-improvement study circles were important. They listened to lectures on general subjects and studied parliamentary law and even child psychology. But the stress was on materials of a Jewish nature: the Bible, Jewish history, and even synagogal music. They had too much pride to tolerate the *Ave Maria* and Christmas melodies in their choir lofts. They even sponsored a book on Jewish music. Their relations with the Jewish Publication Society and the Jewish Chautauqua societies were close; they worked well with the rabbis. At the 1896 convention of the NCJW, one delegate, an ardent feminist, suggested that the circles study the lives of Jesus and Paul; the best of the New Testament, she said, was Jewish. This was radical talk for that decade.

The big philanthropic job the Council performed—and performed well—was helping immigrant Jewesses, primarily those from Eastern Europe. Council women met these newcomers at the ports of entry, escorted them to trains, and greeted them when they reached their destination. The Council feared "white slavery." Jobs were supplied, residential hotels set up, night schools founded; vocational training was given, and social clubs were established. Settlement houses were opened, with libraries, gymnasiums, and variegated programs. Promising students were given scholarships. Delinquents were aided when they ran afoul of the law and had to appear in the juvenile courts. Once an immigrant had settled down, the Council offered aid in the Americanization and naturalization process; they even reached out to women on isolated farms.

A prime interest of the Council sections was the Sunday school, which they chose as a medium to Judaize, educate, and Americanize the children of immigrants. These schools were often called Mission schools, a term borrowed from the Christians, who had established classes among the poor and underprivileged. The Christian schools were both educational and propagandistic; the Jewish Mission schools, too, were cultural and religious, but equally intent on thwarting the conversionist designs of the missionaries. The National Council put its women on the school boards of synagogues. They believed in the importance of a good Jewish education, patterned on the best methods perfected by the Chris-

Rebecca Gratz (1781-1869). A cultured American Jewish woman who made a contribution to general and Jewish communal service in the nineteenth century.

Abigail Minis (1701-1794). Colonial Jewish matriarch of Georgia who was expelled from Savannah during the Revolutionary War for her Whig sympathies.

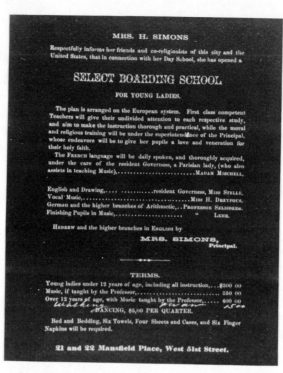

Mrs. H. Simons' "Select Boarding School for Young Ladies." Upwardly mobile German-Jewish girls might well attend an academy of this sort in the nineteenth century.

A PURIM BALL IN NEW YORK CITY
(From Frank Leslie's Popular Monthly, August, 1877)

In nineteenth century American German-Jewish social circles the holiday of Purim was celebrated by masked balls.

Sken-What-Ux, who married a Jewish trader in the latter part of the nineteenth century. She was known as Elizabeth Friedlander.

Courtesy, Maryhill Museum of Fine Arts, Maryhill, Washington

Eugenia Levy Phillips (1820-1902). A fiery anti-Yankee activist, she was expelled from Washington and imprisoned for her political views by General Ben Butler.

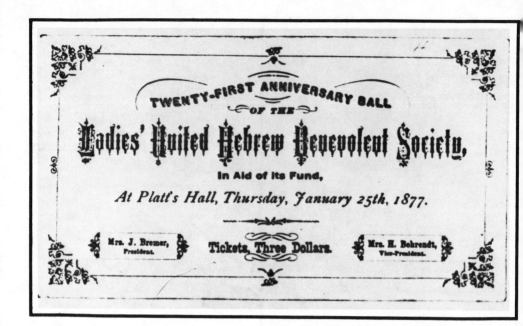

Ladies' United Hebrew Benevolent Society. A direct transplant from Germany, the Society was even listed in American city directories as *Der Israelitische Frauenverein.* It became an important instrument of organized Jewish philanthropic life in America during the nineteenth century.

A landsmanshaft constitution: Kamenets-Podolier Progressive Ladies Association, founded 1908.

The *Landsmanshaftn* were important immigrant self-help associations whose membership consisted of former Jewish residents of the same East European towns or villages. Women, too, had their own *Landsmanshaft* groups.

The World's Congresses
...OF 1893...

PRESIDENT, CHARLES C. BONNEY.

VICE PRES'T, THOMAS B. BRYAN.   TREASURER, LYMAN J. GAGE.

SECRETARIES:

BENJ. BUTTERWORTH.   CLARENCE E. YOUNG.

The Woman's Branch of the Auxiliary.

MRS. POTTER PALMER, PRESIDENT.   MRS. CHARLES HENROTIN, VICE PRESIDENT.

The World's Congress Auxiliary cordially invites you to attend and participate in the deliberations of the Jewish Women's Religious Congress, to convene in the Permanent Memorial Art Palace in the City of Chicago during the week commencing September 3d, 1893, and to attend the Parliament of Religions, September 21st to 26th, inclusive. The favor of an early acceptance is requested.

Clarence E. Young.

Secretary World's Congress Auxiliary.

CHICAGO.

An invitation to attend the Jewish Women's Religious Congress in Chicago. The National Council of Jewish Women, an important national Jewish women's organization, was founded at this congress, held at the 1893 World Columbian Exposition.

Hannah G. Solomon (1858-1942). The first president of the National Council of Jewish Women and an outstanding communal worker.

Carrie Simon (1872-1961). One of the founders of the National Federation of Temple Sisterhoods in 1913, an important organization of the Reform movement. She was an advocate of increased responsibility for Jewish women in religious life.

First page of the first issue of Deborah. (Die Deborah, v. 1. August 24, 1855. p. 1).

Founded in 1855 by Rabbi Isaac Mayer Wise (1819-1900) and published until his death in 1900, the German language newspaper, *Deborah,* was dedicated to the "daughters of Israel."

The first issue of the *American Jewess*, founded by Rosa Sonnes-chein (1847-1932), an early American Zionist who published the message of political Zionism in her newspaper. The *American Jewess* was published from 1895-1899.

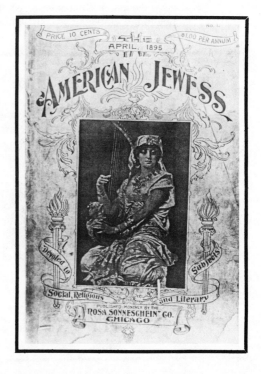

The American Hebrew

The front pages of two leading American Jewish newspapers that devoted whole issues to the American Jewish woman.

The Hebrew Standard

tians in their Sunday schools. The Council was willing to teach Hebrew, but summarily rejected the heder, the traditional Hebrew school, where the sacred language was often taught by an incompetent man in unsanitary surroundings. Julia Richman, the educator, thought that the ghetto heder was not only un-American but "unethical."

Like the congregational sisterhoods, the Council sections were not interested in dispensing charity, friendly visiting, or ministering to the impoverished, but they did render occasional aid to the needy, and did help the blind, the crippled, the unemployed, prisoners, and consumptives. As children of the emerging twentieth century, they believed that the indiscriminate giving of alms degraded recipients. Rather they recommended modern methods to help the poor, advocated the use of trained investigatory personnel, and urged prevention rather than palliation. In general, their programs were akin to those carried on in the Y's, the settlement houses, and the modernized family-service agencies.

Accomplishments of the NCJW

The National Council grew rapidly; by 1896, there were sections in fifty cities and twenty-two states. As early as the third decade of the twentieth century, the Council maintained ten settlement houses and 120 Sabbath schools. It was the largest women's club in both Maryland and Oregon. Working systematically with intelligence and devotion, it was able to help thousands of newcomers. In a programmatic address at the World's Fair in 1893, when the National Council was being established, Sadie American said that this new organization wanted to help American Jewish women educate themselves, exploit their inner resources, and aid the immigrants to find themselves. To a considerable degree, these ends were achieved.

Hadassah

The National Council was oriented to American Jewesses and their opportunities to fulfill themselves as religionists, as Jews, as human beings. Nineteen years after the National Council came into being, a group of women, including Henrietta Szold (1860–1945), founded Hadassah, which ultimately became the Women's Zionist Organization of America. The National Council faced West; Hadassah faced East.

Henrietta Szold was one of the original founders of Hadassah; as later events would prove, she was its most important member. Who was she? A native American, she was one of the many daughters of the Reformist Baltimore rabbi, Benjamin Szold. Her father had no sons, but saw to it that she received a good Jewish and general education. Johns Hopkins was not founded until 1876, Goucher not until 1885, but Henrietta went to high school and in later years audited some courses at the Jewish Theological Seminary in order to improve herself. For many years, she taught in a Gentile private school and volunteered her services in a night school for Jewish immigrants. She had become a Jewish political nationalist even before Herzl wrote *The Jewish State*. In 1893, this exceptional woman became the literary secretary for the Jewish Publication Society. She was well-fitted for the job and functioned—unofficially—as the Society's editor until 1916. It was during this period that she prepared for publication the multivolume editions of the *American Jewish Year Book*, Heinrich Graetz's *History of the Jews*, and Louis Ginzberg's *Legends of the Jews*.

Henrietta Szold moved to New York in 1903; nine years later she and a group of friends, members of a study circle, founded the organization out of which Hadassah soon emerged. Like the original Federation of American Zionists, Hadassah was built from the top down. The founders, most of whom seem to have been native Americans, were thoroughly acculturated, though traditional in bent. Their original goals were simple; they set out to further Judaism in this country and to aid the Jews of the Holy Land. Conditions in Ottoman Palestine were deplorable: the country was languishing under its Turkish overlords; disease, malaria, and trachoma were rife. Romantically, these American Jewesses called their new society Hadassah ("Myrtle"), the Hebrew name of the legendary Persian heroine, Queen Esther, whose exploits are recounted in the Bible. In the course of time Hadassah, over which

Szold presided from 1912 to 1926, became the largest of all the Zionist groups and the largest Jewish woman's organization in the world. In 1978, its rosters listed over 350,000 women.

Henrietta Szold's social station was of importance in recruitment and fund-raising. As a native American of good family, she was able to recruit cultured and wealthy women of the older stock, who lent respectability to the movement at a time when Zionism was summarily rejected by the elite. By 1917, a literacy bill was passed by Congress, and it was rather obvious that it would not be long before America's gates would be closed to Europe's emigrants. Did Szold and her associates sense that sooner or later Palestine would have to serve as a sanctuary for the oppressed Jews of Eastern Europe? Though a fervent Zionist, she was in no sense an extremist; she realized the problem of coping with the country's Arab majority and remained a bi-nationalist throughout her life.

Together with the British and the Zionist pioneers, Hadassah laid the foundations for the medical and social-welfare work that would make Mandate Palestine and its successor, the State of Israel, a livable land with standards acceptable to Western newcomers. Much of the progress made was due to Hadassah. In this respect, the labors of Szold and her associates were extensions of the social work carried on by Jewish women here in the United States. Hadassah began with a nursing service in 1913; by the end of World War I in 1918, a medical unit sponsored by several American organizations, including Hadassah, had reached Palestine. By 1920, already sixty years old, Szold settled in the country and assumed an active role in the medical and social-welfare life of the blighted land. When Hadassah began its work there in the second decade of the century, four out of ten babies did not survive their first year; these American women fought trachoma and malaria, and saw to it that schoolchildren were provided with good milk. In this effort, Szold was influenced by the crusade for pasteurization carried on in the United States by her friend Nathan Straus, the philanthropist. In time, Hadassah brought a degree of hygiene and sanitation into the homes of its clients. It introduced school lunches, provided modern maternity care, established schools for nursing and vocational training, and helped very materially in building Jerusalem's present

Hadassah—Hebrew University Medical Center. As a result, Israeli medical services are said to be the best between Rome and Tokyo. From the day of their inception—and as additional testimony to Miss Szold's vision—these services have been open to all the peoples of the land, Jews and non-Jews alike.

At first, Szold received only grudging cooperation from the male-dominated Zionist establishment; by 1927, her value had been recognized and she was appointed a member of the country's "shadow government," the Palestine Zionist Executive, with the portfolios of health and education. Other honors followed, and in the mid-1930's she was put in charge of youth immigration (aliyah) from Germany. The important accomplishments of Hadassah in education, health, vocational training, and social welfare were now crowned by its successes in Youth Aliyah. Thousands of Jewish adolescents were brought to Palestine from Nazi Germany and prepared for a new life in a new land. Within a few years, the parents of many of them perished in the Holocaust. The first shipload of youngsters landed in 1934; Hadassah assumed formal sponsorship of this "children's crusade" in 1935.

In an eponymous fashion, all the achievements of Hadassah are ascribed to this one American woman, Henrietta Szold. In 1975, the State of Israel memorialized her by engraving her likeness on a five pound note; she had been honored earlier by the issuance of an Israeli postage stamp. Her accomplishments are indeed fabulous, and that is why she is frequently called the Mother of the Yishuv (Israeli Jewry). Still it must never be forgotten that she had devoted help from myriads of Hadassah women, many of them from the humblest walks of life.

Hadassah: What It Did

Hadassah did for Palestine what the American Jewish Joint Distribution Committee did for Eastern Europe. Russian, Polish, and Balkan Jews, it turned out, were kept alive by the "Joint," only to be incinerated by the Germans. Fate decreed that Hadassah would be more fortunate, for the Yishuv, Palestinian Jewry, survived to found the State of Israel. American women helped immensely to rebuild

Palestine materially. Hadassah's social, humanitarian labors in that land are a notable achievement. To accomplish its purposes, it was not unusual for this organization to raise anywhere from $15,000,000 to $30,000,000 a year in the 1970's. These women helped others, and in helping others they helped themselves; they furthered the Zionist movement and thereby developed within themselves a strong sense of self-respect. Here in the United States, Hadassah has stimulated an interest in the study of Jewish life, history, and culture. It publishes a magazine of nationwide circulation; it sponsors an important Jewish youth group, Young Judea. The level of Jewish knowledge and consciousness among many Jewish women in the United States has been significantly raised by Hadassah; this no one can question.

Social Welfare Activity of the American Jewess, 1893—1919

The 1890's marked a radical departure in Jewish life after almost three thousand years. American-born Jewish women continued to stay home, but for many, home served primarily as a base from which to sally forth into the world at large. A number became teachers; others, not a great many, entered the marts of commerce and industry; new opportunities were now opening up to them in the changing world of the early twentieth century. Office help was in demand. Many were now in comfortable middle-class circumstances. They had ample time to follow their inclinations. Homes were full of labor-saving devices; immigrant maids could be hired for a few dollars a week. These relatively affluent, early-twentieth-century matrons were not looking for gainful employment, but they did want something to do, something that would give them a feeling of accomplishment. Desiring to fulfill themselves, many turned to social work. Helping the needy fitted beautifully into the benevolent spirit of the Progressive Era; these women were prepared for the task by an American Jewish tradition reaching back to the year 1819. The collective national desire to succor others was reflected in the rise of the National Council of Jewish Women, Hadassah, the Labor Zionist Pioneer Women, and soon in another mass organization, the Women's ORT.

The period also witnessed the appearance of individuals who made a career for themselves in social service beyond the ambit of the mass societies. Jewish women now had several options; they could turn to the larger general community and disregard the specific needs of their coreligionists, or they could devote themselves more parochially to the Jewish people. If they decided to limit themselves to their own, they could join a branch of a national Jewish organization, interest themselves in a larger communal institution, or attach themselves to one of the smaller traditional charities. Some of the ablest of these women chose to labor on behalf of the American community at large; the Jewish world was too narrow for them.

Who were these women who reached out beyond the Jewish world? What did they accomplish? Some of Margaret Sanger's most enthusiastic supporters in her battle to disseminate birth control information were Jewish women; they helped her organize her clinic and distribute forbidden literature. Others among these Jewish altruists were pacifists; Lillian Wald and Henrietta Szold may be numbered among them. In 1914, after the outbreak of World War I, Rosika Schwimmer came to this country in an effort to stop the spread of the conflict. A Hungarian suffragist and pacifist, she was highly respected by many on the European continent. Here in the United States, she stood in the vanguard of those who organized the Emergency Peace Federation. Their goal was to call a conference of neutrals to reconcile the belligerents, or at least to contain the conflict. Though financed by Henry Ford, she and her cohorts failed; the war to make the world "safe for democracy" continued. Schwimmer remained in the United States, constantly fighting for liberal causes. In the 1920's, her petition for naturalization was rejected—she was damned because of her pacifism—and when she appealed for relief to the Supreme Court, the lower courts were sustained. There were, however, three dissenters on the Supreme Court, Sanford, Brandeis, and Holmes. Justice Holmes, writing the opinion for the minority, implied that Rosika Schwimmer was being punished for believing in the teachings of the Sermon on the Mount.

Sophie Irene Simon Loeb

In the generation before 1920, the country's most effective communal worker and publicist of Jewish origin was Sophie Irene Simon Loeb (1876—1929). Because she wanted to keep families together, she lobbied with legislators to grant pensions to dependent mothers; she found foster homes preferable to orphan asylums. Sophie Loeb labored to secure penny school lunches, lower-priced milk, lower gas rates, more equitable taxation, public play streets, free maternity care for impoverished women, slum clearance, better housing, and the use of schoolrooms as civic centers for immigrants. But she had to make a living, too. In 1913, as a feature writer for Pulitzer's flamboyant *World*, she published a book—*Epigrams of Eve*—whose contents seem hardly in keeping with the social tasks to which she had dedicated herself. A typical selection: "If a woman is a rag, a bone, and a hank of hair, at least there are many willing ragpickers."

The Professional Social Workers

By 1920, it would seem, most paid workers in the charities were men, but there were a few women professionals. It was obvious that there would be some, because women had always carried their share of the charity load. They had been the "caseworkers" during the nineteenth century, and now these female welfare technicians began to appear in many guises. They could be found among probationary officers, teachers in the charity kindergarten, as tenement house inspectors, as administrators of hospitals and orphan asylums. One of them served as the salaried executive of a large New York City Sisterhood for Personal Service. Unlike some of their male colleagues, most of these women cherished the synagogue; they were not hostile to organized religion. Two of them were elected vice-presidents of the National Conference of Jewish Charities. One, Seraphine Eppstein Pisko of Denver (1861—1942), effected a consolidation of the city's general charities, served as president of a Jewish relief society, helped found the National Jewish Consumptive Hospital, and then organized auxiliary groups in many major towns for the hospital's support.

The other vice-president was Miriam (Minnie) Dessau Louis, of New York City. She was a lecturer and district inspector for the New York Department of Education, president of the Hebrew

Technical School for Girls, field secretary for the Jewish Chautauqua Society, chairman of the committee that supervised the Mount Sinai Training School for Nurses, and a Sunday school teacher at Temple Emanu-El. Miriam Louis was one of the founders of the New York City section of the National Council of Jewish Women and a prolific writer of poetry and articles for the press. This list is eloquent testimony to her skills.

Competent women professionals were employed in the several trade schools for girls which had emerged in the big cities of the country. New York City was not the only community to develop such institutions for training the children of the incoming East Europeans. These young immigrant women were taught millinery, cooking, sewing, dressmaking, design. Some of them were given an excellent course in office work. With a broader vision than some of the other schools, the Hebrew Technical School of New York initiated its charges into the world of music, and opened new vistas for them through the social sciences. A few communities set up workshops for indigent women, selling the garments they made. Day nurseries, too, were established for the children of women who were working in the shops. In 1917, there were at least seventeen day nurseries in New York City; most of them were established and run by women. In 1907, the Brightside Day Nursery claimed that, since its establishment in 1893, it had taken care of almost thirty-five thousand tots. Luncheons were provided for five cents. The mothers were gathered together in clubs, and those who wished were given instruction in sewing, embroidering, and millinery. All this sounds very contemporary; today, in the late twentieth century, many working women are keen for the state to fund such infant and child care centers.

The Settlement House

Every community of size in early-twentieth-century America had at least one settlement house in the Jewish ghetto district. Some were established by Gentiles, others by Jews. The settlement house was a social-service center to aid and acculturate immigrants. A typical institution, the Educational Alliance, on East Broadway in New York City, was well-known in the 1890's for the diverse programs which it offered. Its work encompassed educational, social, religious, and even welfare services. For example, the Educational Alliance stood ready to provide legal aid, particularly to women who were faced with the problem of a deserting husband. The plans and schedules of the Alliance included girls and boys, grown men and women; provision was made to assist, educate, entertain, and Americanize all of them. Courses in history, civics, and art were offered; the social program included concerts, lectures, and dramatic presentations. There was a series of clubs, a rabbi led services and gave those who so desired the opportunity to worship.

In one of the Boston ghettos, a favorite resort of some Jewish youngsters was the North End Union, a settlement house sponsored by non-Jews. This institution supported several clubs for Jewish girls; at least one of them was led by Julia Frothingham (d. 1925), a devoted woman who taught the youngsters to appreciate the problems of underprivileged Blacks—in the best tradition of the old abolitionist societies, which had their origin in New England decades before the Civil War. Frothingham taught the girls something about art and read Browning and Tennyson to them, though one sometimes wonders whether a child of ten could appreciate the delicate nuances of these British poets. As the girls grew older, they debated the boys on the subject of equal suffrage. They knew what was going on in the outside world; the ghetto was no ivory tower.

The Maxwell Street Settlement in Chicago's Jewish quarter was run by Ernestine Heller, who, in addition to directing the very busy settlement house, found time to aid the immigrant synagogue across the street, distribute Passover matzos to the poor, keep the records of a slum hospice, and to supervise a nearby day nursery for working mothers. One is tempted to paraphrase Genesis 6:4, "There were (female) giants in the earth in those days."

The Kander Story

No two Jewish settlement house workers were alike. The world knows a great deal about Lillian Wald, whose memory and achievements are now enshrined in the Hall of Fame for Great

Americans. Much less is known about Lizzie Black Kander (d. 1940) of Milwaukee. Mrs. Kander joined the Ladies' Relief Sewing Society, repairing old clothes for immigrants; later she became its president. Because of her ardent interest in helping her fellowman, she would rise at five o'clock in the morning, complete the household chores, and then spend the rest of the day doing social work. She soon became something of an expert on "friendly visiting" among the poor. As a member of the Milwaukee School Board, she helped introduce manual training and domestic science into the public school system. Lizzie Kander was one of the founders of the Milwaukee Jewish Mission, a society which gave children vocational training, including the fine arts. It was this Mission which, in conjunction with the Sisterhood for Personal Service, established the Milwaukee Jewish Settlement House in 1900. Lizzie Kander served as president of "The Settlement" from 1900 to 1918. The Settlement featured clubs, a Sabbath school, and night school classes in history and English. As in all such institutions, a gymnasium and public baths were provided. (Immigrants were always encouraged to bathe frequently.) The girls and their mothers were taught cooking, and in 1901, out of these classes there came forth a modest cookbook, *The Way to a Man's Heart*, prepared by Mrs. Kander and Fanny Greenebaum Schoenberg, an affluent volunteer social worker. Over forty editions have since appeared, the proceeds being used to support a Milwaukee community center. The current edition includes recipes for typical East European Jewish delicacies such as blintzes, matzo balls, kugel, kreplach, knishes, and kishke. Since *The Settlement Cookbook* was initially intended for immigrants, most of whom had come from primitive East European villages, nothing was taken for granted. The cookbook instructed them carefully on how to build a fire, dust a room, and wash dishes. Because most of the Settlement's clients were Orthodox and the institution itself was Jewishly sponsored, no pork recipes were found in the original edition—though recipes for lobsters and frogs' legs were included (the authors were thinking of their own palates): even if forbidden by the Bible, they were so good they just had to be kosher!

Lillian Wald

One of America's most respected social reformers was Lillian Wald (1867—1940), a public health nurse who began her work on the Lower East Side in 1893. A typical social worker of native stock, she was instrumental in bringing uptown women to the downtown ghetto and thereby making it possible for two dissimilar social classes to relate to each other. In order to help the slum dwellers cope with their many problems, she founded the Henry Street Settlement in 1895 with the financial help of Jacob H. Schiff. In less than two decades, she and her associates had a visiting service "manned" by ninety-two nurses who made some 200,000 calls a year in Manhattan. Because of her, the New York City Board of Health introduced public school nursing. Wald's diverse humanitarian activities mark her as a significant figure in the history of social reform; she was a founder of the National Child Labor Committee and a leader of the movement to further the welfare of the very young. Wald agitated for women's suffrage, strove to contain the ravages of tuberculosis, urged the establishment of public parks and playgrounds, spoke against war, and sought to further the goals of the League of Nations. She not only cherished the social ideals of forward-looking clubwomen, she made every effort to effectuate them.

One woman defies description. This was Minnie (Mrs. Charles S.) Guggenheimer (1882—1966). She was neither social reformer nor welfare worker; rather, she was a sociocultural "sport." A "sport" has been defined as "an individual exhibiting a sudden deviation from type beyond the normal limits of individual variation." Once, talking to a huge outdoor audience, she introduced an old beau of hers, Laurence Steinhardt, as the minister to Junkoslavia. This naive, beloved Mrs. Malaprop was the country's best-known unpaid impresaria. From 1918, when she helped found the summer concerts at the Lewisohn Stadium, until her retirement in 1962, she was the chief fund-raiser for the enterprise. Millions of New York music lovers flocked to the performances made possible through her persistent and sacrificial fund-raising efforts. She herself was the most liberal contributor. The open-air concerts she sponsored drew the largest audiences in the world. One could hear a symphony concert for twenty-five cents. Securing sufficient funds was no easy job; it was "forty-four years of blood, sweat, and rain." Here were benevolence, dedication, and cultural impact on a wholesale scale. She embraced all of New York's lovers of melody and harmony when she stepped out of the wings to greet them with her "Hello everybody," as the response rolled back from the assembled thousands, "Hello, Minnie."

Sisterhoods for Personal Service

As the immigrants kept streaming in, the increasing work load facing the old-fashioned ladies' benevolent societies made it difficult for them to cope with the demands confronting them. New women's groups with new approaches arose, and some of the older societies modified and modernized their philanthropic techniques. Possibly influenced by the New York Association for the Improving of the Condition of the Poor, Sisterhoods for Personal Service now appeared. (They are not to be confused with the later National Federation of Temple Sisterhoods.)

In the larger cities, where these sisterhoods were active from the 1890's on, the total area was divided into districts, each assigned to a specific society or synagogal auxiliary. In New York, for instance, the different sisterhoods worked all the way from the New Bowery north to Harlem, and even farther uptown. Of the five thousand cases handled by the United Hebrew Charities in 1917, about a fourth of them were processed by the women volunteers in the sisterhoods. By the late 1890's, these women's groups were so numerous in New York that they were able to form a federation of their own. Later, in 1915, thirty-eight Baltimore societies, with a total membership of over ten thousand Jewesses, came together in the Federation of Jewish Women. Their goal was coordination and increased efficiency.

What did the Sisterhoods for Personal Service do? Were they different from the traditional Ladies' Benevolent Society? In many respects they were often no different than the older benevolent societies of their immigrant mothers. Was it "the same old gal with a different veil"? Or was the new sisterhood another phase in the attempt of a native-born generation to break away from older patterns? The old benevolent societies had always emphasized "personal service" to a fault. Was the renewed emphasis on personal service a reaction to the apparent impersonality of a new breed of social workers? Actually, the sisterhoods which now appeared at the turn of the century were different. The new, acculturated American Jewess reflected the social consciousness of the emerging American clubwoman. Such Jewesses were making a transition from the old-fashioned German Jewish benevolent society to the modern organization, mindful not only of the needs of Jewry, but also of the cultural and welfare demands of the larger America. They were abandoning the religious concept of laying up treasures in heaven and adopting a more scientific approach stressing regeneration and economic independence. Some of these women were more rooted in American than Jewish mores. One worker, disturbed to see an impoverished client eating fish and cake on a Friday night, simply failed to realize the importance and sanctity of the Sabbath meal in the life of a traditional Jew.

In various towns, particularly in New York City, the sisterhoods were miniature social agencies. They opened kindergartens, day nurseries, industrial schools, and workshops; they offered vocational guidance and some training in music; they even searched out jobs for their clients. They founded libraries and religious schools, ran summer camps, provided recreation for their people, and worked closely with the Jewish protofederations then coming into being. In accord with the demands of the newer welfare philosophies, they laid less emphasis on the palliatives, and set out to teach their clients how to budget their modest means—how to work out their own salvation. Obviously the sisterhoods were influenced by the Jewish Y's, the settlement houses, the National Council of Jewish Women, institutional sygagogues, and the exemplary programs set up by Christians laboring to help their own proletarian and lower-middle classes.

Often the sisterhoods became allies of the protofederations, doing legwork for them until the time came when the volunteers were themselves squeezed out by professionals. Female social workers, whether in a settlement house, a sisterhood for personal service, or a relatively autonomous women's charity, helped salvage hundreds, if not thousands, of families.

The Ladies' Aid, 1890—1920

The old-fashioned women's eleemosynary groups persisted into the twentieth century, especially in the smaller towns and cities. Women of the older migrations enjoyed going to the ladies' benevolent society. They loved to meet together, do good, and gossip with their friends. The social aspect was important; indeed, it was a prerequisite if the association was to survive. A philanthropic way of life enveloped the entire family; mother went to the sewing circle, father and son were members of the men's benevolent society, and the daughter frequently volunteered to help wherever she could.

Every women's society had a flavor all its own. The Deborah Unterstuetzungs Verein of Scranton, Pennsylvania, helped the poor, visited the sick, and attended to the needs of its own members. Corsicana, Texas, had a Ladies' Hebrew Cemetery Association; the Young Women's Union of Philadelphia, with hundreds of members, supported a hospice, a day nursery, a kindergarten, a sewing school, and a library; the "best" women in town were on the board: a Fleisher, a Gimbel, a Jastrow, a Muhr, a Friedenwald. The Alpena, Michigan, Hebrew Ladies' Benevolent Society helped finance the temple; it sent money to the National Jewish Hospital for Consumptives, flowers to the sick, and, of course, maintained a Sunday school. Its funds came from dues collected and from the profits of fairs and bazaars. Donations of goods were wheedled out of reluctant wholesalers who did business with their husbands. If Judaism was a tripartite entity of school, prayer, and charity, the Jewesses of America did more than their share, for they ran the schools, raised money to keep the services going, and looked after the needs of many of the community's poor.

The East European Newcomers, 1893—1920:
The "Germans" and the "Russians"

The notable women who graced the Jewish community at the turn of the century—Hannah Einstein, Sadie American, Hannah Solomon, Lillian Wald, Annie Nathan Meyer—represent the old-line native-born and the "Germans"; they are the celebrities who have helped make American Jewish history. Certainly they occupy the limelight; some of them have even won a line or two in the standard one-volume Jewish histories. Yet they represent only a minority of the country's Jewish women; by 1921, these Central Europeans and native Americans were outnumbered at least five to one by East Europeans and their American-born children. Actually, there were two separate Jewish communities, the "Germans" and the "Russians." East European Jews had begun coming to America as early as the seventeenth century; by the 1850's they had a community and a culture of their own in New York City; by the 1890's they dominated American Jewry numerically. Central European Jews looked upon them with suspicion, deemed them uncouth, rejected them because they were "orientals," avoided them because they were Orthodox, detested them because they were Zionists, and held them responsible for the anti-Semitism of the late nineteenth century. The native-born and the arrivés forgot that hotel discrimination was directed not against the impoverished East Europeans, but against millionaires like the Seligmans.

There is some evidence that newcomers here had experienced rejection by their Jewish predecessors ever since the seventeenth century. When the incoming settlers became acculturated, they in turn disdained the next batch of immigrants; one generation of steerage passengers despised the next generation of steerage passengers—it was the Jewish *Mayflower* complex.

Unfortunately for the apprehensive old-timers, the newcomers were also Jews. This meant that—willy-nilly—they had to be helped, and they were helped, sometimes grudgingly, often gladly, even sacrificially. Noblesse oblige? After a fashion. Helping another Jew was not an act of grace; it was a sacred obligation. Still, the relation between the helper and the helped, if not one of love-hate, was commonly a patronizing one. In the final analysis, the prejudice directed against the newcomers was not because they were uncouth (from a Central European cultural point of view), but because they were newcomers. Class and economic status were all-important; ethnic differences were often only a pretext for withdrawal. Nevertheless, differences in European origins encouraged mutual acerbities. The pseudo-Spanish-Portuguese grandees of New York's Shearith Israel looked down on the Rhinelanders and Bavarians; the Bavarians despised the Prussian-Posen-Polack; the Prussianized Polacks kept their distance from all "Russian" Jews; the "Russians" in turn had a descending hierarchy reaching down into the infernal regions. As recently as the second quarter of the twentieth century, a prominent American Jewess—the head of a national Jewish organization and the president of the local symphony board—listened patiently when a friend of hers consoled her because her son had married a Gentile. Her only response was: "At least she isn't a Russian Jewess."

The East Europeans: Economic Survival

The constant problem of the Slavic Jewish newcomers was survival: bread and butter, or, to be more exact, herring and tea. For those in dire need, the established Jewish charities were at hand, but the Russians were loath to turn to the almsgivers; they tried to help themselves. In the course of time they established their own hospitals, hospices, old-folks' homes, and set up women's divisions to support these institutions. The national orders and lodges which the immigrants hastened to organize had auxiliaries offering the women insurance, socializing, and the attractive lure of secret rituals. However, the resources to which the women turned were primarily mutual-aid societies of their own. After the year 1900, there were a great many of them in New York City; for the most part they were hometown and regional associations. It has already been noted that the presidents of such societies were often men because, as with the Germans of an earlier generation, the women had not yet been trained to conduct meetings on their own. As in colonial times, the term of office was only for six months; the president could not afford to give more time; he had to hustle for a living.

In the early twentieth century, Des Moines, Iowa, had three ladies' societies—these in a relatively small Jewish community of about eighteen hundred Jews. Two of them had been organized by the new arrivals. Uprooted from their own European world, these immigrants were looking for "community," for "sisters" to whom they could relate. (Incidentally, having three separate charities in that town made it a paradise for the professional schnorrer, who could exploit them all.) Detroit, a much larger community, had but two women's relief societies—which exchanged lists of their clients. Philadelphia had a Sheltering Home for the Homeless and Aged, a combination hospice and old-folks' home run entirely by immigrant women; they boasted that they had sheltered about thirty thousand strangers. These women were doing a job.

Working Conditions in the Factories and Shops

Most immigrant Jewish women, especially wives, were not employed, although it is estimated that in 1920 about every fifth woman in this country was in the labor force. After marriage, East European women stayed at home and addressed themselves to the task of rearing families. Many of them did keep a boarder or two, and, on occasion, sewed garments for subcontractors. In the 1890's, the women who went out to work were the young ones; they found jobs in the garment industry. How many Jewish girls were employed in such work is not known; not everyone who worked was hunched over a sewing machine. However, it is estimated that over 50 percent of the Jewish women employed in New York were making dresses, waists, and the like.

Working conditions in the factories and sweatshops were not good. They were bad for the men, and worse for the women, who worked just as hard but were paid less. The bosses who exploited them were nearly always fellow-Jews. The hours were long, the wages low. To be sure, exploitation of female mill hands was an old American tradition. The women who toiled in the Lowell textile factories in the late 1840's put in a fourteen-hour day. Pauline Newman, a labor organizer, recalls that as a child she was paid $1.50 for a seven-day week; during the busy season she labored till nine o'clock at night, but there was no overtime pay. In the early twentieth century, Jewish girls fourteen to sixteen years old were paid $3 for every thousand cigarette boxes they turned out, though some women, skilled machine operators, made a great deal more money, especially in season. It is also evident that wherever there were male foremen, there would be sexual harassment. Most shops were dirty and lacked adequate protection against fire. The states had passed legislation governing safety conditions in the shops, but they were observed in the breach. Eight-, nine-, and ten-year-olds were working for New York City's Triangle Waist Company in 1901; when an inspector came in, the children would scamper into a crate under a pile of garments until the officials had left.

Unions? There were no unions of any consequence before 1910, when the women decided to fight for better working conditions. Apparently the times were ripe, for in 1909 these young women in the blouse and dress industry made history in the "Uprising of the Twenty Thousand." Many of these teenagers were of heroic stature. They had been fired up to resist by the impassioned appeals of the young worker Clara Lemlich—at a time when their own male leaders hesitated to take action. These girls persisted despite brutal police, unsympathetic courts, and a hostile press. Hundreds of young women were arrested; some were sent to the workhouse and made to scrub floors for two weeks. The following year saw a series of strikes in the garment industries of New York, Chicago, and other cities; some gains were made. The women among the workers developed a consciousness of the need to join forces to gain their ends.

The 1910 clothing industry strike in Chicago was sparked by a group of girls, among them Bessie Abramowitz (1889—1970) of Grodno, Lithuania. In 1905, a year of pogroms in the Russian Empire, this sixteen-year-old left home and traveled to Chicago, where she found work in the men's clothing industry. Her job was sewing on buttons at two and one-half cents a coat. When the foreman cut her wages, she went out on strike. The company fired her, the industry blacklisted her, and she was forced to leave town; no one would hire her. She came back and found work with Hart, Schaffner & Marx. Again her pay was cut, and again she and several other girls began picketing the plant. The men on the job, among them Sidney Hillman, were also finally induced to walk out. By October 1910, about eight thousand men and women in the industry joined them in the effort to force the manufacturers to give them a living wage. The striking women were aided by the Women's Trade Union League; Jane Addams of Hull House was also very sympathetic.

When, in 1911, a settlement was made with Hart, Schaffner & Marx, Bessie Abramowitz, a leader among the women, urged them to adhere to the terms of the compact. She was a realist; a covenant imposed mutual obligations. In 1914, the garment workers, many of them Jewish, finally became convinced that their own international union, the United Garment Workers, would not protect their interests. They now moved to organize a dissident union, the Amalgamated Clothing Workers of America. Bessie was elected a vice-president of the general executive board, the only woman to be thus honored. Her sweetheart and later husband, Sidney Hillman, became the new president of the ACWA in 1915. Under Franklin Delano Roosevelt, he was for a few brief years the most influential labor leader in this country. This was during World War II. When Hillman died in 1946, Bessie was elected a vice-president and held that office till her death in 1970.

Circumstances conspired to help the women better themselves. The public was more sympathetic to unions in 1911, after the fire at the Triangle Waist Company, when over 140 women died in one of the most tragic disasters in the history of New York City. "The life of men and women is so cheap and property is so sacred," deplored Rose Schneiderman, a leader among the women workers. With the coming of World War I, the government interceded to keep people at their jobs; unions were now encouraged, and Samuel Gompers, head of the American Federation of Labor, was appointed to the powerful Advisory Committee for the Council of National Defense. Several years earlier, when the Jewish and Italian girls revolted in the historic 1909 shirtwaist strike, they had been aided by the national Women's Trade Union League (WTUL), an association of middle-class women of influence and culture, humanitarians determined to befriend girls exploited in industry. The all-inclusive goals of this organization were identical with those of the social reformers; as a trade union league, however, it stressed the importance of unions and worked to win an eight-hour day, a minimum wage, and a clean factory.

Rose Schneiderman

The WTUL also enlisted women workers in its ranks. Among them was one who successfully aspired to leadership: Polish-born Rose Schneiderman (1882/4—1972). As a youngster, Rose went to work as a cash girl in a department store; she put in sixty-four hours a week for which she received $2.16. During the Christmas season, she was required to remain on the job from eight in the morning till ten at night; she received no extra pay and no supper money. Like many Jews of this generation, she educated herself by reading and study. Later, Rose took a job in the garment industry and steadily rose to power as a trade union executive. She and Bessie Abramowitz were among the few women to succeed in wresting authority from male labor leaders, who zealously guarded their privileges. The garment workers' unions tended only too often to treat women as second-class members; women were not taken very seriously. At first, the women activists who served as organizers and business agents were kept down. These devoted workers wanted to play a larger administrative role, but were not encouraged despite their many sacrifices. As late as January 1979, there was not one woman on the executive council of the American Federation of Labor—Congress of Industrial Organizations. Schneiderman's curriculum vitae is very impressive: she was secretary of an international union, was in charge of a general strike, served as chairman of New York City's suffragist campaign, attended European working-women's congresses, ran for the United States Senate on the Labor ticket in 1920, sat on the Labor Advisory Board of President Roosevelt's National Recovery Administration, and for years was secretary to the New York State Department of Labor. She had joined the Women's Trade Union League early in the 1900's; years later she became the president of the national organization and remained at its helm for many years.

Lucy Robins Lang

Rose Schneiderman was no radical; though originally a socialist, she made her peace with Roosevelt's New Deal. There were all kinds of liberals and radicals among the women of that generation, although their numbers were relatively small. The left-wing male leaders paid lip service to equality for women but in practice excluded them from positions of importance. Nevertheless, humanly and historically, they are interesting as Jewish protofeminists, foreshadowing the rise of a new genre of women who fifty years later would assert their right to freedom as they interpreted it. Among the "free" women of these earlier decades was Lucy Robins Lang (b. ca. 1889). Within her group, of course, she was not exceptional. Like most of her Jewish friends, she was Russian-born. After her family settled in Chicago, she became a cigar maker, a very successful one, to be sure. At times she earned $20 a week doing piecework—that was as much as the most skilled male could make; it was a great deal of money; it would buy four hundred loaves of bread.

Lucy entered a trial marriage when she was about fifteen. Her husband studied the piano, while she played the violin: thus they reversed the traditional approach of the ghetto Jews in their choice of musical instruments. The Langs were not impoverished slum dwellers; they were able to rent an apartment with steam heat and a tub. It was such a pleasure to welcome the family and watch them line up for a bath. The Langs came east to New York and moved in both socialist and anarchist circles. They opened a cigar store, where at one time they stockpiled arms destined for Russian revolutionists. From New York, they traveled west to San Francisco, where Lucy and her husband opened a vegetarian restaurant. Their trial marriage had lasted five years; now they decided on a trial separation, but when the press heard of their bold decision, they were bitterly denounced as "free lovers." Lucy was very much disturbed by the unpleasant publicity and notoriety.

Rose Harriet Pastor Stokes and Emma Goldman

Lucy was no notable. Much more widely known, indeed a person of national stature, was Lang's contemporary, Rose Harriet Pastor Stokes (1879—1933). At the age of four, this Polish-born child was already at work, helping her widowed mother sew bows on slippers. They were then living in London. After the family settled in Cleveland, Rose, like Lucy Lang, went to work in a cigar factory. Always of a literary bent, she began writing Yiddish poetry which she sent to New York's *Jewish Daily News* (the *Juedisches Tageblatt*). Rose reached out; she learned to write English poetry in a Friendly Society and became president of the Roses of Zion, a woman's Zionist group. By 1903, the family had shifted east to the American megalopolis, where the ambitious young lady became an assistant editor, writing a column in English for the Yiddish *Daily News*. Rose's column attempted to capture the attention of the younger generation of women. While on a reportorial assignment, she met James Graham Phelps Stokes, a socialist, though of a millionaire family. They were married in 1905.

Rose now became a journalist for the English press, though she still retained her interest in the working classes. In 1918, she was indicted under the Espionage Act because she had attacked the government while the country was at war. She had denounced the Wilson administration for its militarism and its tolerance of profiteers. The courts sentenced her to ten years in prison, a verdict which was later reversed. With the rise of Soviet Russia after the war, she turned to Communism and was divorced by her husband, who had left socialism. Rose continued to walk picket lines for the strikers, and in 1921 ran for borough president of Manhattan on the Communist ticket. She died of cancer in 1933 in a German hospital to which her friends and admirers had sent her for treatment. She had never taken any alimony from her husband. Has she anything to teach us? Did this woman live her life in vain? Her life attests to the capacity of an impoverished immigrant to become an educated, acculturated American; by the same token she documents the efforts of a humanitarian to cope with the evils which, like its merits, are an integral part of every industrial society.

Rose Stokes was a political radical who happened to be Jewish and worked largely with Jews. There were a number of women like her whose first loyalty was not to Jewry but to their own ideals. In New York City, in their own quarter, women of this type frequented the tearooms and coffee houses, where they spent long hours in heated debate ventilating their ideas. Many of them were physically unattractive; they paid no attention to their dress; no one would ever maintain that they enhanced the concept of the feminine mystique. Most of them were very poor; they were totally obscure. From the vantage point of the well-fed, late-twentieth-century observer, they were unfortunate, unhappy women. However, there was one notable exception—the ghetto's outstanding woman radical, Emma Goldman (1869—1940). Incontestably a superior person, this native Eastern European had come to the United States in 1885; she had no desire to remain at home and marry the man whom her father had picked for her. She found work in a Rochester garment factory, earned $2.50 a week, and entered into an unsuccessful marriage. She had little regard for marriage as a conventional civil institution; she was equally unenthusiastic about organized religion.

Goldman was a well-educated, cultured woman, interested in the arts. She became a brilliant and successful lecturer, and for a time helped edit an anarchist journal. Her political philosophy of anarchism, which she had embraced in her twentieth year, impelled her to believe in an ethical cooperative society of equals. She insisted on free speech; she wanted sexual freedom for women; they were not a "sex commodity." By 1890, she was already a fully conscious liberationist, a free soul in every sense of the word. Emma was jailed more than once for her views, for her talks on birth control, for her opposition to the military draft. In 1919, at the time of America's postbellum Red Scare, she was deported with a host of others to Russia, but fled the Soviet regime. She could not and would not submit blindly to authority. Deprived of American citizenship, no longer welcome in this country, she was compelled to spend the rest of her life in exile—for her this was a cruel punishment, for she loved America. On her death in Canada, the United States government permitted her burial in Chicago near the graves of the men executed for the Haymarket killings in 1886. In 1892, the *Nation* wrote that she was one of the "twelve greatest living women." Another writer prophesied that a time would come when people would remember her message of freedom for women. For many, that time came in the 1970's.

Ghetto Tragedies

It is no exaggeration to assert that virtually every ghetto family was faced with a variety of problems. Most of these impoverished East Europeans had departed Russia with few regrets; for them it had been a land of no promise. But here they confronted awesome barriers; here they had to fit themselves for an entirely new way of life. They had come from a primitive agrarian economy to an urban industrial economy, from a land of inferior cultural opportunities to a land of superior secular culture, from a land where the talmudic-rabbinic pattern prevailed to one where a salutary neglect of tradition was inevitable. Reluctantly, they moved from Yiddish to English. They enjoyed the transfer from political tyranny to political freedom, but it was a terribly confusing, very traumatic wrench. For them, the Atlantic crossing could never be peaceful. It left them scarred. They salvaged what they could by building a series of folkish emotional, spiritual, and physical enclaves on the Lower East Side. The need to cope with hard work, apprehension, frustration, and cultural alienation was a constant challenge which often made for unhappy homes and unhappy marriages. Then, too, there were the hazards of sickness, tuberculosis, the death of a husband, the loss of a job and whatever resources they had accumulated. Americanized children drifted away from parents deeply rooted in cherished East European religious traditions. Only too often, husbands who had preceded their wives here were ashamed of them when they greeted them at Ellis Island: the wives were so foreign; they seemed so unattractive, so un-American! Where there are hundreds of thousands of immigrants, there are always a substantial number of ne'er-do-wells and crooks. Some newcomers never found it possible to survive here even in a modest fashion; they were broken on the wheel of fortune. As in the larger general community, desertion was a problem among Jews. Hundreds if not thousands of husbands deserted their families.

A Jewish desertion bureau had to be established by the social workers to locate the absconders and to insist that they assume responsibility for their wives and children. Periodically, one of the Yiddish newspapers would publish a "rogues' gallery" to help identify runaway husbands. Girls and boys from these broken homes were often deposited in orphan asylums. Who can adequately describe the anguish of a deserted wife, left almost alone in a foreign land, a woman ignorant of the new language and faced with the problem of rearing a brood of children?

Prostitution is an inevitable concomitant of, and a familiar phenomenon in, a low-status social group. And prostitution was by no means unknown here among the immigrant Jewish masses. Many years ago, eleven-year-old Jacob Rader Marcus, then clerking for his father, was told by a fellow-clerk that there were Jewish harlots. With all the brashness of a Jewish chauvinist, Marcus turned on his informant: "You're a liar!" An objective historian scarcely even *in potentia*, he was shocked; hence his rude response. The National Council of Jewish Women was also shocked by the extent of the traffic and attempted to strangle its growth. The Council's agents met women at the docks and escorted them to the homes of their friends. For decades, as the immigrants poured in, pimps and panderers beguiled lonely immigrant girls in the dance halls; poverty often induced a girl to turn to a life of shame. Polly Adler, an immigrant teenager, worked in a factory and dated a foreman who raped her; she became pregnant and had to have an abortion. It was the beginning of her career as a prostitute and madam.

Even when there was no broken home, and even when there was a relatively good marriage, hard work and a host of petty annoyances faced every newcomer. Though the misery Jewish émigrés experienced was also the lot of most nineteenth-century Gentile immigrants, one cannot exaggerate the heartaches these Jews suffered and the obstacles they had to surmount. The difficulties which tormented that generation of women and men cannot be glossed over by a phony and maudlin posteventum nostalgia. But this, too, must be said: most of the immigrant women seem to have survived, raised families, and become reasonably contented Americans.

Rise of the East European Jewess in the Social and Economic Scale

A handful of East European Jews, here since the mid-1800's, had in the course of years begun to climb the social and economic ladder; this was particularly true in the states and territories west of the Appalachians. Even among the Jews who had come over since the 1880's, there were quite a number who rose relatively rapidly to wealth, if not to social influence. By 1920, it must be remembered, the East Europeans had been in the United States as a mass group for at least forty years. During that period, they had moved forward culturally, financially, politically—so much so, indeed, that by 1916 they were able to successfully contest the rule of the "German" Jewish establishment.

A substantial minority of the newcomers were poor, but they did not stay poor. The wives and children of lower-echelon white-collar and skilled blue-collar workers and artisans did not have to keep the wolf from the door. Married women often helped their husbands in the shops; girls became saleswomen in the larger stores—even though the pay was poor, the position was considered a prestigious one. Girls who trained at the vocational schools or brought skills from the other side of the ocean became milliners and dressmakers; some did very well. Others, though born abroad or native Americans of East European parentage, underwent training to become typists and secretaries. Still others reached for the top and became schoolteachers. Status was very important to these young ladies; white-collar jobs enabled them to move on to a higher social plane.

It is not inaccurate to maintain that most immigrant housewives, through their husbands or their successful children, were moving slowly upward socially and economically. A few achieved affluence; diamonds were not unknown on the Lower East Side. Unlike the Blacks, Jews were never permanently locked in a ghetto; for most of them it was a bridgehead, a foothold for the next advance. As early as the 1890's, immigrant Jews were moving out of the slums, either because they were forced out by urban renewal projects or because their economic condition had improved. Some crossed the East River to Brooklyn; others moved north into middle and upper

Manhattan, Harlem, and the Bronx. In other metropolises, from Philadelphia west to San Francisco, the attempt was made wherever possible to pattern themselves socially and economically on the resident Jewish elite. The newcomers were determined to become self-employed. Immigrant Jews in the South soon landed on their feet; very few had to appeal to the Jewish charities; acculturation here was a rapid process for both men and women. Though the Orthodox Jews among the East European immigrants throughout the South often affected disdain for the assimilationist native-born Jewish settlers, their prevalent Protestant-like Southern Jewish culture, prejudices, and amenities were tacitly embraced.

On occasion, rarely to be sure, exceptional female newcomers pulled themselves up socially and economically by their own bootstraps. Bertha E. Cohen and Hattie Callner are prime examples. Polish-born Bertha was twenty-two when she landed in America and went to work in a Boston department store. A frugal soul, she saved enough to begin investing in real estate. In 1965, she died a millionaire, the owner of forty-two pieces of property, much of it in Cambridge, where she was known as the "Owner of Harvard Square." Latvian-born Hattie Callner (b. 1864) came to America as a girl of eleven or twelve. In Chicago, where she made her home, she is said to have gone to a technical school for two years. Family tradition has it that she had inherited a sizable sum from a relative who made a fortune in the West. At all events, she turned to the construction industry, and over the years her company built apartment houses valued at about $30,000,000. Apparently some of the city's first apartment dwellings were built by her. As she acquired wealth, she became a philanthropist. Dozens of charities, including the city's famous Hull House, were beneficiaries of her generosity. Callner assumed the presidency of the Kurlander (i.e., Latvian) Aid Society and for many years underwrote the cost of the annual Hadassah fund-raising luncheons.

The American public school system made it possible for the children of the East Europeans to receive a relatively good education; quite a number were able to attend college. In Russia, by contrast, access even to the elementary schools had been exceedingly difficult for Jews in the Pale of Settlement. Not so untypical, perhaps, is the experience of Golda Mabovitch. Born in the Ukraine in 1898, she came here as a child, studied, received her certificate at a normal school, and became a schoolteacher in Milwaukee. She married a man by the name of Myerson. Golda, a devoted Labor Zionist (Poale Zion), soon became a good orator in Yiddish and English; later she would add Hebrew. In 1921, at the age of twenty-three, she settled in Palestine, where she carved out a distinguished career for herself. After the establishment of the State of Israel, she was appointed minister to Soviet Russia; in 1969, as Golda Meir, she became Israel's prime minister. Obviously, her basic training was American. Little Golda Mabovitch had come to the United States as a child of eight; her contemporary, Paula Munweis, arrived when she was thirteen. She grew up in this country, studied nursing at Newark's Beth Israel Hospital, and in 1917 married a Polish-born Palestinian Zionist pioneer then living here, David Ben-Gurion. In 1948, one of Paula's teachers at the Beth Israel Hospital addressed a class of nurses at the Hadassah Hospital in Jerusalem: "Study hard, mind what the doctors tell you, and then one day you will get a diploma and can marry a prime minister." Paula Ben-Gurion, who was in the audience, strode up to the front and responded vigorously: "I didn't marry a prime minister; I made one."

Even for the older immigrant girls who worked in the factories, education was always available. They could attend night schools and take classes at settlement houses. If they were truly ambitious and determined, they could study on their own. A few did and enriched themselves culturally; some achieved a degree of recognition. A handful became Yiddish journalists; others, not many, devoted themselves to the socialist and anarchist movements, which led them to read and think—the Marxist dialectic is, after all, no pabulum for sluggish minds. Almost without exception, East European Jewesses, whether anarchists, socialists, or Orthodox traditionalists, were America-oriented. Even the Orthodox Jewess, piously reading her Yiddish petitionary prayers, always thought America superior to despotic czarist Russia. Mary Antin, the immigrant girl from Polotsk who wrote the euphoric *Promised Land*, was an impassioned lover of everything American. She loved its shops, its houses, its public buildings, its engines, its George and Martha Washington, its ideals.

Judaism, the religion? That assumed no primacy among her loves; she was not attracted to the religion of her ancestors.

By the first decade of the new century, a number of women of East European stock were dentists, physicians, and lawyers. Medical internships for women were a problem. As late as 1908, only three female interns were tolerated in all of New York City; two were at Mount Sinai Hospital. Counsellor Esther Kunstler, a diminutive little woman of twenty-two—she looked like a child—opened an office on Rivington Street and dedicated herself to the needs of East Side Jewesses. She had no problem making herself understood; she spoke six languages. Some of the newcomers were actresses on the Yiddish stage; a scattered few were even found uptown on Broadway. Ambitious girls and wives pushed their sweethearts and husbands into the world of the professionals; at times they supported them through school, making it possible for them to study and graduate. One of these immigrants who made a name for herself as an American writer was Anzia Yezierska—though hers was certainly no rags-to-riches story. Almost every year since her arrival from Poland as a young woman was a year of struggle. For a time she worked as a cook in an immigrant's home; after that she put in a twelve-hour daily stint in a sweatshop. Determined to become a writer, she went to night school. In 1919, when she was almost thirty-five, one of her stories was selected as the best story of the year. *Hungry Hearts*, a collection of her tales, brought her fame. For a brief period she worked in Hollywood, but failed to make good there; she returned to New York, where she salvaged a degree of emotional satisfaction in writing and self-expression. Drawing on her own years of toil and disillusionment, she addressed herself realistically to her basic theme, the impact of American life on the East European newcomers. She died as she had lived, on the edge of poverty. Her influence was, on the whole, limited; readers tend to recoil from intensity, from a monotonous harping on hunger and loneliness. But it was indeed an achievement for an immigrant to come here as a young adult and to accomplish what Yezierska did in literature.

It is a far cry from Anzia Yezierska to Belle Lindner Israels Moskowitz (1877—1933), a native New Yorker, the daughter of a Harlem watchmaker. Her studies took her to Teachers College at

Columbia, but she was not destined to spend her life teaching youngsters. She was married twice, fortunately for her to men who were sympathetic to her work. By 1900, the Educational Alliance, a downtown settlement house, had put her on the staff at an annual salary of $500. This relationship with Jews and Jewish institutions was never severed in a career that made her one of America's most prominent, influential women. Taking on a number of important assignments before she found her métier, she worked on the *Survey*, handled grievances as a manager of the Labor Department of the Dress and Waist Manufacturers' Association, served as secretary of the New York State Reconstruction Commission and later as a public relations counsellor for the Port of New York Authority.

By this time, she had found the assignment that was to distinguish her; she had become the confidante and advisor of New York Governor Alfred Smith as he moved to implement his social-welfare programs. It was she, together with other Jews, who helped him develop his social vision, and when he ran for president, she served as his publicity manager. Yet, though occupied with challenging public tasks, she managed to maintain a good home life and conducted what was in effect a salon for her intimates. In a way, Belle Moskowitz's career came to an end when Alfred Smith turned to the right, and the new leader who appeared on her horizon, Franklin D. Roosevelt, chose not to consult her. She is notable as one of the first Jewesses in this country, possibly the very first, to make a name for herself in a world which looked askance at women in important public posts.

The Personal Life of the East European Jewess

With few exceptions, the women of East European stock were not intent on making careers outside the home. Marriage was all-important for them. Young men and women made their own marriage arrangements, often to the dismay of the parents and many times with disastrous results. The marriage broker, the shadchan, time-honored in Slavic-Jewish Europe, found slim pickings here. The prospect of marriage often brought problems for young women.

Some of them, well-read, had intellectual aspirations; the men, often involved in business, had limited cultural interests. The girls did not want to step down in taking a partner for life; they wanted husbands of equal intellectual stature. Even in the ghetto, intermarriages were not unknown. Here in the metropolitan enclaves, the rigorous social controls of the European villages had begun to break down. In 1899, Charles K. Harris, one of the country's leading songwriters, wrote "A Rabbi's Daughter." The story was simple: a rabbi's daughter fell desperately in love with a Gentile, her father would never permit her to marry the man she loved, so she lay down and died—a typical turn-of-the-century tearjerker. In 1922, *Abie's Irish Rose*, which deals with the marriage of a Jewish boy and an Irish girl, ran over twenty-three hundred performances on Broadway. Why did the Jews flock to see it? After two thousand years, were they weary of being men of sorrows, of being despised and rejected? Was intermarriage a solution to their millennial miseries? What a pleasant way to solve the Jewish problem, vicariously, in two hours! All's well that ends well—on the stage. In the real life of the Lower East Side, parents were bitterly opposed to intermarriage.

Despite the absence of modern forms of entertainment like motion pictures, radio, and television, newcomers to America had a full social life both in and out of the home. For matrons—and some of the younger married, too—there was always the local female mutual-aid society. Whether the settlement houses in the big cities were sponsored by Jews or Gentiles, they were always host to a number of attractive Jewish clubs. These social groups gave individuals the sense of intimate fellowship which they craved. Jewish women did not have to stay home and twiddle their thumbs; there were engagement festivities, weddings, balls, picnics, graduation parties, bar mitzvahs, and circumcision collations (with yellow sponge cake de rigueur). Even before 1900, before Herzl and what the unsympathetic called his "madman's dance" and his "prostitution" of Judaism, there were numerous societies for the Daughters of Zion. Hadassah grew out of one of these small circles. By now, literary clubs—which in fact offered more talk than literature—had also begun to make their appearance. One could always visit the family and kinsfolk, enjoy a glass of good Russian tea, taken from a little red tin box and sweetened with red raspberry preserves, unless, of course, one preferred the tea Russian style: holding a lump of cone sugar in one's mouth and sucking the beverage through it. Yiddish theatres were well-attended, though three theatres for several hundred thousand Jews on the Lower East Side and thousands of others in the secondary areas of settlement were not so much to brag about. Even so, the women who went there had a good cry—they loved the Yiddish melodramas depicting ungrateful, rebellious children.

The consolations of religion? The recollection of a European Jewish way of life, yes; prayers, transcendental meditation, spiritual ferment, no. Only those women deeply rooted in European traditions were moved to pour out their hearts in prayer. After all, when had women ever been encouraged to play much part in the Orthodox synagogue? Since time immemorial it had been a male institution. Marxist-minded Jewesses would have no truck with religion; they despised the synagogue and its beliefs and looked with contempt on its male cohorts entrenched in tradition. Politically radical women were often schismatic Jews: anti-religious, anti-Zionist, they were perilously close to being anti-Jewish.

The Natives and the Newcomers: A Brief Review and Some Afterthoughts

By the 1880's, for the first time in American history, Jewesses were entering industry on a large scale as workers, principally in the garment trade. Theirs was a sad lot. Their own people exploited them, and initially there was little that these new arrivals could do to protect themselves. They had no education, no training, no knowledge of English. Where else could they turn? It took a full thirty years before they organized to help themselves, managed to strike successfully, and began winning a shorter work day and better pay in a cleaner, healthier factory. For American Jews, the years after 1881 were to usher in a unique epoch, a strange interlude in their economic history. Once this generation faded away, Jewish women would never again go back to the factories. Jewish garment workers were neither the daughters of proletarian mothers nor the mothers of proletarian daughters.

Let there never be any doubt: the years these women toiled in the factories were years of suffering, unhappiness, even poverty. Following patterns already established among the men, the immigrant Jewesses both at work and at home, set out to cope with the problems of financial insecurity and their own fears. They organized mutual-aid associations which guaranteed a modicum of insurance and offered opportunities to meet one another socially. It is worth noting that they created few credit unions; they were not prepared to go into business on their own, even on a modest scale, but they were eager to borrow a few dollars to buy a daughter a coat or to help papa and mama still languishing in the Old Country (Discreet, the Ladies Hebrew Free Loan did not tell the husband when his spouse made a loan.) Despite their particularistic female landsmanshaften, these women did succeed in entering the mainstream of American culture; they wanted to think, dress, and act like Americans. It did not take them long to create a way of life which synthesized the culture of Slavic-Jewish Europe and the American metropolis.

The acculturated Central Europeans looked askance at the new arrivals; the "Germans" seemed indifferent to the fact that they themselves had already been here for over a generation and were fortunate in having come from lands culturally more comparable to America. The transition, the adjustment for the Central Europeans was much easier than for the Jews from autocratic, primitive Russia. The Russian women suffered more than their German sisters, who rarely went into the shops as working women. Fortunately, many, if not most, of the women of the Lower East Side were not fated to remain forever in the Manhattan ghetto which was their first home in America; they began to move out and up; creature comforts were in prospect; life came to an end for them in an apartment with a bathtub.

The rise to relative financial security was quicker in the hinterland; housing was often better; husbands and fathers became businessmen, if only on a modest scale, and the daughters, almost completely enveloped by an overpowering American culture, had many opportunities for a good education. High school or college training gave a girl a profession—teaching, a passport into the world of American respectability. This was a hope devoutly nourished. Away from

New York City, an ambitious Jewess had a good chance to marry a man who was not an artisan or a factory worker; her husband might be or become a businessman with a place all his own. It all took time, of course, but a generation after the first poverty-stricken pogrom victims landed, they and their children had already created a network of charities which extended all the way from Boston to Los Angeles. In Chicago, in 1912, with the aid of Julius Rosenwald, they had succeeded in establishing a philanthropic federation of their own, one whose institutions observed the sacrosanct dietary laws. This was a symbolic Declaration of Independence.

Some of these immigrants made careers for themselves in the land of unlimited opportunty. An Emma Goldman taught a minuscule minority to think, to seek spiritual and intellectual emancipation from both rabbinic and Victorian standards of conduct; a Rose Schneiderman helped thousands in their struggle to make a livelihood; a Sophie Loeb spearheaded the enactment of legislation which enhanced the lives of hundreds of thousands of women and children. It is no small thing that thirty years after Russian refugees began flooding these shores, women flocked to create Hadassah, the organization which fostered Jewish education and culture in this land and provided modern medical care for Palestine and Israel. It is a notable achievement; the impoverished women of 1881 were, by 1912, ready to extend their largesse and love to thousands in a faraway land.

Again, it is beyond doubt that the years 1841 to 1920 mark the domination of American Jewry by the "Germans." It is to the credit of the incoming "Russians" and their children that the women among them were, by the end of the second decade of the new century, ready and able to go out on their own, to create their own institutions, and to emancipate themselves from the leading strings of the "Germans." Yet, culturally they patterned themselves almost slavishly on the German women because they deemed them an elite group; these earlier settlers were "Americans." Even after a generation in America, the newcomers were lacking in self-assurance. Despite the anti-"German" hostility which rankled in the bosoms of many East European Jewesses, they looked with envy upon the women of the earlier migrations. However, it cannot be said that such respect and envy were undeserved. More and more native-born, children of Central Europeans, were being educated in institutions of higher learning. This schooling, reinforced by perseverance and natural ability, carried some of them far. They became physicians, researchers in the natural sciences, devout worshipers at the altar of English literature. Individuals here and there, not a great many, to be sure, had already begun emerging as competent literary craftsmen.

The Young Women's Christian Association made a limited but not insubstantial impress upon mid-nineteenth-century Jewish ladies. In New York City, the Young Women's Christian Association had already come into being by 1858. Basically evangelical, and oriented toward orthodox Christianity, it comprehended a world of commitment—testimony, prayer, and Bible study—which inevitably left the typical postbellum American Jewess untouched; psychologically, she was not attuned to that type of religiosity. Thus it was structurally, and not religiously, that the growing YWCA influenced American Jewish women. Jewish girls had already begun entering the Young Men's Hebrew Association in one way or another as early as the 1860's; by 1888, a YMHA women's auxiliary had been established in New York; in 1902, an autonomous YWHA made its appearance. In the Jewish women's Y's, literature, learning, sociability, and gymnastics became a harmonious whole. Up to the 1890's, these Y auxiliaries were directed primarily toward Jewesses of German origin. By the early twentieth century their goals had already shifted; now they tended to become Americanization agencies, concerned with the problems of the incoming East European Jewesses. Like the Clara de Hirsch Home for Working Girls and the Hebrew Technical School for Girls, the YWHA emphasized vocational training, the Anglo-Saxon amenities, English literature, religious education, and physical fitness. In the early twentieth century it was a favored undertaking of Sephardic Shearith Israel. Curiously enough, while the Christian women's Y's and the contemporary Christian Endeavor Movement enjoyed great vogue, the YWHA's achieved only modest growth and never captured the imagination of American Jewesses. Many of these young women were ready to go off on their own—but not into the YWHA. Was it too "Christian" for them?

By 1920, Jewesses of mid-nineteenth-century American vintage were indistinguishable from their Gentile neighbors in terms of external appearance; they ate the same foods, wore the same kind of clothes, went to the same plays on the Rialto. All this they wanted. As Jews, they did go to synagogue but certainly not too often; they attended formal worship services less regularly than the Protestant women whom they admired. Their Christian neighbors were often ready to accept them socially, though not without reservations. Christians could never, and would never, forget that the Cohens and Levys were Jews—that they were different. But when emotionally touched, the Christians could be very considerate. In Wichita, Kansas, the good citizens of the town were so sorry for Captain Alfred Dreyfus, who was suffering in France, that they elected a hometown Jewish girl, Sadie Joseph, Queen of the Street Carnival.

The new twentieth-century generation of Jewish women, alive to the demands of the time, found their forte in civic and social work. The Progressive Age was ushering in two decades of idealism and humanitarianism. Influenced by women like Jane Addams and Lillian Wald, Jewish girls joined others in going down to the ghettos to educate, to Americanize, and to help. How much of this was "feminine consciousness," how much was an almost detached, nonethnic humanitarianism, how much was Jewish identification and sympathy, it is difficult to determine. Some of these women, American-born Jewesses for the most part, worked through the settlement houses; others, especially in the metropolitan centers, revamped the women's charitable societies, fortified them with new "scientific" notions of social welfare, and transmuted them into Sisterhoods for Personal Service. In the smaller communities, social work was carried on by the female benevolent societies which had begun decades earlier. What these older associations lacked in sociological perspective and theory, they made up in sympathy, loving-kindness, and an intense desire to be of help. True, the clients were patronized; this was all but inevitable. As social workers, Jewish women often fluttered about on three levels: some were found in the traditional, unsophisticated, Ladies' Aid and Support societies; others, Jewish clubwomen, were happy in the National Council of Jewish Women and unconcerned with palliative relief for individual clients; still others, stalwarts of the religious sisterhoods, were content to limit their activity almost solely to temples and their schools. The social-welfare interests of the synagogue woman were minimal—possibly in reaction to their rivals, the National Council sections, which operated well outside the ambit of the synagogues.

In emancipating women, Reform Jewry was in the vanguard. The men in the movement had been quick to make their obeisance to the American tradition of chivalry to the women of one's own social class. Notable American Jewesses began preaching by invitation from temple pulpits. Several Reform synagogues accepted women as outright members; occasionally, the ladies served on the board of the school and even of the synagogue itself, but on the whole the liberation of Reform women was more verbal than real. This was true in the larger American Jewish community as well; the committee appointed in 1905 to commemorate the 250th anniversary of the settlement of the Jews in North America had no female representative. Poor Ricke Nounes; no one remembered her and the other women who had landed at New Amsterdam in the autumn of 1654. When the National Association of Jewish Social Workers met at Baltimore in 1915, the thirty-one speakers were all males. Minnie F. Low, of Chicago, protested vigorously. Despite being compelled to drop out of high school as a freshman, she worked as a professional in the field for years. Up to her death in 1922, she was an outstanding social worker in both her city and state, dividing her time between Jewish and non-Jewish philanthropic agencies. People in Chicago referred to her as "The Jane Addams of the Jews." Minnie Low's brilliant career was crowned in 1914 with election to the presidency of the National Conference of Jewish Charities. This Conference was conscious of the importance of women, at least to a degree.

Two other national institutions had accorded women consideration as early as 1900—the Jewish Publication Society and the Jewish Chautauqua. Mrs. Solomon Schechter was even accepted as a member of the executive council of the United Synagogue of America, the Conservative religious union, despite the fact that Conservatism still maintained a quasi-Orthodox stance. These episodes represented a real advance. There was a special stirring of female consciousness on the part of at least one woman, who began modestly, if not lustfully, to cast her eyes on the rabbinate as a potential profession for herself.

In general, the women of the two communities—the natives and the Central Europeans on one side, and the East Europeans on the other—would remain separate and unequal until most of them died off after having wandered in the Wilderness of Prejudice for a generation. It was probably more than prejudice which lay behind their mutual insistence on separatism: the women in both groups, beginning to find themselves, wanted to be on their own; some may have seen the threat of a leveling influence in the amalgamation between Germans and Russians. Occasionally, benevolent societies of Jewesses even refused to join the philanthropic federations set up by their own husbands; these wives did not want to be swallowed up in male-dominated enterprises. Thousands of women joined the auxiliaries established by the national orders because they enjoyed associating with other Jewesses. This drive to control their own activity was symptomatic of an emancipatory sentiment.

The years 1900 to 1920 may be looked upon as an age when women documented their presence both quantitatively and qualitatively. They were found in many fields; they were reaching out and many demonstrated competence. They had come out of the "kitchens" in the 1870's and 1880's, and blossomed as independent, self-conscious human beings in the 1890's. But advances in a man's world continued to be slow: of the approximately 320 biographical sketches of American Jewish communal workers published in the 1905–1906 *American Jewish Year Book*, only about 24 percent were those of women.

During these decades, individual Jewesses were interested in helping Margaret Sanger impart knowledge of birth control. Like Sanger, they believed that a married woman should not be denied the right of deciding how many children she would bring into the world. From a traditional Jewish point of view, this was heresy; socially, it was revolutionary. Jewesses of the older stocks wanted to make this a better world for all human beings. As women—and for some it may have been subconscious—they were determined to be somebodies. Their humanitarian striving to serve the immigrants and others in need, too, were to find expression in the programs of the National Council of Jewish Women. The old-line women leaders stood ready to help their East European sisters, who were oppressed economically. The vote, so many believed, would ameliorate prevailing economic disabilities. It is curious that when in 1917 the New Yorkers were challenged on woman's suffrage, the Jewish East Siders, bourgeois Orthodox and unionists alike, cast their ballots for equal rights. On this issue their voting record was as good as that of the silk-stocking assembly districts. When the cards were down, the East Side masses were on the side of the angels! Immigrant women close to the labor movement wanted the franchise because, in a realistic sense, they hoped that it would bring higher wages, fewer hours of toil, and a cleaner shop for those struggling in the garment factories. With the aid of the Wilson administration, labor leaders had made measurable progress in this direction by 1920.

A number of Jewish women distinguished themselves in many areas of endeavor during the thirty years before 1920. Justly or unjustly, formal recorded history recognizes only outstanding achievers. Jewesses had succeeded in gaining recognition for themselves in the performing arts, social work and welfare legislation, politics, and education. They had gone far, very far, since the early nineteenth century, when most Jewish women were tied to their homes, their husbands, and age-old taboos. The women of the early nineteenth century had the brains, but neither the freedom nor the opportunity.

Even by 1920, female notables were numerically few. Is it proper to say that their deeds constitute the history of America's Jewish women? The real history of the American Jewess is the history of the "mass-woman." What part was this woman now playing in the tripartite structure of Judaism—worship, study, and good deeds? Administratively, she now had a foot in the door of the synagogue; her Jewish classes in the National Council of Jewish Women, Hadassah, and the Labor Zionist Pioneer Women had become increasingly important, although for the National Council, general culture and education were probably as important as Jewish indoctrination. It is likely that in the area of philanthropy, the women were as important as the men—maybe even more important. Despite the fact that men were at the top of the philanthropic heap, much of the actual work load in almost every community was still borne by women. Thus the history of the American Jewess was being made by this "mass-woman." As late as 1920, out of ignorance or indifference, she took little interest in remedial legislation, sex education, international peace, women's suffrage, hospitals for the insane, or protective laws for children and their mothers. These larger issues were beyond her ken. The typical Jewess, whether affluent or impoverished, was concerned with her home and husband, her children, their education and their religious identity. In synagogue attendance she was often negligent, but there could be no question where her religious loyalties lay.

One fact is all—important in summarizing the lives and achievements of the women of this generation: they survived Jewishly. The families they reared moved forward economically, socially, and culturally. In many instances, they reared children who would be heard from in the generation that was yet to come.

· 5 ·

The Era of Enlargement and Expansion, 1920—1962

Women Make History

I N April 1783, Mordecai Sheftall wrote his twenty-one-year-old son Sheftall Sheftall, deputy quartermaster general of issues for the State of Georgia, to announce the end of the war with Great Britain: "We have the whole world to begin againe." Now having won the right to vote in 1920, women could not be blamed for thinking that they too had the whole world to begin again. Actually there were few changes. Mother would continue to help in the store, or, if business was good, take time out to busy herself at the Ladies' Aid. She could work for the synagogue, the Sunday school, for Zionism, international peace, even for birth control. In 1925, an overenthusiastic liberal rabbi, Joseph Leiser, thinking only of Reform, proudly announced to the world that the Jewish woman of his day was prepared to serve mankind and Jewry; she was freed from the "tyranny of domestic and marital domination." Women, he said, now had equality with men. This was of course an exaggeration, though it is true that for the first time many women, Jewesses among them, were beginning to emancipate themselves from traditional morality and conventional mores. They began to smoke, drink, talk openly of birth control, and to enjoy sexual freedom.

Few women could doubt that there were opportunities for them in the professions, in education, in the arts and sciences, in com-

merce, in music, or on the stage and screen. With learning and training came jobs. There was hardly any type of activity in which Jewish
women were not found. In 1925, Mrs. Elaine Rosenthal Reinhart
won the triple crown as the Western Women's Golf Champion.
Slowly, small numbers continued to drift into law and even
medicine, where they faced a de facto quota; most women opted for
jobs as teachers in the public schools; a number became librarians.
Whatever the cause, more and more women were being added to
the labor force. After 1920, they began competing in the job
market; by 1957, it is estimated that about a third of America's
workers were female. That percentage was to increase substantially
by the late 1970's. The number of Jewish girls in the garment industry declined relatively rapidly; marriage and death reduced their
percentages in the trades and in the unions. They deserted the
Lower East Side in large numbers; the year 1930 found about one-
third as many Jews there as in 1916. The daughters of the blouse,
dress, cloak, and suit workers flocked to the schools. In 1920, only
16,000 women received a bachelor of arts or an equivalent degree in
the United States; in 1957, 116,000 women earned degrees.
Thousands were going to college, acquiring polish, the amenities, a
degree—and often a husband.

By 1918, Jews, particularly the males, were pushing for higher.
education; about one in five Jews attending college was a woman;
among Gentiles the percentage of women was higher—one in three.
What did these Jewesses study? In descending order, they opted for
commerce and finance (bookkeeping?), teaching, law, dentistry,
pharmacy, and medicine. As early as 1923 there were already
twenty-four Jewesses teaching at the college level. A survey made of
Jewish students enrolled in college in 1934 shows that an increasing
percentage were women. By that year proportionately more Jewish
women attended college than their Gentile counterparts. In New
York City about 52.1 percent of all female students in the city's colleges were Jews. In other cities of mass Jewish settlement, there was
also a disproportionately high percentage of Jewesses seeking to
prepare themselves to enter a profession. It was a veritable educational explosion. Of all women in American schools of higher learning, 6.28 percent were Jewesses. This impressive percentage was due

to the fact that Jews were an urban people, that they were moving rapidly into the middle class, and that higher education was good and cheap in New York City, where so many were settled. But even then more Jewish men were going to college than women.

Ruth Sapinsky Hurwitz (1889—1961) was one of the sixteen thousand women who earned bachelor's degrees before 1920. She was born in Scottsburg, Indiana, and graduated from Wellesley. Ruth remained well within the Jewish sphere, for she was married to Henry Hurwitz, the founder of the Intercollegiate Menorah Movement and the editor of its journal. After leaving school, she wrote stories, articles, and book reviews, introduced art and music into the Jewish Sunday schools where she was employed, taught history and English to immigrants, and lectured on child guidance and psychology to classes at Teachers' College, Columbia University. The societies which she joined are an eloquent commentary on the interests of cultured Jewesses of the mid-twentieth century: the Wellesley Club of New York City, both the French Institute and the English-speaking Union, the League of Women Voters, the American Civil Liberties Union, and Hadassah.

Elizabeth Gertrude Leven Stern (1890—1954) was another young woman who received her bachelor's degree in the early twentieth century—from the University of Pittsburgh. Born in Poland in 1890, Elizabeth came to this country as a child; her father was a hazzan. Occasionally using Eleanor or Leah Morton as pseudonyms, she became a writer, journalist, and social worker of some distinction. She was employed in New York settlement houses and with the Jewish Immigration Bureau, which routed East European newcomers through Galveston, Texas. She was a teacher and principal of night schools in several cities and a devoted worker on behalf of prisoners, Blacks, Spanish Loyalists, and Jewish exiles from Germany. As a journalist and columnist, she wrote for newspapers in New York and Philadelphia; she was the author of well over a dozen books, one of them, *I Am a Woman—and a Jew* (1926). Her efforts to come to terms with herself as a "Jew" were far from simple: her husband was a Gentile; she refused to identify herself religiously as a Jew, although she vigorously proclaimed her oneness with the Jewish people. Anti-Semitism offended this ardent advocate of social justice. In her later years, she found a spiritual haven in the Society of Friends; she embraced the Quaker faith wholeheartedly and was buried in a Quaker cemetery.

Ruth Sapinsky, we have noted, studied at Wellesley; Elizabeth Stern attended the University of Pittsburgh; Selma Evelyn Fine Goldsmith (1912—1962) matriculated at Cornell and earned her Ph.D. at Radcliffe in 1937. Goldsmith was an economist and statistician; by the time of her death in 1962 she was recognized as one of the country's leading authorities on national income. She had been chief of the Income and Statistics Branch of the Bureau of the Census. In 1956, Dr. Goldsmith was the only woman among the sixteen who received prestigious Rockefeller Public Service Awards; she was given a similiar citation by the Department of Commerce. Her writings in the area of economics established her reputation as one of America's leading students in the fields of economics and statistics.

Selma Goldsmith, Ruth Hurwitz, and Elizabeth Stern were all married women with families to raise; they were not "professional" Jews. Fanny (Fannie) Goldstein (1888—1961) was librarian of the West End branch of the Boston Public Library. In her later years, shortly before retirement, she was appointed citywide curator of Jewish books. Fanny was the originator of Jewish Book Week, which became the nationally observed Jewish Book Month. She lived in an immigrant Jewish quarter where boys and girls all but devoured books; she taught them to read books dealing with their people and their history. Indeed, she has been referred to as the "Conscience of Boston Jewry." Yet she was not parochial in her interests. At her library, she initiated an annual interfaith party—a Christmas-Hanukkah celebration. Her goodwill innovations were reinforced by Negro History Week, Catholic Book Week, and Brotherhood Week; in the spring season of 1955, she mounted an exhibition of "The Christs of the Artist." In the final analysis, though, her ultimate mission in life was to encourage Boston Jews, indeed Jews everywhere, to read Jewish books; her efforts were applauded and met with a degree of success.

None of the standard histories of American Jewry record the name of Sophie (Sophia) Moses Robison (1888—1969). There is no special reason why they should. She neither gave millions nor won a Nobel Prize, but she was a technician, a scholar of unusual capacity, and a noble human being. True, Robison could have bragged about her American roots, which reached back into the 1820's. She, too, went to Wellesley (1909), supporting herself, in part, by lighting fireplaces; on graduation she studied in Germany and then returned to take a master's degree at Columbia. The career on which she subsequently embarked made her one of America's most respected criminologists. In all probability, she was the country's leading authority on delinquency. For years she occupied the chair of professor of sociology at the Columbia University School of Social Work. She taught at ten other colleges during her career and was respected not only as a student of crime, but as a writer, statistician, educator, and social activist. She encouraged Margaret Sanger in her birth control work and as far back as the 1930's was fighting on behalf of the Blacks.

Sophie Robison's bibliography of works, articles, reviews, and research studies is very impressive. Her researches spanned the spectrum from "The Jewish Population of Trenton, 1937" to "The Christ Type in Modern German Literature," her master's thesis at Columbia. She did not earn her Ph.D. until she was almost fifty; she needed that degree to get a job, and she needed a job because the family fortunes were shattered during the Great Depression. Living in Mount Vernon made it necessary for her to commute to New York City. She usually had to run to make the train, but she made it—she had been on the track team at Wellesley.

Her ties to the Jewish people were close: she worked for the National Council of Jewish Women, edited a series of valuable statistical studies for the New York Conference on Jewish Relations, served on the board of the New York Chapter of the American Friends of the Hebrew University, and supported the social-minded American Jewish Congress. On Friday nights her home was a salon where brilliant young people, Jews and Gentiles, gathered to talk and to enjoy the Robisons' hospitality. Widowed at a relatively early age, she raised and educated a family of five. A biographer has said of her that she was "a person of uncommon greatness."

Successful and Generous Women

A few exceptional women made their presence felt in the world of commerce and economic enterprise. By 1925 Jewish women were recognized as America's leading designers of women's clothes. They determined what the ladies would wear. Their salaries were huge; one or two, it would appear, made close to $100,000 a year. Individuals among them combined designing and manufacturing; they owned their own businesses. Beatrice Fox Auerbach (d. 1968) inherited a large business in Hartford, and under her guidance G. Fox & Co. became one of the great department stores of New England. Born in Austrian Poland (Galicia), Jennie Grossinger came to this country as a child and went to work in a factory sewing buttonholes at the age of thirteen; she made $1.50 her first week. Her father, a tailor, suffered a breakdown and bought a rundown farm near the town of Liberty in the Catskill Mountains; there was a seven-room farmhouse on the place. The family was never able to work the farm—it was not fertile—so they took in boarders at $9 a week. The little family-run summer resort that they started was built up by Jennie's husband Harry and herself. After Harry's death in 1964, Jennie became sole owner of what in the course of time had grown into a resort empire—actually bigger than the principality of Monaco. The Grossinger premises include some twelve hundred acres, over thirty buildings, enough rooms for fourteen hundred guests, and a dining hall seating about seventeen hundred people. As many as 150,000 guests come to Grossinger's annually, and each year the receipts run in the millions. The kitchen of course is kosher, for the Grossingers were Orthodox and catered to people who wanted a kosher table. Many of their guests, however, were non-Jews; they liked Jewish food.

Jennie Grossinger, who died in 1972, was a philanthropist who gave to many causes. She was not, as such, exceptional among Jewish women. Over a century earlier, Rosanna Osterman of Texas left much of her substantial estate to charity; Judah Touro was obviously in her mind as she wrote her will. The twentieth-century Jewesses who have given away substantial sums were interesting people. One of them was Vivian Straus Dixon, whose philanthropies were centered around an institution for unwed mothers. Mrs. Dixon was a daughter of Isidor and Ida Straus, the devoted couple who went down on the *Titanic* in 1912. Among Isidor's many benefactions, not the least was the endowment fund of the Jewish Theological Seminary, to which he had contributed liberally; his daughter Vivian was buried in 1967 out of St. Bartholomew's Episcopal Church on Park Avenue. Mrs. Arthur Lehman (d. 1965), born a Lewisohn, aided the orthopedically handicapped, and found time to become a champion tennis player. Mrs. Florence G. Heller (d. 1966), of Chicago, gave $1,000,000 to Brandeis University to found the Florence Heller Graduate School for Advanced Studies in Social Welfare. In 1964, she was elected president of the National Jewish Welfare Board. During the 1960's men began realizing that women must be accorded recognition; the ladies had begun to make their presence felt. Blanche Frank Ittleson (d. 1975), a truly generous and thoughtful philanthropist, lived to be ninety-nine. In her was fulfilled the biblical promise: "Charity (Righteousness) delivereth from death" (Proverbs 10:2). She was very much concerned with problems of mental health, particularly the needs of emotionally disturbed children. In 1930, Caroline Bamberger Fuld and her brother gave $5,000,000 to establish the Institute for Advanced Study at Princeton.

Politics

It has been said that the nineteenth amendment, which extended the vote to women, was the climax of the Progressive Age. Women could no longer be ignored. The franchise certainly opened doors for them, but Jewesses, it would seem, took little immediate advantage of their opportunities. Either they were not interested, not competent, or unable to surmount the rampant anti-Jewish prejudice of the 1920's. In later decades, the picture would change. In 1965, Katherine Elkus White, daughter of Abraham I. Elkus, President Wilson's ambassador to Turkey, was appointed United States ambassador to Denmark. Mrs. White was no novice; in the 1950's she had been elected mayor of the New Jersey resort town of Red Bank.

Years later she would chair the New Jersey Highway Authority, the agency which administered the $300,000,000 Garden State Parkway. Was she a good Jew? She was a member of her synagogue sisterhood and Hadassah. In New York City—where Jewish votes count—politicians genuflected in the direction of women. In 1959 Caroline Klein Simon (b. 1900), a lawyer, was appointed New York State's first female secretary of state. Four years later she became a judge of the Court of Claims.

One woman was fortunate enough and wise enough to seize time by the forelock and make a truly great career. Before Anna M. Rosenberg (b. 1900/1902) ceased to play a role on the stage of business and politics, the United States government awarded her the coveted national Medal of Merit—the country's first woman to be so recognized. What had this Hungarian immigrant done that her adopted land selected her as the woman whom it delighted to honor? Anna Rosenberg was the child of a Hungarian family which arrived here with some means in the early years of the twentieth century. While still in her early twenties, she had the courage to start a business of her own that was one day to prove very lucrative. She was essentially a businesswoman who worked as a personnel consultant and labor mediator; when her country needed her she did duty as a public servant. She was "Mrs. Fix-It." Franklin Roosevelt, who had rejected the politically astute Belle Moskowitz, sponsored Anna Rosenberg. From the 1930's into the 1960's she accepted important assignments in New York and Washington. She held high office in the National Recovery Administration, and sat on both the Social Security Board and the War Labor Board; in 1950, President Truman called on her to serve as an assistant secretary of defense. It was her job to help draft the Universal Military Service and Training Bill and to provide the pool of millions who would keep the wheels of industry turning; she had to make sure that the armed forces were always at full strength during the Korean War. No American Jewess had yet risen as high as she in government service; indeed, in all American history, few women have occupied posts comparable to hers.

Jewesses soon entered the legislative assemblies in at least three states; one, Florence Prag Kahn, took the oath in the United States

House of Representatives and became Congress' first Jewess. Born in Utah in 1868, Florence Prag moved with her family to California, went to college, and made a living teaching high school. She married Julius Kahn, who served many terms in Congress between 1899 and 1924, most of the time as a member of the powerful Committee on Military Affairs. She succeeded him in Congress at his death. Mrs. Kahn was damned as a "political hack," but this was condemnation, not evaluation. She was unquestionably an accomplished politician, for she had served as her husband's secretary since 1899. A rock-ribbed Republican from a Republican district, she lived in an age when many substantial Jewish businessmen believed that the country could only survive through the party which provided a full dinner pail, the party of Abraham Lincoln. She was bitterly opposed to Prohibition and motion picture censorship, was a firm believer in military preparedness and, like her husband before her, sat on the Committee on Military Affairs. In April 1929, the speaker of the House, Nicholas Longworth, asked her to take the chair for a day. Years earlier, after her marriage to Congressman Kahn, President McKinley had invited the couple to dinner. They walked to the White House; a carriage would have cost them a dollar. "In what country," said German-born Julius Kahn, "could two poor Jews be on their way to dine with the head of state?" Like many other Republican stalwarts, Florence Kahn was defeated in the Roosevelt landslide of 1936. A generation later, a new breed of Jewess was to enter Congress—New York and Brooklyn would not be denied.

Religion

Rabbi Joseph Leiser was simply too sanguine about the freedom and privileges to be enjoyed by women in Reform synagogues. As late as the turn of the century, no woman was appointed to any committee or served on any board of the Union of American Hebrew Congregations. Disabilities persisted, though many faded away with the passing of time, and women were admitted to most administrative posts in the Reform congregational structure. It was not until 1923 that they were declared eligible for membership on the executive board of the Union of American Hebrew Congregations. The late 1940's were a watershed, at least for Reform Jewesses, because Reform congregations began calling women up to the Torah and encouraging them to become bat mitzvah. This ceremony was taken over from the Reconstructionists and other liberals within Conservative Judaism. In the 1950's, a few Reform Jewesses began serving as presidents of congregations; by then one or two women had also unofficially assumed rabbinical duties, though only in smaller Reform congregations like Trinidad, Colorado, and Meridian, Mississippi.

Influenced possibly by the National Council of Jewish Women, the socially-minded thinking of a new generation of native American Jewesses, and by the pressure of their own aggressive, liberal leadership, the Reform movement's National Federation of Temple Sisterhoods expanded its programs. The traditional chores of synagogue and Sabbath school support were continued and extended, but the sisterhoods now manifested an interest in art and music; they opened kindergartens for disadvantaged minority children and taught remedial reading in the public schools. The emphasis was now on social justice and world peace. The sisterhoods grew; recruits, girls reared in traditional homes, found it hard to resist the appeal of synagogue services in a liberal format. These newcomers enjoyed family pews, choral music, intelligible liturgy, and the intellectual freedom characteristic of Reform Judaism, a "denomination" which seriously attempted to harmonize modern thought and freedom of conscience with the religious practices and the ethical traditions of the past.

As Orthodoxy began losing women to the Reform and Conservative movements, it took stock of itself. It saw the handwriting on the wall as early as the 1930's, when one of its leaders, Rabbi Joseph Hyman Lookstein, became principal of the Hebrew Teachers' Training School for Girls. Actually one-third of all the students securing a Jewish education during that decade were girls. All Jewish denominations were beginning to count on their women. Loyal traditionalists could not and would not change the Law, the halakah, but it could and occasionally did shift its emphasis radically in the 1950's and early 1960's. Orthodoxy was obviously on the defensive;

it was fully conscious of the seductive appeal which advanced education had on its young women. Orthodox women could no longer be ignored or neglected. Stern College for Women was opened at Yeshiva University to give them a sound Jewish and general education. There was even talk among the Orthodox of giving women administrative responsibility on the boards of synagogues and national commissions. The new apologetics stoutly maintained that women were not inferior in matters religious, but owing to their psyche and physical characteristics, women had been assigned a different role by the Bible and the rabbis of old. The Orthodox conceded, of course, that women are the intellectual equals of men. Even the ultra-pietist Orthodox, the Hasidim, now insisted on the need for giving their womenfolk a thorough grounding in Jewish lore. A new sensibility showed itself in Orthodox circles.

From the 1920's on, the Conservatives profited by American Jewry's irrepressible turn to the left. They were determined to save their women for a Judaism which they saw synthesizing the best in Orthodoxy and modernism. The Conservative movement was successful, for by the third quarter of the century it had become, and it still is, American Judaism's largest denomination. Its Women's League, in 1979, had eight hundred sisterhoods and 200,000 members. Conservatives were characterized by an enlightened opportunism: Friday night services, the use of the organ, family pews, the English sermon, and the bat mitzvah ritual all became more or less standard in Conservative synagogues. Decorum was maintained, and the old "commercialism" of auctioning off synagogal privileges was eliminated. Women were loyal to this new movement because it courted them. The Conservative Jewess, frequently a college student or university graduate, could participate in a dignified service which was in many respects comparable to what Reform Jews and Christians enjoyed. True, during the 1950's, women of this centrist group were in no sense deemed religiously equal to their men, but for the time being they were quite content. It would not be until the 1970's that some among them would rise up with radical demands.

All three major American Jewish denominations were able to recruit young people in the years following World War II because of a strong undertow of romanticism and flight into the past, a flight set in motion by the sufferings of Eastern European Jewry and the devastating German massacres which destroyed most of the Jews of Europe. Reform Judaism turned to the right ritually and theologically under the impact of anti-Semitism and the closing of the world's ports to Jewish refugees. Latter-day political nationalism, Zionism, had now become an integral part of Reform. Attendance at services in most Reform synagogues was pitifully small, yet religion was coming into its own. Ideologically and emotionally, though not structurally, American Jewish youth started moving closer to one another. Some of the youth were friendly to the synagogue and its institutions; many were indifferent; the actual number of those who were hostile was small. Thousands of young American Jews flocked to the summer camps established primarily by the Reformers and the Conservatives. It was almost possible to speak of a spiritual renascence among the youth. In the eyes of the Gentiles, Judaism now assumed respectability; it was accepted as a coequal in the American trinity of Protestantism, Catholicism, and Judaism—a recognition which enhanced its appeal in the eyes of the children of Israel.

The Gentle Revolution

The Jewish "Camp Movement," in which the girls played their part along with the boys, was in no sense an aspect of the women's liberationist movement; it was not a manifestation of an assertive feminine consciousness. And yet, the mid-twentieth century did witness and did document the rebirth of the Women's Declaration of Independence, first enunciated at Seneca Falls, New York, in 1848. Unquestionably, the rise of the National Council of Jewish Women in 1893, of Hadassah in 1912, the sisterhoods in 1913, and the Women's League in 1918 had marked a gentle, yet very real revolution. Overtly, these national associations were either Jewish sociocultural societies or religious or Zionist auxiliaries. In fact, they were much more. Women were determined to follow their own bent. They may not have been set on making history, but they made it by being what they themselves wanted to be. The drive toward self-determination was intensified as these female organizations grew and prospered. They were joined by the B'nai B'rith Women, the Women's Labor Zionist Organization of America (Pioneer Women), the women's division of the right-wing Agudath Israel of America, and the Hasidic Agudas N'shei U'bnos Chabad ("The Association of the Wives and Daughters of the Chabad"). An impressive newcomer among these national associations was the Women's American ORT (Organization for Rehabilitation Through Training), founded in 1927. Today ORT is an international body which finances and supports vocational schools in New York City, South America, Europe, North Africa, Iran, and Israel. It is the boast of these ladies that they are the fastest-growing Jewish women's group in the United States. Theirs is essentially a worldwide philanthropic association supplementing the work of the male-controlled American Jewish Joint Distribution Committee (JDC). By the 1960's, the several America-based Jewish women's organizations could muster almost a million members, nearly a fifth of the entire American Jewish community. The growing influence of women in this country was documented in 1978 by the admission of Hadassah and Women's ORT into the National Jewish Community Relations Advisory Council. The National Council of Jewish Women was already a member of this prestigious umbrella defense organization.

Women Leaders

Among this million or so women, who were the notables? There were hundreds, if not thousands, of exceptionally able and dedicated women—doers and activists. In this instance, comparison and selection is certainly difficult. May Weisser, born on the Lower East Side to a family of Russian-Rumanian immigrants, went to work for the Hebrew National Orphan House as a volunteer when she was fourteen (1914). At fifteen, she was given a paying job by the orphanage; at twenty-three, she was superintendent of the Israel Orphan Asylum of New York City, which ultimately sheltered two hundred orphan children. She married her boss, the founder of the asylum, Judge Gustave Hartman.

Fanny Fligelman Brin (1884—1961) was also born in Rumania,

though she was reared in Minnesota, where she went to college, earned a Phi Beta Kappa key, taught school in Minneapolis, and soon became an active worker in a number of civic and Jewish associations. Fanny labored tirelessly to aid refugees fleeing from Germany. She devoted many hours to the League of Women Voters and the peace movement. Her vigorous opposition to militarism can best be summed up in an address she made in New Orleans in 1935: "A nation which spends four-fifths of its income on war and preparation for war cannot advance the civilized arts of life." Yet only five years later, the German threat to democracy compelled Mrs. Brin to change her anti-war stance. In 1932, she was elected president of the National Council of Jewish Women and served until 1938. In 1934, her efforts on behalf of peace, democracy, women's rights, and Judaism prompted Carrie Chapman Catt to name her one of America's ten most eminent women. Well over a generation ago, Fanny Brin said: "Today's world is a difficult one for women to find their place. But some day there will be a truer integration of women's abilities and contributions . . . and it will be a better world."

These two women, May Weisser and Fanny Brin, are singled out not because they were exceptional but rather because they are typical examples of mid-twentieth-century American Jewish activists. In almost every town and city which had a Jewish community, there were at least one or two women who were exemplary leaders. Their general level of achievement was so high that few individuals stood out. Leadership, in fact, is exceedingly difficult to define in a community where one finds numerous women of culture and administrative capacity. Had they lived in earlier generations, many of America's twentieth-century social activists would have been lauded to the skies.

An increasing percentage of these female "movers and shakers" came from families of East European immigrant stock. Actually, by 1960, many of these newcomers were no longer aware of the national provenance of their parents; if they did not know they often did not care. Whether papa or grandpa had come from Berlin or Bialystok was a matter of complete indifference to them. Ever since 1931, when the anti-Jewish, anti-Catholic, anti-Slavic, and anti-

Mediterranean immigration acts of the 1920's finally took effect, American Jewry had been well on the road to homogenization. The "German" and "Russian" Jews were dying out; from now on there only would be "Americans."

Refugee German Women in America

Even the thousands of German émigrés who had escaped the crucible of Europe were soon reasonably well acculturated. The highly educated women among them, European Jewry's elite women, brought a new dimension to the Jewish communities here. Like the men, they were "émigrés de luxe"—a term once employed by the late Isaac Max Rubinow in a denigratory sense, since many German refugees of the 1930's displayed a very healthy respect for themselves and their Germanic background. American Jewish leaders did everything they could to help them, but rather frowned on their mannerisms in much the same way as they had fifty years earlier frowned on the pronounced Yiddishkeit of the East European greenhorns. After the persecutions began in Germany, a meeting was called in the Hebrew Union College chapel in Cincinnati to orient the city's German Jewish newcomers to the American way of life. Max Hirsch, a member of the Cincinnati Jewish elite, a philanthropist and social worker, tended to look askance at those immigrants who read German newspapers in the streetcars. The chairman of Cincinnati's Jewish Community Relations Committee, the American-born son of a Russian Jew who had come to the United States in the 1880's, turned to Hirsch and said to him quietly: "Max, look at these newcomers; they are the grandparents of our grandchildren." Max Hirsch blinked.

The phrase "émigrés de luxe" is employed in this history of the American Jewess in a positive, complimentary sense. Mrs. Jakob Michael (d. 1964), a scion of the Frankfort-on-the-Main Sondheimer metal-trading magnates, served as the head of the women's division of the New York United Jewish Appeal Drive, a very prestigious post. She and her husband gave generously to some American Orthodox Jewish institutions. Dr. Julie Braun-Vogelstein

(d. 1971), scion of a very distinguished German family, received her doctorate in art history and Egyptology. Hildegard Lewy (d. 1967) taught Assyriology at the Hebrew Union College; her doctorate was in physics, but she later studied Assyriology in order to assist her husband, Julius Lewy, a very well known orientalist. Like the Lewys, Dr. Frieda Wunderlich was a fugitive from Germany; she had served in the Prussian parliament and been looked upon as an outstanding social scientist. An economist, sociologist, and authority on labor, she served from 1939 to 1940, as dean of the Graduate Faculty of Political and Social Science of the "University in Exile," the New School for Social Research. She had been elected unanimously by her colleagues. Erika Perlmann (1912—1974), a native of Czechoslovakia, became a professor of biochemistry at the Rockefeller Institute; Mrs. Bela Fabian (d. 1964) had been a member of the anti-German and anti-Russian underground at a time when the Germans and later the Russians occupied her native Hungary. Helene Deutsch (b. 1884), a Polish-speaking Galician Jewess, is one of the pioneers of Freudian psychiatry; Baroness Lili Hatvany (1890—1967), a playwright and screenwriter, was a well-known author and dramatist before she fled to the United States. Her family, sugar industrialists, were patrons of Hungary's National Rabbinical Seminary. Like the baroness, writer Vicki Baum (d. 1960) was a native of the Austro-Hungarian Empire. This talented woman, a fine musician, was the author of the best-seller *Grand Hotel*, a novel, and later a screenplay, which brought her fame, wealth, and notoriety. She once told an interviewer: "You can live down any number of flops but you can't live down a success."

All these women were Central European immigrants who had escaped the Holocaust and found a home here in the United States. The most notable of the lot was undoubtedly Hannah Arendt (1906—1975), the political scientist, writer, and editor. Like Frieda Wunderlich, she taught at the New School; her field was political philosophy. After fleeing from Germany, she took refuge in France, but when the Germans occupied that country, she fled to the United States, where she finally found a secure haven. It was years before she received due recognition as a seminal thinker dealing with the complex problems of Nazism, Communism, totalitarianism, anti-

Semitism, imperialism, war, and revolution. Here in the United States she took on odd jobs, working for the Conference on Jewish Relations and other Jewish organizations. For a time she was the chief editor for the Schocken press. As had been true in France, where she was an executive for Youth Aliyah, the Jews here always saw to it that she had a job. Once her talents were recognized she advanced rapidly. She taught at a number of universities; Princeton made her its first full-fledged female professor; Denmark singled her out for her contribution to European culture. She was awarded several honorary degrees, some by this country's greatest universities. Arendt's works brought her extravagant praise; she was recognized as one of the outstanding intellectuals of the mid-twentieth century—and attacked for the startling conclusions which characterized some of her studies. Many resented her critical view of the European Jewish leaders of the pre-Holocaust period. Like most other Jewish refugee intellectuals, Arendt had no ties to the Jewish religion.

Postscript

In general, Jewesses of the pre-1960 decades were distinguished for their education, their drive for recognition in the economy, their solid achievements, and their determination to "make it" in a man's world—but no matter what they did it was still a man's world. The forty years between 1920 and 1960 saw the rise of thousands of women who had escaped the Egypt of enthrallment without even the guidance of a female Moses. Their revolt was low-key, but nevertheless real. If divorce is a form of liberation, then those rebels broke their shackles; most divorces emanated from the wives, not from the husbands. A very substantial minority were no longer immured in the kitchen, in religious traditions, or in time-honored social imperatives; yet it was not all peaches and cream for the American Jewess. Many would have applauded the bitter outburst of Bertha Pappenheim, the founder of Germany's League of Jewish Women: "If there is justice in the world to come, women will make the laws and men will have the babies." Popular prejudice against women was strong; Jewish husbands, like most males, thought of themselves as masters of their households. Women in traditional Jewish homes could not hurdle the talmudic barriers erected in Mesopotamia fifteen hundred years ago. Judeophobia—already centuries old when Jesus preached—persisted in the Gentile world. Despite these hazards, however, women made their way. Of the forty-six biographies of deceased Jewesses in the authoritative *Notable American Women*, forty had lived in the years from 1900 to 1950.

The new recognition accorded women in the synagogues and their spiritual, ethical, and cultural advances in these decades of ferment are adequately documented. In 1958, the rabbi of Cincinnati's Rockdale Temple asked the girls and boys in his confirmation class to write ethical wills. This was purely a pedagogical device. They did. The high level of intelligence evidenced by the fifteen-year-old youngsters was startling. It may well be that they were an unusual lot, for they were all from middle-class and upper-middle-class families and each attended a college preparatory high school or went to an elite academy. In any case, what they wrote revealed an unusual degree of sophistication and intellectual ability. Their emphases were ethical, humanitarian, and compassionate. The American Jewish girls of 1958 had come a long way since 1779, when the fifteen-year-old Rachel Gratz wrote to her "Honored Farther" from wartorn Lancaster: "I have just begun to cipher and I am very much delighted at it."

·6·

The Women's Revolt and the American Jewess, 1963—1980

America's Women Begin to Come into Their Own

I N 1848, when the feminists met at Seneca Falls, very few American women of working age had a paying job; by the late 1970's, at least 50 percent were in the labor force, and the percentage was increasing steadily. Present-day historians of American women focus on the rebirth of the women's liberation movement in the 1960's; the 1848 women's Declaration of Sentiments, the original "revolt," had been little more than a brave and, on the whole, futile gesture. The Uprising of the 1960's, however, was an effective one that would bring about almost shocking changes in all of American life; it directly affected some 2,000,000 Jewish females.

The women's revolt was in part stimulated by the rise of the New Left, a spontaneous mass outbreak (some would say, hysteria) led by American college youth. This emotional upheaval, somewhat reminiscent of the medieval crusades, was sparked by the courageous protests, marches, and boycotts of Blacks in the 1950's and early 1960's, when they battled for an extension of their civil rights. In turn, their heroic rebellion fired a campus revolt of American youth, who fought for a larger voice in the conduct of public affairs. They opposed the military draft and the Vietnam conflict; they worried about the horrors of nuclear war and feared that they were living in a civilization fated to destroy itself. The young men and women of the 1950's and 1960's were shocked by a society which they saw only in the darkest of hues. While they did despair of the future, they were not resigned to it; their desperation only drove them on to passionate protests, even to violence. Their mood, if not their philosophy, was evangelical. They were not looking for "pie in the sky by and by"; they were seeking a better world for every human being here and now. But they had no plan—they had no effective leadership.

The turmoil which the New Left brought to American campuses involved women as well as men. The revolts were exemplary for the women. Society at large cried out for salvage because of its evils. Despite the fourteenth and fifteenth amendments, Blacks were still oppressed and had to be liberated once and for all. It was but a step to demand liberation for an even larger group, women, who had been suffering disabilities since the dawn of history. In 1963, amid national and international upheavals, Betty Friedan's *Feminine Mystique* made its appearance. It was an appeal on behalf of a group which, however marginal, happened to be the world's largest majority: women. The theses of this Jewish free-lance writer were simple: ensconced on a pedestal, women were cherished, while in reality they were disabled; they were not permitted to make important decisions; their opportunities to advance in an attractive world of challenge were limited; they were tied to home and children and treated as inferiors. Women did want a home and children, but they did not wish to be denied careers; they demanded that men treat them as partners in every aspect of life; they wanted to fulfill themselves completely, totally.

The Feminine Mystique quickly became a best-seller. The book created a stir; over two million copies were sold. The ground had already been prepared not only by the spirit of revolt then sweeping the campuses, but by the appearance of the English translation of Simone de Beauvoir's *The Second Sex* (1953), which described the disabilities to which women were subject, and by Eleanor Flexner's *Century of Struggle: The Woman's Rights Movement in the United States* (1959).

After the appearance of *The Feminine Mystique*, many women

became acutely conscious of the handicaps to which they were subject, the price they had to pay for being "feminine." They now
began reaching out for the good things of life which had been denied
them: political and economic opportunity, national office, real
equality. They knew that they were as well-educated as men, and
believed themselves to be just as capable. Thus it was that a feminist
movement of some consequence took shape. The patriarchal system
which put them in second place, even if an honored second place,
would have to be radically modified. Family, home, religion were
dear to them, but there was still another world outside—a warm,
alluring, beckoning place. It was an attractive universe of politics,
science, commerce, prestige, and reward, a world of freedom, even
of sexual freedom, which had always been denied them. Women are
human beings. They do not want to be defined and circumscribed
by sex; they insisted on equal human status despite their physical and
psychological distinctiveness. This quiet, nonviolent feminist revolt
of the 1960's now became a reality—it was a social revolution.

Feminist Arguments and Goals Spelled Out

America's predominantly male Congress did not realize what it had
let itself in for when it passed the Civil Rights Act of 1964, pro-
hibiting discrimination because of race, color, religion, sex, or national origin. With the doors wide open, women rushed in to secure
privileges they had long sought by creating an organization for that
purpose. NOW, the National Organization for Women, made its
appearance in 1966; its prime purpose was to implement the Civil
Rights Act. The feminists were by no means of one mind in their
demands, but they were agreed that they had a right to all the
political, economic, social, and religious privileges hitherto pre-
empted by men. There was talk of contraceptive information
centers, the right to safe and legal abortions, of the need for paid
maternity leaves. They asked that working parents be accorded tax
breaks for child care; they pleaded for government-funded child-care
centers for women on the job, shelters for battered wives, acceptance
of lesbians as full members of society, more rights in divorce, admis-

sion of women into the hierarchy of religious officiants, more females appointed to public office. Husbands, some wives said, must share equally in housekeeping and child-rearing. In 1971, the Women's National Political Caucus was organized to assure the effective emancipation of women by a constitutional Equal Rights Amendment. The amendment was passed by Congress in 1972; as of the date of publication of this book, it had not yet been ratified by the requisite number of state legislatures.

The Jewish Female Revolt in the 1970's

Moderate and conservative feminists wanted the same rights as men and were prepared to cooperate with them; radical liberationists called for a social transformation involving the possible restructuring of home, family life, and society. Thus, there evolved two basic programs for the emancipation of women, both with Jewish leaders and followers. Gloria Steinem stands out among the conservative feminists. She is the granddaughter of Pauline Perlmutter Steinem, a prominent clubwoman and communal worker. One might venture to say that Gloria came by her leadership qualities honestly. Grandma Pauline Perlmutter, born in Poland, reared in Germany, spent most of her life in Toledo, where she stood out as a Progressive. She was a follower of Samuel Milton ("Golden Rule") Jones. Within a few years after her settlement in town, she became a leader in the general and in the Jewish community. Her primary interest was in ethics. This explains her membership in the Christian-oriented Golden Rule Mothers' Club, in theosophy, and in Reform Judaism. She was president of the women's auxiliary of the local Reform temple. By 1904 Pauline was a leader in six women's organizations. That was the year the voters put her on the school board, the first Toledo woman to hold elective office. Four years later she became president of the Ohio Woman's Suffrage Association and president of the town's Jewish Free Loan Association. She was a determined Progressive reformer—and a Jewish activist. Women, she believed, were entitled to political rights, but the man was "the head of the

The Henry Street Settlemen. Founded by Lillian Wald (1867-1940), one of America's most noted social reformers, the Henry Street Settlement was organized in 1895 to help the hundreds of thousands of Jewish immigrants in New York's Lower East Side cope with their difficulties in adjusting to American life. (From a drawing by Abraham Phillips)

Striking women from the Amalgamated Clothing Workers Union. A large percentage of the workers were Jews.

Alla Nazimova (1879-1945). A great Russian Jewish actress, she came to America in 1905 and was known for her presentation of characters in plays by Ibsen.

Helena Rubinstein (1871-1965). A truly remarkable American Jewish businesswoman, she was one of the principal founders of the lucrative cosmetics industry.

Judge Caroline K. Simon (b. 1900). New York's first woman secretary of state, she became a judge of the Court of Claims in New York.

Anna M. Rosenberg (b. 1902). A distinguished public servant, she held a number of important posts, highlighted by her appointment in 1950 as an assistant secretary of defense, the highest position yet attained in government by an American Jewish woman.

Courtesy, U.S. Army photographs

Beatrice Sanders (b. 1900). In 1952 she became one of the first women to assume the presidency of a temple congregation. Upon the death of her husband, Gilbert, who had served for many years as the lay-rabbi of Congregation Aaron in Trinidad, Colorado, she became the lay-rabbi of the congregation.

Bess Myerson (b. 1924). A talented musician and a former beauty queen, she was appointed New York City's commissioner of consumer affairs in 1969.

Roberta Peters (b. 1930). She is one of the most famous opera stars in America, and was the first American recipient of the prestigious Bolshoi medal presented by the Soviet Union.

Courtesy, Cincinnati Enquirer

Hannah Arendt (1906-1975). A refugee from Nazi Germany, she was a brilliant political philosopher and her book, *The Origins of Totalitarianism,* has become a classic in its field.

Golda Meir (1898-1978). She came to America as a child and received her formal education in this country. In 1921 she settled in Palestine and was a long-time Israeli political leader after the creation of the Jewish state in 1948. She became the country's prime minister in 1969. (Sculpture by Ruth Lee Leventhal, New York City)

house." This remarkable immigrant was a Jew, a German, a fighting liberal, a homemaker. When Grandma died in 1940, little Gloria, the future feminist and editor of *Ms.*, was only six years of age.

Why have individual Jewish women been so prominent in the forefront of the movement? It is after all a fact that the actual number of Jewish women in this country is probably not much more than 1 percent of the total population. There are many diverse drives pushing these Jewish feminist theoreticians. Jews hate injustice because of the harassment, prejudice, and mass murders to which they have been exposed for over two thousand years. For many Jews, the German Holocaust has been the climactic trauma. They have never been able to forget that they were once slaves in Egypt, as both the Pentateuch and the *Haggadah*, the ritual for the Passover feast, spell out in detail. Jews are a minority that has always been disabled. Since most of them believe that they are still subject to disabilities, they have tended to ally themselves with liberals in the modern state in their quest for equality. They are ambitious and crave recognition; they exhibit an intense need for status. Jews, men and women alike, are fully aware of their ability and intelligence. They have pushed forward and succeeded largely because many are convinced that they possess leadership qualities. A movement like women's liberation had a powerful appeal for many mid- and late-twentieth-century American Jewesses.

The outstanding American feminists who happened to be Jewish were not the leaders of a Jewish female "revolt," as such. Actually, this "Jewish uprising" was, in organizational terms, of little consequence. Jewish women, remaining well within the realm of Jewish commitment, had been slow to rebel; by the 1960's, Jews had become one of the most affluent middle-class groups in the United States. Did the typical American Jewess have anything to gain by voicing objection to the order of things? Nonetheless a Jewish feminist protest did surface in the 1970's. The protestors were often traditional Jewesses. Time brings perspective and suggests that Jewish feminism is not altogether new in American Jewish history. Past generations have known individuals with a sense of feminine self-esteem, women quite conscious of their accomplishments and the value of their work. Even a Victorian like Julia Richman lashed out at men who looked upon women as inferiors, or mere housekeepers. Beneath her starched blouse there beat a rebellious heart.

When the present-day Jewish feminists made their appearance on the scene, they bespoke a tendency which had never been entirely absent—but what did they want? Who were they? As with non-Jews, their basic drive was fulfillment within the realm of their own particular way of life. Perhaps no one can really fathom what these Jewish petitioners of the 1970's were seeking; each individual is a unique personality with her own desires, needs, and ambitions. Affluent women are not primarily concerned with their economic future; they want respect in their role as homemakers. Indeed, for many, home is not the final answer to their needs; they look for recognition in a larger sphere. They will not be gainsaid. Undoubtedly, the many thousands of Jewish women now employed in commerce and trade have built-in problems if they are married. They must come to terms with their husbands, children, and their obligations as housekeepers; they need help if they are to cope with all their responsibilities. Because they provide such a substantial portion of the family income, they ask for, and often receive, the right to participate in all important decisions.

Beyond the home are the Jewish community and the synagogue. What does the "new woman" seek from these? That depends upon her interest in her fellow-Jews and in Judaism, the religion and the culture. In general, the affiliated Jewess resents being looked upon as a second-class citizen; she expects equality, an appointment to the federation hierarchy or to the boards of welfare agencies. Her amour propre prods her to make a career for herself in the community of her religious peers. Among the Reformers, there are few worlds left to conquer. Women, now gladly accepted as members of the synagogue, are frequently elected to its board, though even at this late hour not in proportion to their numbers. Still, more and more women are being elected presidents of Reform congregations. By 1978, about 150 Reform and Conservative Jewesses had occupied that office. Women rabbis in growing numbers have already graduated from the liberal seminaries and are entering the rabbinate. Young women, fascinated by the prospect of a rabbinical career, of mounting a rostrum and talking down to a throng of respectful listeners, are flocking in large numbers to the Hebrew Union College— Jewish Institute of Religion and the Reconstructionist Rabbinical College. Of course, it is still too early to determine whether congregations will accept them and accord them the courtesies showered on male officiants. Female rabbis are still very much of a curiosity. A guest at a wedding, noticing that the rabbi was heavy with child, exclaimed: "A pregnant rabbi—I just can't believe it."

The concessions made in the 1960's by the Orthodox bear watching; their bright girls are encouraged to study the rabbinical writings, traditionally always a male preserve. In 1979 a brilliant young woman was studying at Yeshiva University for a doctorate in Talmud. These traditionalists continue to talk of finding a place in the structure and administration of Orthodox Judaism for their womenfolk, but to date there has been no amelioration of the difficulties facing Orthodox women in the area of marriage, remarriage, and divorce. The wording of the restrictive laws is precise; the inherent problems are apparently insurmountable. Not a few Orthodox women are resentful that no change for the better has yet been effected in their status.

Conservative Jews, always more alert to the needs of the time, have already begun moving to the left. They have been engaged in a continuous process of adjustment for well over a half a century. In a number of synagogues the women were granted male prerogatives, recognized as members of a praying quorum (1973), and invited to read from the Law (1955). It is likely that male-oriented laws of marriage and divorce will be perceptibly modified to accord equality to women in the foreseeable future. Conservative women who still revere tradition are hoping to be admitted as witnesses in courts of rabbinic law; the liberals among them have asked for the acceptance of women as cantors and rabbis. Ultimately, pressure from the left will probably induce the Conservatives to ordain women. The liberalism of the Reformers, and their rejection of the authoritativeness of religious codes, compels the Conservatives and even stimulates the Orthodox to take action lest they lose adherents. Girls of Orthodox and Conservative parentage are as well-educated, and intellectually alert, as the daughters of Reform congregants.

Jewish Feminist Organizations, 1972—1980

In order to reach their goals, Jewish feminists created organizations, media, and instrumentalities necessary for their purposes. The initiative did not come from the left; the followers of Reform felt no need to take action, since they had been making advances slowly but consistently since the 1840's. The first remonstrances came from women in Conservative synagogues, women who believed it was imperative to bridge the gap between the talmudic and the modern world. They were slow in getting started; it was almost a decade after the publication of *The Feminine Mystique* before they bestirred themselves.

In the 1960's, as the amorphous, multifaceted New Left movement developed, two diverse Jewish trends stood out. The one—aberrant, anti-Zionist, anti-Israel, cosmopolitan—was probably not untouched by self-hatred. This group never formally organized. The other, intensely Jewish, set out to establish small communities of young adults, fellowship retreats, havurot whose historical antecedents reached back to pre-Christian times, though the modern college youth probably never knew this when they first turned to self-containment. It is very questionable, too, whether these contemporary Jewish communes have been influenced by the more than three thousand collectives that dotted the American landscape from Massachusetts to California during the 1970's. Uncomfortable in the conventional assemblies of their peers and elders, these dedicated young men and women met together for prayer, study, companionship, cultural and religious edification, and mutual reassurance. They emphasized personal involvement. They wanted to be Jews on their own terms. A number of havurot remained well within the sphere of a congregation. Some fellowships were family-centered groups unhappy with Jewish congregational and communal establishments and bureaucracies. Their members were "searchers," part of a larger drive of Jewish youth and adults, too, for spiritual peace, and an acceptable way of life. During the 1970's, these havurah initiates were content to stay in the Jewish fold: a haunting awareness of the Holocaust, the persecution of Soviet Jews, constant fears that Israel would fall victim to massacre—saw to that. Many were historical romantics who embraced the Law and its minute prescriptions as their own treasured possession. Their sympathies for Jews and Judaism were rich and lasting. All told, the havurot of the 1970's probably never included more than a few thousand associates.

The women and men who sought spiritual refuge apart from conventional Jewish organizations were only one aspect of the Uprising of the 1960's; another was a demonstration by a handful of women at a convention of Conservative rabbis in 1972. These petitioners, Conservative Jewesses, had already created an organization of their own, Ezrat Nashim. By a purely fortuitous quirk of the Hebrew language, the phrase Ezrat Nashim can be translated either "Help for Women" or the "Female Enclave." (Whether the founders had this double-entendre in mind is uncertain.) Ezrat Nashim was one of the first, perhaps the very first, Jewish female group to come into being under the impact of the New Left ferment. More immediately, Ezrat Nashim was probably influenced by the North American Jewish Students' Network, an umbrella service organization founded in 1969 by students who wished to emphasize their identity as Jews. The network was all-embracing, for its assortment included Zionists, socialists, Yiddishists, and religionists.

These Conservative women religionists sought complete parity with men in the practice and principles of God's Law. Ezrat Nashim marked the beginnings of the revolt among those women who, unhappy though they might have been, had refused to throw off the yoke of the Law. Their appearance in 1972 may possibly have been influenced by the imminent ordination of Sally Priesand, the first woman in history to be ordained by a rabbinical seminary. In February 1973, the Students' Network convoked the National Jewish Women's Conference; in June they published an anthology, *The Jewish Woman*, whose purpose was to stimulate women's concern for themselves. Some impact seems to have been made by them and by the liberals in the Conservative rabbinate, for in September 1973, the Rabbinical Assembly declared it permissible—though not mandatory—to count women in a minyan (a praying quorum). This was a significant change from past practice. The following year, probably in imitation of the older nondenominational National Organization for Women, the Jewish Feminist Organization (JFO) made its appearance. Its program was a reflection of the demands of Ezrat Nashim: equality with the men in matters religious.

By the 1970's, then, women were no longer inclined to submit to male domination. A number of women were serving as congregational presidents; others had already received Reform and Reconstructionist ordination. The Conservatives, too, were inching to the left; a woman was permitted to finish the prescribed course in the Conservative cantorial school—though, to be sure, she was denied a diploma. But, mirabile dictu, the Jewish Theological Seminary had a woman on its staff teaching Talmud. Ultra-right-wing Orthodox, like Agudath Israel, look askance at feminism, though they too are prepared to offer their womenfolk more opportunity to study the traditional classics. They are opposed to the Equal Rights Amendment for fear that the traditional wall between the sexes will be breached, leading to immorality. The Chabad Hasidim, who run an exceptional public relations program, were giving their parochial-school girls the skills to make a place for themselves in the commercial-industrial world. They are not bent on compelling them to remain secluded in their homes. Evangelical in spirit, the Hasidim were vigorously recruiting women for their fundamentalist religious philosophy and establishing Chabad houses, where questing or unhappy young women could find themselves. Chabad was, incidentally, demonstrating that feminism is not necessarily liberal or leftist; its essence is the right of women to come to flower. Chabad's efforts are feminist in that they want their female neophytes and womenfolk to enjoy peace of mind and happiness—but the basic goals of the Hasidim have not changed: woman's place is in the home. Furthermore, let no one be in doubt: the world of the Hasidim would remain completely male-dominated, God Himself had so decreed: "He [Adam] shall rule over thee [Eve]" (Genesis 3:16). When the Golden Wedding Anniversary of the Hasidic Rebbe was celebrated in 1979, the women were all curtained off from the men.

By the late 1950's, the Chabad women had already begun publishing a Yiddish magazine of their own, *Di Yiddishe Heim* ("The Jewish Home"). In the 1970's Jewish feminists issued an English-language quarterly, *Lilith.* The name is intriguing; one rabbinic source has it that Lilith was created by God when He made Adam, even before He fashioned Eve. When Adam began asserting his overlordship, Lilith answered: "We are both equal because we both come from the earth." She was a crude creature, determined, demonic. Did the Jewish feminists of the 1970's hope that her spirit would fire the movement? Like Lilith, they too were rebels; they refused to be passive, submissive—however beloved—bondwomen.

Even as late as 1979, no sizable community had given women as a group the authority or the power their work merited. A survey made in 1976 indicated that only three out of fifty-five Jewish communities had women as presidents of their federations; 22 percent had female vice-presidents, but these were women who represented constituent women's associations. While it is true that women were being chosen to fill important honorary offices in a few of the smaller towns, it is very questionable whether even these presiding dignitaries were part of the elite who pulled the strings behind the scenes. Only 13 percent of the people delegated to raise funds were women; 16.5 percent of all executive committee members were females. About 15 percent of the monies raised by the United Jewish Appeal in 1975 was collected by women, but this percentage would be radically increased if women were credited with one-half of the millions given by their husbands.

In 1979, women were not well represented at either the honorary or the salaried executive level in the Jewish community's formal institutional structure. Traditionally women were rarely accepted as leaders. Men resisted sharing power, because women were now seen as rivals. Few men wanted affirmative action in their own Jewish world, where at least one-half of the potential aspirants were female. Of 234 organizations of national significance listed in the 1979 *American Jewish Year Book*, only 26 have female presidents or chief executives. Out of 300 Jewish communal associations, only 3 percent had women directing their organizations—and this at a time when almost 80 percent of the actual labor force was female. Even the most important Jewish women's magazines are still edited by men. Nevertheless, it is evident that women are creeping forward; they are finally beginning to receive recognition. This is true in social-welfare agencies, where women serve as both paid executives and representative lay leaders. One of the reasons women have advanced in the communal hierarchy is that they have more time than most men and can come to the meetings during the daytime. Nevertheless, almost everywhere, the final, the important decisions are made by an elite group of men.

The American Jewess Moves Forward

There can be no question that American Jewesses have moved forward since the 1890's, when they first took the bit between their teeth. They stubbornly and steadily continued their advance in the twentieth century, even though they were not given their due. On occasion though, some individuals were. It is a relatively simple exercise to determine who these individuals were and why they were recognized—one need only examine the obituaries published annually in the *American Jewish Year Book*. Very few scholars have been memorialized, not because they did not exist, but because, in most instances, their visibility was low; they had no national organization to commemorate them. In a way, these vignettes are not truly representative of the achievements of American Jewish women, for one suspects that many of them were singled out solely because their death notices appeared in the *New York Times* and other metropolitan newspapers. With New York still the center of Jewish organizational activity in this country, it is understandable that the hinterland might be neglected. The portrayal of the achievements of notable women outside of New York City is thus necessarily inadequate, for about half of America's Jews do not live in the megalopolis or its environs. If these *Year Book* obituaries are augmented by others not included by the *Year Book* editors, a more detailed picture of the accomplishments of America's outstanding Jewish women may emerge.

Quite a number of the women whose lives are epitomized in the *Year Book* were executives who worked on an intermediate level. They held important positions in the American Jewish Committee and other national organizations. Executives on a lower level were ignored because they were thought of as hirelings. Volunteers who served at a high level in national Jewish associations were always given recognition, particularly if they led the National Council of Jewish Women or female auxiliaries established by the Reformers, the Orthodox, the Conservatives, the Reconstructionists, and the Zionists. Recognition here was virtually built in. Every decade of the twentieth century has had its abundance of civic-minded women. If they were wealthy and made generous contributions, they were always acclaimed; some of them were remembered more for their generous gifts than for their actual civic accomplishments. A few served secular universities—one was a trustee of a Catholic college—but as a rule they devoted themselves to Jewish institutions. Women have been very active as philanthropists, in the Mount Sinai School of Medicine, the Albert Einstein College of Medicine, Brandeis University, the Hebrew Union College, Gratz College, Dropsie University, and a number of other Jewish schools. Due deference has always been paid to the memory of women who worked for the United Jewish Appeal and New York's Federation of Jewish Philanthropies; large sums were expected here and were forthcoming.

These notables of the last generation were to be found everywhere: in schools of music, on the boards of symphonies and chamber music societies, in prison and parole work, in the American Red Cross. They sponsored art museums and homes for the aged. All in all, the list of their beneficiaries is very impressive. While elderly, insecure widows of wealth have a tendency to plead poverty and practice parsimony, the accumulatively large sums donated by them offer eloquent testimony that the "widow's syndrome" has not always been in evidence. Israel appeals to women; they support its welfare and cultural institutions like the Hebrew University, the Weizmann Institute of Science, and the Hadassah Hospital. It would seem that nationalism is the motivation which impels them to give. These distinguished female philanthropists not only support the United Jewish Appeal, a preponderance of whose millions go to Israel, but also the female American Zionist societies, such as Hadassah and Pioneer Women.

Helena Rubenstein (1871—1965) was a philanthropist of sorts who extended her largesse to Israel. The Tel Aviv Art Museum was a beneficiary of her generosity. In some respects she was America's most remarkable Jewish businesswoman. Rubenstein was one of the best-known contemporary American Jews: she was a very successful cosmetician whose career in the commercial and industrial world was notable. This was a self-made woman. As far as one can garner from the obfuscatory reports of her origins, she was born in Polish Galicia of humble parents and then moved on to Australia where, after years of struggle, she made a small fortune manufacturing a cold cream for women. Later she immigrated to London, where she opened a beauty salon. Within a few years she established branches of her business in Paris and other cities and became one of the continent's leading entrepreneurs in her field. The year 1914 saw her settled in the United States, where she became very wealthy as a manufacturer of beauty products. An exceptionally able and shrewd businesswoman, she sent salespersons on the road to demonstrate the proper use of makeup. Rubenstein certainly merits a place in history because she stands out as one of the principal founders of a large and lucrative industry. In the 1960's her firm had annual sales of about $60,000,000. Her personal estate of about $100,000,000 included a very valuable art collection. Several years after her death the business was sold to Colgate-Palmolive Company for over $142,000,000 in stock.

Helena Rubenstein was one of a very small number of Jewesses who competed successfully with men in the world of big business. Like Rubenstein, Mrs. Vivian Beaumont Allen was also very rich. She was, however, more fortunate in one sense—she had a millionaire for a father. The Beaumonts, originally Shoenbergs, were part of the May Company department store clan. Her father, Joseph E. Shoenberg, had begun modestly in the retail clothing trade at Leadville, Colorado, during the late 1870's. His store was known as "Cheap Joe's." Thus Mrs. Allen was in no sense self-made, but, as she boasted, she knew how to "add" and "subtract," how to make money, and how to give it away. She was a good investor, and increased the millions her father had left her. The $3,000,000 Vivian Beaumont Theater at New York's Lincoln Center for the Performing Arts was part of the process of "subtraction." On her death in 1962, she, too, like Vivian Straus Dixon, was buried out of St. Bartholomew's on Park Avenue.

There were very few American women in the third quarter of the twentieth century who were good enough or lucky enough to head large corporations. A 1973 *Fortune* survey of sixty-five hundred corporations revealed that a bare handful were run by women—among them, however, there was a disproportionately large number of very capable Jewesses. One, the owner of the *Washington Post*, got off to a good start by inheriting her job. Two others co-founded multimillion-dollar businesses with their husbands: one in the toy business, and the other in fabric design. Three others were the sole architects of their fortunes. One had a hobby of making organdy pinafores for children, a hobby she turned into a business grossing $3,000,000 a year. Another, who had earned her Ph.D. at Columbia University in chemistry, established a successful research laboratory; a third founded a company which grew and canned a special type of tomato—its annual sales ran into the millions. In 1966, its proprietor sold her business for close to $9,000,000.

A very substantial number of the women among the hundreds memorialized in the annual issues of the *American Jewish Year Book* were outstanding social workers, volunteers for the most part. They held positions of leadership, or would not have merited notice in the *Year Book*. They have this in common: they wanted to be of service to the Jewish and larger general community. The list of organizations for which individual women have labored, and at times have stood at the helm, includes immigration aid groups, settlement houses, community centers, camps, Jewish nursing schools, the Community Chest, city blood banks, child-guidance societies, crime prevention groups, civil rights agencies, and vocational guidance associations. These women have worked for the blind, under-privileged youth, the Council of Jewish Federations, and Women's American ORT. A former president of the National Council of Jewish Women, a woman from Louisiana, lent a helping hand to the National Association for the Advancement of Colored People in her state. The late Susan Brandeis Gilbert, the daughter of Louis D. Brandeis, was active in the National League of Women Voters. The hope of aiding others inspired some women at a very early age. In a bat mitzvah talk at the Washington Hebrew Congregation of Washington, D.C., Justice Louis D. Brandeis' thirteen-year-old great-granddaughter lauded her ancestor for his career as the people's attorney and his efforts to better working conditions for women; it is her intention to follow in his footsteps.

Relatively few of the worthies recorded in the *Year Book* necrologies were Orthodox; a greater number were adherents of the Conservative movement, the majority were Reform Jewesses. The reason for this is clear: Reform Jews were recruited primarily from older settlers who had been engaged in communal and welfare work for generations and thus enjoyed a degree of social status which induced the socially prominent Gentiles to co-opt them. It is interesting to note the appearance of a number of social workers who came to the United States as German refugees; after only a few decades on American soil, they became executives of note.

Notable Contemporaries

The above description of the work done by outstanding women has been based on a large number of necrologies, but inasmuch as the 1970's have been years of radical change, notable living Jewesses seem to have had more interesting careers than the deceased. Barbara Tuchman, for instance, a pro-Zionist member of the Morgenthau-Wertheim clan, has won two Pulitzer Prizes and in 1979 was elected president of the American Academy and Institute of Arts and Letters. She is the Academy's first woman presiding officer. These living worthies have captured the public's imagination. Three of the four to be described in detail below are feminists. Two are academicians, the other two are politicians. Lucy Dawidowicz (b. 1915) is an historian, a college professor, who has written an excellent book on the Holocaust. An observant, committed Orthodox religionist, she is drawn—somewhat defensively—to the traditional Hebrew prayers and classical Orthodox service. The *mehizah*, the physical barrier which separates women from the menfolk in the synagogue, permits her to concentrate on her prayers. Dawidowicz loves the warm atmosphere of the old-fashioned synagogue, although she deprecates the gossip. (The men love it *because* of the gossip. Their Father has many mansions, and they are very much at home in every one of them.) Dr. Dawidowicz is "modern" enough to desire a decorous service, but she would never be comfortable with the sepulchral silences of a classical Reform temple.

The flamboyant, colorful Bella Abzug (b. 1920) is more vibrant than Lucy, but then, she is a politician. Someone has even called her "Battling Bella." Abzug, a lawyer, served three terms in Congress during the 1970's. Congress was no paradise for her: she was not made very welcome, for she was a woman, a Jew, a New Yorker, a feminist. She had four strikes against her before she even entered the Capitol. Abzug is a strong advocate of international peace, an ardent champion of civil liberties for Blacks and Whites, a Zionist, and a religionist. Once Orthodox, she has since moved over to the left; she is now an adherent of Conservatism, but no longer keeps a kosher home. There is very little doubt where this woman stands; she is a left-wing Democrat.

Elizabeth Holtzman (b. 1941), another liberal Democrat, is altogether different from Mrs. Abzug. Despite the opposition of the Democratic machine, her followers in Brooklyn threw out Emanuel Celler, a leader of nationwide prominence who had served his constituents for almost fifty years. This was something of a revolution. At thirty-one, she was the youngest woman ever sent to the House of Representatives. Her brilliant career at Radcliffe was crowned with a Phi Beta Kappa key. She comes from a family of achievers; her mother teaches Russian at Hunter College. Elizabeth, who studied law at Harvard, was appointed to its Board of Overseers only eleven years after her graduation. A prestigious law firm in New York City invited her to join its staff. Like Abzug, she is an articulate liberal, very much concerned with the welfare of women, children, and the underprivileged. In 1978, the Consumer Federation of America said that she was the only liberal in Congress who consistently voted to protect the masses against "corporate greed." In this the Age of Awards, more than one agency has proclaimed her Woman of the Year. Her Jewish interests? Hadassah, of course.

There are signs that Jewesses, like other American women, are slowly beginning to make their way politically, though no Jewess has yet served in either a presidential cabinet or the United States Senate. Ever since the 1920's, Jewish women have sat in state legislatures and served in municipal and state courts. In 1978,

Dianne Feinstein, daughter of a Jewish father and a Catholic mother, became mayor of San Francisco. Though given a Catholic religious education, Dianne opted for the faith of her father and has lived as a Jewess. In recent years, two Jewish women have been appointed to federal judicial posts; one to a district court, the other, Phyllis Kravitch, to the higher circuit court. Phyllis, who is now on the Court of Appeals in the Fifth Circuit, had looked forward to a career in the law ever since she was a child. She is the third woman in American history to sit on the appeals bench, the first Jewess to be accorded this honor. In 1975, she became president of the Savannah Bar Association; the National Council of Jewish Women gave her their coveted Hannah G. Solomon Award because she has always held high the ideals which have distinguished this prestigious association.

Like Dawidowicz, Rosalyn S. Yalow (b. 1921) is an academician. She is also an important scientist, who won a Nobel Prize for her work in radioimmunoassay. She herself is a third-generation American; her father was born on the Lower East Side. She is obviously an intellectual; she was reading books even before she entered kindergarten. When she grew up, she developed an interest in chemistry, mathematics, and physics; by 1945, she had a teaching assistantship in physics at the University of Illinois and finally received her Ph.D. in nuclear physics—quite an achievement for a woman in those days. She was the only female on the staff of the College of Engineering, and her career was not untouched by subtle discrimination. To please her husband, she keeps a kosher kitchen. Yalow is a feminist; she does not like "ghetto" jobs or "ghetto" awards, those which single out women. Speaking for women, she has said that "if we were ever to move upwards we must demonstrate competence, courage, and determination to succeed and must be prepared to challenge and take our place in the Establishment."

Yalow's bold words only echo the battle cry of thousands of Jewesses who are determined to make careers for themselves in a man's world. Today there is hardly a profession or an aspect of business in which these women are not engaged; a substantial number, literally thousands, are succeeding in their chosen callings. They can look forward to help from the federal government; the

1964 Civil Rights Act forbids denial of opportunity to women. In Cincinnati, in September 1978, a group of Jewish women, all professionals, held a discussion on the subject "Pushing Up or Pushed Around." Among the speakers at this colloquium were an attorney with one of the most prestigious law firms in town; a mechanical engineer with Procter & Gamble, the internationally known soap firm; an administrative secretary in the Department of Student Affairs at the University of Cincinnati; and a vice-president of marketing services for a large realty concern. Lunch was served at this panel discussion, and the dietary laws were observed.

The *World Almanac* for 1979 lists the twenty-five women whom it deems to be the most influential members of their sex in the United States; six are Jewesses; two others have Jewish fathers. The remarkable growth in opportunities and jobs for American Jewish women has not yet found a place in the histories of American Jewry, but it merits mention. This growth is important not because of the achievements of individuals, and not because of any profound impact they have made on the American economy and culture, but rather because their deeds are irrefutable evidence of the rapid progress made by Jewish women in recent decades. The process of moving into a man's world, which began at the turn of the century, has now accelerated markedly. Today, numerous Jewesses make their living as artists, writers, novelists, literary critics, journalists, columnists, historians, scientists, physicians, psychiatrists, lawyers, and civil servants. Thousands more are social workers and public school teachers; an increasing number hold teaching positions in the colleges and universities of this country. Individuals have been appointed to important posts in the public school system of New York City and have served as deans of women in some of the city's colleges.

While the new "affirmative action" has helped a few Jewesses secure appointments in colleges and universities, the same device also threatens to reduce their number in public school systems, particularly in New York City. Able, competent Jewish women have been denied teaching positions because they must yield to others who are given preferential treatment based on racial or ethnic origin. Reacting to what they deem an injustice, these Jewish women have come to believe, rightly or wrongly, that they are victims of anti-Semitism and, consequently, have adopted a more cautious attitude to civil rights. Attacked by some Blacks as racists, they have retreated within themselves—their universalism dampened—but their ethnic particularism has been strengthened and their Jewish identification intensified. The concern these teachers show for their people, a responsiveness characteristic of most American Jewesses today, has been heightened by their sympathy for Soviet Jewry and by their wish to see Israel secure. When Israel is threatened, they feel threatened.

Careers Incarnate

The numerous occupations in which women are found in the late twentieth century would amount to a mechanical listing unless these categories are seen incarnate in the lives of human beings. There is so much variety, there are so many gifts. Many of the women who grew up in the years after 1920 carved out notable careers for themselves when opportunity beckoned and they had the courage to respond. Not all were reaching out; most were willing to become housewives. Mrs. Abraham Beame, the wife of New York City's first Jewish mayor, would have gladly recorded herself in the census questionnaire as a "housewife." She was no liberationist: she loved having her husband minister to her needs; she expected a man to open the door for her; she neither drank nor smoked; she frowned on television violence and pornographic movies. When her husband left the house in the mid-1970's to be sworn in as mayor, he asked her what he ought to wear, a raincoat or a topcoat. "Wear the raincoat," she said, "take the topcoat." He did what she told him. This Lower East Side girl had gone to work as a bookkeeper to help support the family. Her only ambition was to maintain a good home for a good husband; she nursed no pretensions.

Ida Rauh Eastman, who died in 1970, was a founder of the Provincetown Players. A sculptor, painter, and poet, she was interested in the stage, art, and women's rights. Though once arrested and found guilty of obscenity after passing out pamphlets on birth control, she managed to stay out of jail; her sentence was suspended. Peggy (Marguerite) Guggenheim (b. 1898) was an important collector of modern art and a patron of men like Muro, Chagall, Klee, Dali, Calder, and Moore. She opened art galleries in London and in New York. Once, when bringing modern metal sculpture into London, Peggy barely escaped having to pay duty on her treasures; the customs officials saw the pieces as junk, scrap iron, raw materials. Russian-born Louise Nevelson is one of America's best-known sculptors; the Hebrew Union College—Jewish Institute of Religion conferred an honorary degree on her in 1977, and Artists Equity elected her as its president.

As in the past, a number of Jewish women are active on the stage and screen; one of the most successful of all contemporary lyricists, Dorothy Fields, had at her death in 1976 written nearly four hundred songs for Broadway musicals and been elected to the Songwriters' Hall of Fame. Roberta Peters (b. 1930) and Beverly Sills (b. 1929) are two of the country's most famous opera stars; each has sung at the Metropolitan. Brooklyn-born Sills was three years old when she made her debut on radio as Bubbles Silverman on *Uncle Bob's Rainbow House.* Thus she got off to a good start at an early age; her classmates in public school acclaimed her as Most Likely to Succeed, and Harvard gave her an honorary degree. Peters, the daughter of a shoe salesman, dropped out of high school to study voice. This petite coloratura, a bit over five feet tall, wears a size six dress, weighs 110 pounds, and is the mother of two grown boys. The Federation of Women's Clubs liked her well enough to name her Woman of the Year when she was only thirty-four; she was the first American recipient of the Soviet Union's Bolshoi medal.

By the 1970's, Jewish women had already been known as writers and authors for about a century. There was this difference, however: the early craftsmen were not able to support themselves through their writings, while many of our contemporary authors have lived comfortably, if not luxuriously, on their royalties. Laura Keane Zametkin Hobson (b. 1900) seems to have been successful from the very start. After leaving Cornell, she worked as an advertising copywriter, newspaper reporter, and short-story writer and novelist. She was once promotion director for *Time.* Whatever she put her hand to succeeded. In 1947, she wrote *Gentleman's Agreement*, a novel portraying the experiences of a Gentile journalist who pretended to be a Jew in order to study anti-Semitism. The novel sold more than 2,000,000 copies and, when translated to film, won the Academy Award for best motion picture of 1947. At one of the parties she attended, a guest who was not overly fond of the Chosen People blandly informed the group that some of his best friends were Jews—to which Mrs. Hobson responded: "So are mine; my father and mother." Her father, Michael Zametkin, had been an editor of the Yiddish *Jewish Daily Forward;* her mother had run for assemblywoman on the Socialist ticket. Laura was an agnostic. As *Gentleman's Agreement* implies, anti-Semitism annoyed her exceedingly; she despised such idiocy.

Some of Lillian Hellman's plays have known success on the screen as well as on the stage. Hellman (b. 1905/1907), a very gifted dramaturge, is probably the country's leading woman playwright. Like Mrs. Hobson, Hellman is a liberal who is sympathetic to left-wing movements and was courageous enough to inform the chairman of the House Committee on Un-American Activities that she would not testify against her friends. She referred to herself as a writer, a Jew, and a friend of labor. Mrs. Phoebe Wolkind Ephron, who died in 1971, also wrote plays for the stage and screen. Refusing to be catalogued as a housewife who wrote in her spare time, she indignantly informed an interviewer that she rarely went into the kitchen except for ice cubes to cool her drink. A working woman, she had an office and kept regular hours. Among the smart set, few women were better known than Dorothy Rothschild Parker (1893—1967), who was a drama critic, book reviewer, poet, short-story and screenplay writer, a contributor to the *New Yorker*, and a satirist known to all young men—and to some not so young—for her famous miniquips, such as: "Men seldom make passes at girls who wear glasses." This may explain why she never wore her spectacles in public, though she was very nearsighted. She also taught English at a Los Angeles college: "The students read things and then they fight. It's called discussion." She, too, was a political leftist; the bulk of her estate was left to Martin Luther King, Jr., and the National Association for the Advancement of Colored People. One wonders whether her tombstone bears the epitaph which she once dashed off: "Excuse my dust."

When it came to the reading public, Dorothy Parker, Lillian Hellman, and Laura Hobson could not hope to compete with Sylvia Porter and the twin Friedman sisters. Sylvia Field Porter (b. 1913) writes a financial column, "Your Dollar," appearing in over three hundred newspapers. She received an excellent education at Hunter College, where she earned a Phi Beta Kappa key, and then worked on Wall Street, where she gained an insight into the economics and mysteries of the stock market. She exerts an influence on the American economy because she is read by millions of people who appreciate the simplicity and lucidity of her English style and her obvious grasp of business and commerce.

The Friedman sisters, born in Sioux City, Iowa, in 1918, are both journalists who give advice in their syndicated columns to teenagers, parents, and millions of assorted readers. Both use pseudonyms. Pauline Friedman Phillips writes under the name Abigail Van Buren, "Dear Abby." Her column appears in eight hundred newspapers here and abroad. She is a hard worker. "When I learned how to say 'no' graciously, life became immeasurably more productive." Her sister, "Ann Landers," Mrs. Jules (Esther) Lederer, writes for hundreds of newspapers—including one in the Fiji Islands. At times, Ann receives a thousand letters a day; she has eight secretaries to answer this huge mail. The readers' letters she reproduces are authentic, not fabricated; the columns that appear in the newspapers are written by her, not by her staff. Most of the letters sent to her come from middle-aged people and deal with an almost infinite variety of subjects: sex, alcoholism, and the benefits of bacon are three examples. This last culinary recommendation brought a howl of protest from seventeen rabbis. It is estimated that she has some 60,000,000 daily readers. Both sisters have been active in Jewish organizations: Pauline was once chairperson of the Minnesota-Wisconsin Council of the B'nai B'rith Auxiliary; her sister Esther was the head of the Minnesota-Wisconsin Council of the Anti-Defamation League of B'nai B'rith.

Katherine Meyer Graham (b. 1917), daughter of a very important Washington executive during World War I, is chairman of the board of the influential *Washington Post*, which won the coveted Pulitzer Prize for its detailed reports on the Watergate scandal. On her father's side, she is descended from a distinguished Jewish family which included a scholarly Grand Rabbin of France. (There is very little reason to believe that Mrs. Graham has evinced any interest in Jews or Judaism.) Rose Greenberg K. Cannon (d. 1968), a native of Rumania, was manager of a Communist newspaper; Anita Cahn Block (d. 1967), Barnard graduate, writer, and lawyer, read foreign plays for the Theater Guild and helped found the socialist *New York Call*, which she served as drama critic and editor of the women's page. Her readers were not regaled with recipes or fashion notes; she limited herself to serious discussions of social and political problems. The *Call* was probably the first paper which gave a hearing to Margaret Sanger's appeal for birth control. The Marxist Anita Block has no interest in Judaism: "My ideal is to wipe out all religions, all race consciousness, and to create a United States of the World in which the true brotherhood of man shall prevail." Gertrude Blumenthal, employed by Simon and Schuster to direct one of their publishing divisions, edited a series of biographies for young people. When she died in 1973, she left nearly 240 volumes in print. Following in the footsteps of her grandfather Jacob and her father Mortimer, it was inevitable that Dorothy Schiff (b. 1903) would manifest an interest in social work. Thus she lent her name to the Women's Trade Union League, the Henry Street Settlement, and Mount Sinai Hospital. In the early 1940's, she assumed control of the liberal *New York Post* as owner, editor, and publisher.

Dorothy Schiff was not an active welfare worker; hundreds of Jewesses were and still are. In a way, helping others is as much the métier of modern social-minded Jewesses as it was of their grand-mothers. To scan the newspapers and necrologies of the 1960's and 1970's is to read of numerous humanitarians: one was interested in a reformatory for girls; others gave their time, energy, and skills to the New York Guild for the Jewish Blind, an agency which toils annual-ly to aid more than fifteen hundred men, women, and children deprived of their sight. With her husband's help, Mrs. Melanie Tokaji Rothenberg founded one of the first commercial interracial camps in this country. This was as early as 1927. The Jewish Big

Sisters Society engaged Annis Chaikin (d. 1970) as its first social worker. After earning her B.A. with honors at Nebraska University, she pursued graduate studies in Greek and Latin. She was a pacifist and a feminist. Her husband, Christian Sorensen, a Gentile, served as the state's attorney general; her numerous children were social activists and respected public servants. One of her sons, Theodore Chaikin Sorensen, a close associate of John F. Kennedy, was an unsuccessful candidate for the United States Senate from New York.

It comes almost as a shock to record the changes in the opportunities now accorded women in the world of science. When the century dawned, they were not at all welcome in the research laboratories; a generation later, one dared not ignore them. Four examples, picked at random, are in a sense quite typical. As chief of the chest clinic for children at the Bellevue Hospital Center, Edith Maas Lincoln (d. 1977), a clinical professor of pediatrics, was one of America's pioneers in employing drugs to cure tuberculosis. Libbie Henrietta Hyman (d. 1969), a native of Des Moines, Iowa, turned to the study of invertebrates after receiving her Ph.D. degree at the University of Chicago. Hyman, who was one of the country's leading authorities in her field, published six volumes on the subject. Though she suffered from Parkinson's disease, she continued her research even when compelled to work out of a wheelchair. Sophia Josephine Kleegman (d. 1971), clinical professor of obstetrics and gynecology at New York University's school of medicine, was the first woman given a staff position at Bellevue Hospital. She was active in the Planned Parenthood Federation and served as president of New York's Medical Women's Association.

Edith Lincoln, Libbie Hyman, and Sophia Kleegman were natural scientists, concerned with the physical world and its phenomena. Hortense Powdermaker (1900—1970) was a social scientist. She studied human society—the individuals who make it what it is. Powdermaker grew up in Baltimore and earned her B.A. degree at Goucher College. Before going on to graduate work, she threw in her lot with the Amalgamated Clothing Workers of America, then struggling to establish itself in Baltimore. While still at school, she spent several weeks working in a shirt factory and became interested in the labor movement. Powdermaker gave four years of her life to this union and then went to London to study cultural anthropology under Bronislaw K. Malinowski. Receiving her Ph.D. from the University of London in 1928, she sailed for the Melanesian Islands in the Pacific, where she studied the culture of primitive natives who were just emerging from cannibalism. On her return, she taught at Yale. Years later Powdermaker moved on to Queens College, where she established and headed the department of anthropology and sociology. In the meantime, she had spent a year in a Mississippi town where she analyzed the social system of segregation and the interpersonal relations between Blacks and Whites. In the late 1940's, Dr. Powdermaker went to Hollywood to study the cinema and its social influence. Speaking of the Hollywood executives, she said that she found them as interesting—culturally and anthropologically, of course—as the cannibals of the South Pacific. Powdermaker, the author of six major works, was a recognized and respected scholar.

For women, the opportunities in the social and natural sciences have been matched by those in the world of politics. After women were granted the vote, politicians courted them. By the time of the November 1978 elections, more than 10 percent of the seats in American state legislatures were occupied by women, six were lieutenant governors, ten were secretaries of state, six state treasurers, and one woman was elected to the United States Senate. Jewesses, too, are beginning to assume appointive and elective offices. In fact, they have been filling political posts for decades; many of them were lawyers, and thus well-qualified to serve as legislators, judges, and administrators. Jeanette G. Brill (d. 1964), born on the Lower East Side, was the first Brooklyn woman to be appointed a magistrate. She began as a teacher, and when her friends at school learned that she wanted to be a lawyer, they helped raise the money to finance her legal education. They no doubt were as dismayed as she by the hostility evinced toward her by judges and male associates. Frieda B. Hennock (1904—1960), a native of Poland who came here as a child of six, graduated from the Brooklyn Law School and practiced in New York City until her appointment to the Federal Communications Commission in 1948. A cousin of Supreme Court Justice Louis D. Brandeis, Nanette Dembitz, was appointed by Mayor John V. Lindsay to serve as judge of a New York

City family court in 1967. It was Lindsay, too, who asked Mrs. John L. Loeb to accept a position as New York City commissioner to the United Nations. This is a hostess job. She was expected to help the mayor and his wife welcome the new members of the United Nations and Consular Corps. Loeb was the only woman in Mayor Lindsay's cabinet.

Mrs. Loeb was an aristocrat, a scion of the Lehman-Lewisohn banking and mining clan. The Lehmans had first come to this country in the 1840's. Anna Moscowitz Kross, born in Eastern Europe in 1889/1891, was brought here as a child and went to work at the age of eleven. Her father was a buttonhole maker. She struggled to get an education and finally became a lawyer, but did not attend her own graduation exercises—she could not afford to buy a dress for the occasion. Years later, after holding office as a New York City magistrate, she was honored with the ranking post of commissioner of correction. Her memberships in numerous organizations offer mute but eloquent commentary on the role of a successful American Jewess: the National Council of Jewish Women, Hadassah, and the American Association of University Women

None of these female politicians were professional feminists. Karen Lipshultz DeCrow (b. 1937) was. She went to law school, ran for mayor of Syracuse, and joined the National Organization of Women (NOW). In 1974, she became the president of this society which has led in the struggle to abolish discrimination against women in employment, educational aid, housing, and credit. NOW is equally determined to improve the lot of all females—ethnic minorities, lesbians, housewives, and office workers—rich and poor.

These brief and very selective mini-biographies of Jewish women in the professions suggest that individuals are finding niches in diverse areas of commerce and culture. While it is true that many gravitate toward teaching, social work, law, and medicine, there are, in reality, few fields of endeavor from which they are totally absent. The government's listing of occupations for the economically active population of the mid-twentieth century includes over fifty different basic professions, techniques, and skills. It would not be too difficult to unearth Jewish women in at least forty of them; it might take some digging to find Jewish women who are employed as airplane pilots, radio operators, surveyors, foresters, and funeral directors. In medieval and early modern times, Jews nibbled at every type of business; now, in the late twentieth century, Jewish women nibble at almost every profession. Dora Brahms, who died in 1970, would have fitted easily into the professional category of "designer." More than once she was called to the White House to decorate various chambers, including the Oval Office. Hers was big business; refurbishing a room or a series of rooms for a client might well run into the hundreds of thousands of dollars.

It would be difficult to determine just where Jean Rosenthal (d. 1969) belonged in the government's list of technicians. She was one of the country's most distinguished lighting designers. She planned and arranged the lighting for more than two hundred Broadway and operatic productions. It was her job to eliminate stage shadows, and to help bring out the best in the ballets, operas, and theatrical performances. Through her lighting effects, she created the atmosphere which is so important if a stage performance is to come alive.

In 1974, a Brooklyn Jewess operating a successful brothel in Nevada (where prostitution is legal) was an unsuccessful candidate for the state legislature. In her own way, she was a skilled administrator, though this type of work is not specifically included in the government's statistical data. Gertrude Schimmel, a native of the Bronx and a Phi Beta Kappa graduate of Hunter College, where she majored in English, was the first woman in New York City to reach the rank of inspector on New York's police force. Inspector Schimmel is active in the Society of Jewish Police Officers and brags that she helped "liberate" the city's police department. Bess Myerson (b. 1924), another New York City girl, studied music, organized an all-girl orchestra, played as guest soloist with the New York Philharmonic, and even enrolled for a master's degree at Columbia. In 1969 she was sworn in as New York City commissioner of consumer affairs by Mayor John V. Lindsay. Years before, in 1945, this beautiful girl had been acclaimed "Miss America." While doing a War Bond tour in Wilmington, Delaware, she overheard her Gentile hostess saying: "We cannot have Miss Myerson at the country club reception in her honor. . . . We never had a Jew in the country club." Miss Myerson immediately packed her bag and left the house. The incident helped make a "good" Jewess out of her. In 1976, Barbara Walters (b. 1931) signed a contract to broadcast news over a major television network at a guaranteed salary of $1,000,000 a year. What a far cry from the days when Jewish girls in department stores worked from sixty to eighty hours a week for a total salary of less then $3.

American Jewish Women and the Golden Age

Since these brief descriptive sketches testify that women also are attaining distinction in the area of higher education, it is reasonable to inquire what the social scientists among them are doing to further academic studies in the Science of Judaism—the critical study of Jewish history, life, culture, and religion. The chief present-day laboratories for the discipline are Israel and the United States. During the last two generations, the advances in the field have been so noteworthy here that it is proper to suggest that a Golden Age is already in progress. What has made it all possible is the size of America's Jewry; over 40 percent of the Jews in the world live here. Secular learning has become the rule; some 80 percent of all Jewish women and men will attend a university or school of higher learning. This is the world's most affluent Jewry; the leadership it manifests is documented not only by the exercise of its political influence and its many philanthropies here, but by its ardent interest in aiding Jewish communities abroad and in furthering them economically, socially and culturally. It is moot as to whether the State of Israel could survive without the wholehearted support of American Jewry.

Intensive Jewish studies both in Hebrew and the vernacular are prerequisites for a Golden Age. The Talmud—the most important of all Jewish books and more authoritative religiously than even the Bible—Maimonides' *Guide for the Perplexed,* the writings of Martin Buber and Leo Baeck were all written in the vernacular, not in Hebrew. Furtherance of Hebraic studies in the United States is fostered by seminaries, Jewish colleges, and training schools for teachers; there are, all told, dozens of such institutions. The United States now supports hundreds of "secular" colleges and universities where Jewish subjects are taught. Excellent libraries of Hebraica and Judaica are attached to Jewish colleges, a number of universities, and to some public libraries in large cities. There are national societies furthering study and research, several periodicals of scientific caliber, and a relatively large number of internationally reputable scholars who work in the Jewish field. Over the years, hundreds of Jewish books of scientific merit have rolled off the presses of American publishers.

What is the women's contribution, if any, to this discipline? There were a number of female Jewish scholars in the mid-twentieth century; most of them were European-trained refugees. Despite the fact that American Jewish women had already begun to move into the Science of Judaism after the Feminist Revolt of 1963, less than 20 of the 236 articles published in *Jewish Social Studies* during 1964—1978 were written by them. Before 1970, there were barely a half-dozen American-born Jewesses in this branch of study. Female Jewish academicians, teaching primarily in the social sciences, then began evincing an interest in the Jewish aspect of their professional studies; a few started by reviewing Jewish books. In the 1970's, the newest breed of rabbis—women—all had some training in this specialized scientific domain. Even earlier—almost two decades earlier—Jewish religious denominations were already emphasizing the need for women to study Hebrew intensively and to acquire Jewish learning. Now, for the first time, in the mid-1970's, women in this field—not many, to be sure—received appointments at universities, colleges, and even at seminaries. Jewish girls, graduate students in collegiate institutions, were writing theses on Jewish subjects. Some of them were studying in Israel; others were preparing themselves here in the United States for serious academic work in this specialty. In a sense, women turning to the Science of Judaism were reacting feministically. What right had men to monopolize Jewish learning? According to Deuteronomy 33:4, "Moses charged us [*all* of us] with the Teaching as the heritage of Jacob"—not merely the males!

By the late 1970's, an increasing number of women were becoming Jewish scholars; their names are found on the rosters of the Association for Jewish Studies, a professional organization. In 1978,

16 percent of the members of this society were females. By 1979, these women were beginning to make their presence felt. Few have as yet published monographs in the weightier scientific journals and serials like the *Hebrew Union College Annual* and the *Proceedings of the American Academy for Jewish Research,* but there is no reason to doubt that in another decade many more female Jewish scholars will have made their appearance.

Jewish Women and Feminism

Are the thousands of women currently found in nearly all the professions necessarily feminists and liberationists? While the number of women who belong to Jewish feminist organizations is all but insignificant—these minuscule groups play little part in American Jewish life—it is no less true that there is hardly a knowledgeable Jewess in this country who has not been profoundly influenced by the emancipatory spirit of feminism. Most Jewish women are well aware of the benefits that have accrued to them through the feminist drive; they are sympathetic to those liberationist goals which will bring more autonomy to all females. Liberationism, espoused by Jewesses with religious and ethnic loyalties, is an aspect of their drive to come to terms with contemporary American culture and mores—they seek to harmonize Judaism and modernity. They are confronted by a dual challenge: they want to emancipate themselves within Judaism, not from Judaism, and at the same time they yearn for complete equality with the men in all religious practices. Ambitious and knowledgeable women who are affiliated with Reform Judaism are primarily interested in advancing themselves not in the synagogue, but in the structured Jewish community; the leftists among the Conservatives are pushing for religious equality within the framework of the Law; percipient Orthodox women, subservient to the ancient traditions, wish to further themselves culturally and to make sure that their personalities as women are accorded a larger degree of autonomy. Some of them, it would seem, are no longer placated by a glib recital of Proverbs 31: "Who can find a virtuous woman, for her price is far above rubies."

Women demand recognition in the larger world of trade, industry, and higher education, but also insist on more rights within the Jewish community and religion. When men persist in keeping Judaism a man's religion, the "gentler" sex is quick to remind them that the Jewish faith has been perpetuated by women. There are mature, cultured women who resent the fact that they are not accorded the religious privileges of a naive thirteen-year-old boy who has just become bar mitzvah. In the late 1970's, few Jewesses failed to question the traditional role assigned women in the home. While many believe that they have yet to be granted equality in the home, they have by no means repudiated this oldest of all institutions. Most unmarried feminists and liberationists have not abandoned the hope of a place of their own with husband and children. Even women who opt to remain housewives and refrain from taking jobs in the market are not cut off from the world outside; they are joiners, the backbone of the National Council of Jewish Women, Hadassah, Women's ORT, and the female lodges. In a way these women have the best of both worlds: an improved wifely status at home, and the joys of "sisterhood" outside.

·7·

Retrospect and Prospect, 1654—2000

IN colonial and early national America, younger women looked for husbands, while wives kept house, raised a Jewish family, performed the home rites and ceremonies, and, to judge from the evidence available, accentuated the ethical. They were pious enough, but there is little evidence that they were particularly submissive or passive. From 1819 on, "sisterhood" manifested itself; from then on, if only modestly, women sought to be on their own. They emerged as organized groups; they enjoyed themselves. This mild assertiveness has continued down to the present day. In 1820, the first American Jewish female association numbered at the most a hundred members; today Hadassah alone counts its members in the hundreds of thousands. Antebellum Jewesses created their "Ladies' Aids" because there was a job to be done and they set out to do it. The men in their shops and stores were too busy, so the women stepped into the breach; it was good work, God's work, and they enjoyed the side product: female consciousness-raising—an unwitting benefit to be sure. As immigrants or daughters of immigrants, they were too insecure to think in terms of social reforms, woman suffrage, or feminism. Their sense of sisterhood was socially and religiously oriented, not politically. They were not bold innovators; they were content with their lot and their bourgeois ambitions.

Was there a collective women's history before 1890? Yes—after a fashion. There were women of culture and personality who were not without influence; there were local charity societies, and many devoted social workers. Moreover, in the history of a people, can the authentic historian properly refuse to acknowledge the preponderant social importance of the home? The first real break came in the early 1890's, with the founding of the National Council of Jewish Women: that is the watershed, inaugurating a new era for American Jewesses. Two disparate groups of Jewesses now emerged to make history. The first was composed of the native-born and the acculturated of Central European birth. Many of them, as children of middle-class parents, had received a passable education, which they employed either to gain a livelihood or for their own delecta-tion. As Jews eager to prove themselves in a Gentile society, they were determined not to remain submerged and unnoticed. Nonetheless, they tended to pattern themselves on the Gentiles, whose influence was all but overwhelming. The Jewesses of that generation stood out for the social-welfare services they rendered their fellow-Jews.

The second group of women was composed of the East European immigrants. They had been coming to America in large numbers ever since the 1880's, and were quite visible by the 1890's. Im-poverished, uneducated, and arriving at a time when industrialism was in full swing, they had no choice but to crowd into the garment factories, if only for one generation. They were among the "ac-cidents" of American Jewish history. Never before and never since have large numbers of Jewish women worked in American industry as laborers. The years they spent hunched over their sewing machines in factories and sweatshops were a sad interlude, a bad dream in a history reaching all the way back to the mid-1650's. Their Americanization was rapid—it began the day they landed— because they had no desire to be rejected by their fellow-Jews as greenhorns. These newcomers eagerly patterned themselves on the Jewish settlers who had preceded them. In the generation that followed, their children and grandchildren made their mark as social and communal workers, as competent professionals, and on occasion even as distinguished scientists.

No matter what their lineage, American Jewesses were different from their fellow-Americans; they were the only "infidels" among some 75,000,000 nominal Christians. How American were Jewish women at the turn of the century? The native-born were very well, even totally, acculturated, and because they were prone to be exuberant and demonstrative in their loyalties, it is no exaggeration to say that they were 125 percent American. At times, it was difficult to detect anything overtly Jewish about them; but to draw the conclusion that they had no interest in their traditions would be false. Most were irrevocably committed to Jewry and to Judaism, even if their professions of faith were not ardent.

By the 1960's, a social revolution was underway in America. Jews, men and women alike, were prime beneficiaries of the revolt. For reasons that are not always clear, anti-Jewish social barriers began breaking down even before the 1950's. The social ferment of the postwar decades only speeded up the process of tolerance and acceptance. Fraternities and sororities, exclusive resorts and hotels, discriminatory urban clubs, were now open to Jews; large industrial complexes began to employ them as executives, if only in token numbers. How were Jewish women affected? Young American women, major participants in the campus upheavals of the 1960's, became passionate liberationists, and as feminism made gains, Jewesses, too, advanced themselves. A number of the highly visible outstanding leaders of the new feminist movement were Jewish women. These women, however, did not represent the distaff side of American Jewry; the radicals among them had no real following among their female coethnics. But feminism as a movement, certainly in its more moderate expectations, did exert considerable influence upon Jewesses, even upon those who were Orthodox in practice.

Urban Jewish women, fully cognizant of contemporary cultural and social currents, had long been aware of feminism and its implications. As early as 1915, a Chicago Jewess, who was a social worker and communal leader, likened feminism to a glacier pushing its way forward, carrying all before it—and had used the word "feminism." Despite the fact that the Jewess of the third quarter of the twentieth century was rarely a registered member of any feminist organization, she was in sympathy with the emancipatory aims of those intent on improving the status of women. Notwithstanding her customary conservatism, the Jewish woman yearned to be someone; she wanted equality with the men, and freedom as she defined it. Consciously or subconsciously, she looked forward to a world beyond the confines of her home; she wanted to emancipate herself, in part at least, from the restraints imposed by parents, by husband, and socioethnic taboos.

Feminism encouraged her to satisfy her ambitions, and she *was* ambitious. She wanted to get ahead financially, to provide for herself and her family, to climb ever higher into the upper-middle class. But no matter what her instinctual longings were, no matter where she worked and what she did, she still believed that the home was basic. Her identification was multifaceted. She was one with womankind in their efforts to find fulfillment and close in spirit to all Jews—women as well as men. This woman was always concerned with the fate of her people, the Jewish people. The typical Jewess of 1980—that is, the woman who did not hesitate to acknowledge her Jewish origins—wanted to be part of a closely integrated Jewish community. Being Jewish gave her a comfortable feeling of well-being and security which she was determined to maintain. At times she was almost inclined to pity her less fortunate Gentile neighbors. What was behind it all? Arrogance? Chauvinism? Reality? "Community"?

What Will Happen to the American Jewess?

What will happen tomorrow to the American Jewess who demands a larger measure of equality and opportunity in synagogue, home, the Jewish community, the job market? It is hard to say—prophecy is hazardous: an ancient Jewish sage said sarcastically that since the destruction of the Temple, prophecy had been taken away from the prophets and been given to madmen and prattling infants. Since the Orthodox as well as the Conservatives, influenced by the Reformers and the feminists, are making concessions to women, the cry has been raised by some that the synagogue is being feminized, that the

American Judaism of the future will be a gynecocracy. This is an old plaint. As early as 1902, Hannah Solomon denied that there would be a "feminizing of the synagogue." There is little danger of this: Judaism is still a man's religion, even among the Reformers. The synagogue and the larger Jewish community will be enriched when women assume a more important role in religion, in the federations, and in the administration of all local institutions. This wider, more intensive participation may in part compensate for the continuing widespread indifference, intermarriage, defection, and assimilation to which American Jewish life seems prone. At this juncture, however, it is necessary to emphasize that of the thousands of Gentile women who marry Jews every year, a very substantial number adopt a Jewish way of life. Indeed, they become formal converts and are distinguished for their zeal and devotion.

It is well over a century since the first Protestant female was ordained in the United States, but there are still very few large American churches where women serve as senior minister. Female rabbis? They are already pouring out of the liberal seminaries in rather substantial numbers. Jobs? If the experience of female Protestant pastors is any guide, women rabbis will not meet with ready acceptance by synagogal heads. Many female congregants prefer male rabbis. Even for them, God is a man. At best, women rabbis will be shunted off to the smaller cities or to secondary positions and assignments. For them, the Messiah is still around the corner tarrying. However, the experience of instructors in the seminaries indicates that by and large women are intellectually as competent as men in research and scholarship. There can be no doubt about it: critical studies will profit markedly from the writings of an increasing number of brilliant females.

The problem facing Amerian Jewry today, a problem to become ever more acute, is what will happen to the traditional Jewish home? There are women for whom this is no real problem. They are prepared to jump down from the pedestal upon which they have been held captive by gyneolatrous men who insist on paying homage to the feminine mystique. Whether or not they are liberationists, for these women a career comes first; they do not insist on creating or maintaining a home. They are joining the increasing number of singles, divorcees, widows, and assorted maiden ladies reaching out to create a meaningful social world of their own. Subconsciously at least, many of these liberationists are, in reality, patterning themselves almost slavishly on men. Most womenfolk, however, want a home, a husband, at least one child, and a career. These are the women who will continue to swell the labor market. They are faced with dilemmas. It is difficult to maintain a home, bear and rear children, work at a job, and keep the family together. Tensions are bound to rise where women contribute materially to the support of the ménage. Few men are prepared to accord equality in the family to a wife, let alone recognize her as the major partner. Men's egos bruise easily, for after all they have been the prime providers for millennia. Who will look after the children now? Makeshift devices are being concocted to maintain the "home," to harmonize the needs of children, husbands, and care of the house. Will the family structure ultimately have to be modified because of radical changes in the domestic way of life?

The problem of maintaining a home and meshing in dual careers is no bogie conjured up by neurotics; it is very real. Fannie Hurst had to cope with this hurdle all her married life; her musician-husband was very sensitive. "Every career woman with a private-lifemate," she wrote in her autobiography, "is faced with this problem in one form or another: the dignity of her mate." When a husband and wife are both professionals and one is called out of town to fill an attractive post, the remaining spouse must pull up stakes, sacrifice his or her position, and seek a new berth—or else refuse to leave and thereby risk breaking up the marriage. These confrontations are now daily occurrences. In her very useful *America's Immigrant Women*, Cecyle S. Neidle cites a case in point. Dr. Ruth Weiner, an Austrian refugee, member of a family which has produced physicians for generations, is a mother of four. Both she and her husband are chemists. He teaches at a college in Denver, but male prejudice made it impossible for her to secure an appointment in Colorado which befitted her talents. Then she received a call offering her tenured employment in Miami, Florida. She and her husband discussed their problem. He cannot or will not leave; she was determined to take the job for which she was trained. Their final decision was that the husband would remain with two of the children; she left for Miami with the other two. Theirs was a Solomonic decision; they decided to cut the "baby" in half.

It may well be that this exposition of a threatened home is alarmist, positing problems that do not exist for the Jewish mass-woman. There are many men who are willing to grant equality to their wives; most Jewesses have rejected liberationism. Despite the problems that do in a very real sense exist, women do not want to tamper with the family structure, though they are determined once and for all to maintain their gains in the outside world. In view of the government's insistence on equal opportunities for women, it is reasonable to assume that the next decade will see additional thousands of Jewish women pouring into the job markets. They will go into business, colleges and universities, and, judging from what they have already achieved, will enrich the cultural and scientific world. American Jewish history books will have to take women into account. Up to now, historiographically, the American Jewish woman, with some exceptions, has been a nonperson.

Whether they work at a job and keep house or have opted solely for homemaking, a substantial percentage of Jewish women would seem content with their lot. They are reasonably well satisfied with their work in the office; they are well-ensconced in the comforting embrace of their family, their faith, and their people. A study made at the University of Maryland in 1971 demonstrates that although 56.5 percent of the Jewesses were preparing to take master's degrees in order to enter the job market, they had a higher level of religious and ethnic identity than males. They were "good" Jews. The new generation of American Jewesses will become increasingly important. In the past, Judaism has survived as much through its women as through its cocky minority of men who still rule the roost. Women have always been the invisible majority.

There is a talmudic tradition that the emancipation from Egyptian slavery owes everything to that generation's female activists, the "pious women." Without them, there would have been no Exodus and no salvation. It is an intriguing statement, one which presents a significant challenge to the Jewish women who now face the twenty-first century.

Bibliographical Note

Introduction

This book, *The American Jewish Woman, 1654—1980,* is not a chronicle of Jewish feminism, although one can in no wise tell the story of the American Jewess without linking her emergence to the present-day female liberation movement. For the Jewish woman who identifies with her people, feminism is the struggle to achieve equality in the Jewish secular and religious communities. There is a growing literature on Jewish feminism, less published data, unfortunately, on the actual history of the American Jewess. In this bibliographical note the effort will be made not only to record the sources and literature employed in the present work but also to make a few suggestions for those students who wish to carry on research in the field.

In many respects, American Jewish history is one of the most challenging areas of present-day study; the study of the American Jewess is even more inviting. There are, however, relatively few books and articles which deal specifically with the history of the American Jewish woman. Published material is sparse; the data however, are available; one has to dig for it. There is no area of civic, communal, associational, economic, cultural, and religious activity from which Jewesses are completely absent. In one form or another their participation can be documented. Several years ago, students of general American history declared that there was very little available material on the history of the American woman. However, a National Endowment for the Humanities and University of Minnesota study disclosed that there are at least eighteen thousand collections of primary source material here in the United States which throw light on the history of the American woman. Students who have a specific subject or individual in mind will do well to consult Philip M. Hamer (ed.), *A Guide to Archives and Manuscripts in the United States* (New Haven, 1961) and *The National Union Catalog of Manuscript Collections, 1959—1961* (Ann Arbor, Mich., 1962). Later volumes, through 1970, are published by the Library of Congress. They would also do well to consult the *Directory of Archives and Manuscript Repositories* published by the National Historical Publications and Records Commission (Washington, D.C., 1978).

Bibliographies on the History of the American Jewess

There is no comprehensive bibliography of the activities of the American Jewish woman from 1654 to 1980. Aviva Cantor has compiled *A Bibliography on the Jewish Woman: A Comprehensive and Annotated Listing of Works Published 1900—1978* (Fresh Meadows, N.Y., 1979). It is helpful. The American Jewish Committee has prepared *The Jewish Woman in the Community: A Selected Annotated Bibliography* (New York, 1976). This brief selection was edited by Cyma M. Horowitz. The Hebrew Union College Library, Cincinnati, has the following two typescripts on file: "The Jewish Woman: A Partially Annotated Bibliography" (1976?), the work of some Buffalo, New York, women; and Dorothy Steiner, "They Achieved and Went Beyond: An Annotated Bibliography of Biographies of Remarkable American Jewish Women" (Los Angeles, 1977).

Archival Materials

As suggested above, manuscript materials abound in the general archives. For example, the Court of Ordinary in Savannah has the long and very informative will of Esther Sheftall; the Charleston, South Carolina, probate records contain the poignant ethical will of Deborah Moses, the mother of Major Raphael J. Moses of the Confederate Army. Etting and Gratz letters are available in the files of the Historical Society of Pennsylvania; Mordecai family papers are found in the Library of Congress, in the North Carolina Department of Archives and History, and in the collections at both Duke University and the University of North Carolina. There are also Gratz papers in the library of the University of North Carolina at Chapel Hill, a Mendes Cohen Collection in the files of the Maryland Historical Society, John Lawe papers in the library of the Historical Society of Wisconsin in Madison (the Canada Franks family), and an extensive cache of Lopez papers in the Newport Historical Society.

All synagogues have archives. The older congregations have rich collections; Shearith Israel and Temple Emanu-El of New York, Mikveh Israel of Philadelphia, and Beth Elohim, Charleston, have not yet been adequately researched for their references to women. The libraries of the Leo Baeck Institute, the Yivo Institute for Jewish Research, the Zionist Archives and Library, the New York Public Library, the American Jewish Committee—all in New York City—have manuscripts and documents important to the study of the American Jewish woman. With few exceptions, the city, regional, and state Jewish historical societies have begun assembling data on women. The American Jewish Historical Society has among its collections papers on Rebecca Gratz and Grace Seixas Nathan. The documents now assembled in the American Jewish Archives in Cincinnati are described in the five-volume publication: *Manuscript Catalog of the American Jewish Archives, Cincinnati* (Boston, 1971—78). The references to Jewesses in its semi-annual periodical, the *American Jewish Archives*, are now recorded in detail in Paul F. White's *Index to the American Jewish Archives*, vols. 1—24 (Cincinnati, 1979). See the entries "Ladies" and "Women." The "Nearprint" files of the American Jewish Archives contain very substantial collections of data on Jewish women's societies, Jewish female notables, and many other subjects relating to the history of Jewesses in the United States.

Source Books

There is as yet no published actual source book on the history of this country's Jewish women. There are readers, cooperative essay collections. Rudolf Glanz, however, has written two narrative volumes which incorporate data of a source character. They are: *The Jewish Woman in America: Two Female Immigrant Generations, 1820—1929* (2 vols., New York, 1976), vol. 1: *The Eastern European Jewish Woman*; vol. 2: *The German Jewish Woman*.

Other American Jewish source books are of a more general character, but they all contain some documents which deal directly with the women of this country. Among them are the following works of Jacob Rader Marcus: *Early American Jewry* (2 vols., Philadelphia, 1951—55); *Memoirs of American Jews, 1775—1865* (3 vols., Philadelphia, 1955—56); *American Jewry—Documents—Eighteenth Century* (Cincinnati, 1959), and *On Love, Marriage, Children. . . . And Death, Too* (Cincinnati, 1965). Joseph L. Blau and Salo W. Baron are the editors of *The Jews of the United States, 1790—1840: A Documentary History* (New York, 1963). Many facets of the life of this country's Jewesses are reflected in this interesting and valuable collection. Another useful source book for American Jewry is Morris U. Schappes's *Documentary History of the Jews in the United States, 1654—1875* (New York, 1971). Schappes is accurate and critical in his approach; his notes are particularly helpful.

Encyclopedias and Other Jewish Reference Works

In a way, source books are limited in their scope; they are subjective in their choice of documents. Encyclopedias are far more embracing, for they envision, or should envision, all aspects of the topics, institutions, and individuals that lie within their scope. Unfortunately the *Jewish Encyclopedia* (12 vols., New York, 1901—1906)—the oldest and the best of all the Jewish reference books—contains very little data on American women. This excellent reference book was compiled in a day when Jewish scholars and their patrons were not interested in the history and status of women. There is, however, a sound article on the "Council of Jewish Women" by the indomitable Sadie American. Far more useful for our purpose is the *Universal Jewish Encyclopedia* (10 vols., New York, 1939—43). By the 1930's women had begun to come into their own. This reference work, sociologically and Americanistically oriented, does not altogether neglect women.

The article on "Woman" in the *Universal Jewish Encyclopedia* is helpful to the historian, for it lists American Jewesses who were active in their respective communities. To be sure, not all were notables; this is to the good. We are interested in the "average" woman. Lists can be supplemented by the earlier article of I. George Dobsevage, "Jews of Prominence in the United States," *American Jewish Year Book*, vol. 24, 1922—23 (Philadelphia, 1922), pp. 109 ff. The relatively few women included by Dobsevage were deemed important in the first quarter of the century. The sixteen-volume *Encyclopaedia Judaica* (Jerusalem, 1971—72) is a very useful tool for the historian concerned with the advance of women and the development of their institutions since the 1940's. Volume 1, a concordance-type Index, is a valuable aid for the student of American Jewish history. There are also a number of *Encyclopaedia Judaica Year Books*. Much smaller and more specialized is the two-volume *Encyclopedia of Zionism and Israel* (New York, 1971), edited by Raphael Patai. There are good articles here on Hadassah and on Henrietta Szold and many other American Zionist women leaders.

Two other reference books have proved to be particularly useful for research in the history of the American Jewess. The one is *A Jewish Calendar for Fifty Years*, by Jacques J. Lyons and Abraham De Sola (Montreal, 1854); the other is *The Jewish Communal Register of New York City, 1917—1918* (2d ed., New York, 1918). The *Calendar* includes a list of the most important Jewish women's organizations in the United States in 1854 (pp. 148 ff.); the *Register* lists and describes in some detail the New York societies and institutions as of 1918. The significance of these two works is obvious.

Periodicals and Serials

By the last quarter of the nineteenth century, the American Jew in general became news, and talented women like Emma and Josephine Lazarus, Nina Morais, and Lee C. Harby were invited to write articles, stories, and poems for general (non-Jewish) national magazines. Emma Lazarus defended Jewry in the *Century Magazine*, 1882 and 1883; Nina Morais wrote on "The Limitations of Sex" in the *North American Review*, vol. 132 (1881). By the turn of the century, non-Jewish English metropolitan newspapers were to become very important sources of information for the Jewish historian. The obituaries of notable American women were now detailed and informative. For New York, the *Times*, the *Tribune*, and the *World* are particularly useful. The *Tribune* sent its reporters down to the Lower East Side to write genre stories about the Jews; a number of them have been reprinted in Allon Schoener, *Portal to America: The Lower East Side, 1870—1925* (New York, 1967) and in Jacob R. Marcus, *The American Jewish Woman: A Documentary History* (New York, 1981). Not infrequently, twentieth-century national magazines published articles that throw light on the history of the American Jewess. Wyndham Robertson's piece, "The Ten Highest-Ranking Women in Big Business," *Fortune*, vol. 87, April 1973, pp. 81 ff., is a case in point. *Nutrition*, vol. 4, September-October, 1941, a trade paper issued by the Quaker Oats Company, includes an autobiography of the pioneer dietician Frances Stern. *Ms.*, a feminist magazine, occasionally prints articles reporting the experiences of various types of American Jewish women (vol 3, July 1974, pp. 76 ff.). One of the founders and editors of this magazine is Gloria Steinem, granddaughter of an early Jewish feminist.

Far more useful, of course, are the American Jewish newspapers, magazines, and annuals published in English, German, and Yiddish. All these serials contain news items, articles, letters to the editor, and reports on organizations which treat directly of the life and work of Jewish women. These periodicals are listed annually in the *American Jewish Year Book*. Curiously enough, nineteenth-century European Jewish periodicals are also helpful because the transatlantic magazines frequently reprinted tidbits from the American press, or employed American correspondents who, on occasion, sent in data on women. Exotic items appear constantly in the European Jewish press; American Jewish women were an object of interest because of the greater freedom they enjoyed. The *Occident* of Isaac Leeser and the *Israelite* of Isaac M. Wise both concern themselves with women. In his German *Die Deborah*, Wise wrote of the American Jewess as early as the 1850's. David Einhorn's German *Sinai* occasionally reprinted reports of American Jewish women's societies (vol. 6 [1861—62], pp. 381 ff.), and the *Jewish Messenger* of New York City welcomed letters to the editor on the problems faced by the postbellum American Jewish ladies. New York's *Hebrew Standard* ran special women's issues on April 5, 1907, April 10, 1908, May 7, 1909, May 20, 1910, May 26, 1911. These annual issues of the *Hebrew Standard* are very informative. The *American Hebrew* (vol. 117, Nov. 6, 1925, pp. 811 ff.) ran a special Women's Number describing how the "women are taking hold of the world's work." Thus, by the first decade of the new century, women had attained a degree of recognition. No later than 1900, practically every major town had a Jewish weekly. Over the decades, these papers record the slow rise of the Jewess in the hierarchy of the Jewish community.

In the late twentieth century, the following Jewish weeklies, monthlies, and quarterlies frequently carried articles on the American Jewess: the *Jewish Post and Opinion*, the *Jewish Spectator*, *Present Tense* (American Jewish Committee), *Moment*, *Judaism* (American Jewish Congress), *Midstream* (Zionist), *Jewish Currents* (Marxist), the *National Jewish Monthly* (B'nai B'rith), the *Congress Monthly* (once *Weekly*, and *Bi-Weekly*), the *Reconstructionist*, *Sh'ma* (independent, liberal, Reformistic), and *Di Yiddishe Heim* (Lubavitch Hasidic women). The local weeklies draw heavily on the *Jewish Telegraphic Agency Daily News Bulletin* for news items which often include annual reports of national Jewish women's organizations. Obviously the house organs of the large national women's associations are excellent sources for any valuation of the twentieth-century American Jewish woman. As a rule these periodicals are very well edited.

The *Menorah Journal* published articles by Ruth Sapin (Sapinsky) Hurwitz on the American Jewess (vol.2, pp. 294 ff., vol. 35 pp. 111

ff., vol. 38, pp. 220. ff.) Her study in the *Menorah Journal*, vol. 2, pp. 294 ff., is an analysis of the American Jewish college woman, based on research that was carried on in 1915. In the spring of 1978, the Anti-Defamation League devoted an entire issue of *Face to Face: An Inter-Religious Bulletin*, vol. 5, Spring 1978, to women. The New-Jewish Left in magazines like *Davka* and *Genesis II* has always emphasized equality of the sexes in the Jewish community, and it was *Response*, an affiliate of the Jewish Student Press Service, which published *The Jewish Woman: An Anthology*, in the summer of 1973. The religious house organs of the Reform Jewish laity are the *Proceedings of the Union of American Hebrew Congregations* and *Reform Judaism*. Since the publication of the first volume of the *Proceedings* in 1873 (?), these reports have always carried data on women. The addresses on the sisterhoods carried in the *Forty-First Annual Report of the Union of American Hebrew Congregations* (Cincinnati, 1915), pp. 7680 ff., are illuminating.

In recent years, the rabbis of all denominations have had to concern themselves with the religious demands of women. Indeed, the Reform rabbis' yearbooks of the Central Conference of American Rabbis confronted the issue of equality for women as early as 1892 (vol. 3, p. 40). The Indexes to the CCAR yearbooks are helpful in locating information on women (*Central Conference of American Rabbis, Yearbook, Index*, vols. 1—50 [n.p., 1941]; vols. 51—60 [n.p., 1951]; vols. 61—80 [New York, 1972]). The Reform rabbis also publish the *Journal of Reform Judaism*, formerly the *CCAR Journal*. The Conservatives, in their *Proceedings of the Rabbinical Assembly of America* and their magazine *Conservative Judaism*, have not failed to confront the issue of women's "rights" in normative Judaism. The laymen in Conservatism have recorded their decisions on the position of women in the halakah in *Proceedings: The United Synagogue of America, 1973 Biennial Convention, Kiamesha Lake, N.Y., November 11—15, 1973*. The Rabbinical Council of America, the instrumentality of the middle-of-the-road Orthodox, employs the magazine *Tradition* to express its attitude toward the religious status of women. The Orthodox lay religious authorities have made known their liberalistic approach to women's place in religion in the *Resolutions Adopted by the Union of Orthodox Jewish Congregations of America,*

76th Anniversary Biennial Convention, 13—17 Kislev, 5735, November 27—December 1, 1974 (Boca Raton, Florida). Right-wing Orthodoxy, the Agudas Israel of America, has never failed to support the time-hallowed laws which still assign a very specific role to females. Its periodical is the *Jewish Observer.*

Formal Jewish history is presented in the *Publications of the American Jewish Historical Society* (later the *American Jewish Historical Quarterly,* now *American Jewish History*) and in the *American Jewish Archives.* Both these periodicals contain much data on the American Jewish woman, describing her activities since Ricke Nounes was sued by Asser Levy on September 14, 1654 (*PAJHS,* vol 18, p. 70), a few days after the first Jewish community in New York was established. Typical of the new interest in Jewesses is the article on Jewish businesswomen in the *American Jewish Historical Quarterly,* vol. 66, pp. 137 ff. The *American Jewish Archives* for April 1979—"History is the Record of Human Beings: A Documentary"—has not failed to make adequate provision for the Jewess.

The annuals which were published in this country in the last quarter of the nineteenth century nearly all have pertinent data for the historian of the America Jewess. Thus the *American Jews' Annual for 1893—1894* (Cincinnati, 1893, pp. 91 ff.) has an article on the literary efforts of this country's female Jewish writers. The *Jewish Book Annual,* published since 1942, is replete with information. For instance, vol. 35, pp. 97 ff., has an essay by Blu Greenberg on "Recent Literature on Jewish Women." The most useful of the annuals is the *American Jewish Year Book* (1899 to date). Unfortunately, the excellent Index (Elfrida C. Solis-Cohen, *American Jewish Year Book: Index to Volumes 1—50* [New York, 1967]) does not actually disclose the wealth of detail on women found in these first fifty volumes. Volume 1 records in some detail every major Jewish society in the country; volume 22, pp. 383 ff., supplies statistics on professional tendencies among Jewish women students for the scholastic year 1918—19; volume 24, pp. 109 ff., lists some ninety women of prominence among some fifteen hundred Jewish men in this country. Twenty-six of the ladies were writers; seventeen, actresses. In volume 33, pp. 165 ff., Rebekah Kohut describes the "Jewish

Women's Organization in the United States." Most volumes of the *Year Book* carry epitomes of the lives of Jews and Jewesses who died in the preceding year or two. These obituaries are an important biographical source.

When Isaac M. Wise began to publish *Die Deborah* in German, he certainly had all German Jewish readers in mind, not merely the women. By 1888, there was a weekly Yiddish *Weibersche Zeitung* ("Women's Paper"). The United Order of True Sisters was publishing the *Ordens Echo* ("The Order's Echo") since 1884, and a Philadelphia entrepreneur published a short-lived monthly, the *Jewish Woman*, in 1892—93. By 1895, Rosa Sonneschein began to edit the *American Jewess* (1895—99). Its issues reflect the modest goals of women as they set out to secure some recognition in a man's world. This magazine has been described, not altogether adequately, in *American Jewish History*, vol. 68, pp. 57—63. Hadassah has issued a *Newsletter* and the *Hadassah Magazine* since 1921; the Pioneer Women and the National Council of Jewish Women have published English bulletins and house organs since the first quarter of the twentieth century. In 1913, some New Yorkers issued *Die Frauen Welt: The Jewish Ladies' Home Journal* and in 1922—23 brought out a Yiddish-English *Yiddish Women's Journal* (*Der yidisher froyen zhurnal*). The Lubavitcher Hasidim, the most alert of the traditionalists, began to publish *Di Yiddishe Heim* ("The Jewish Home") in Yiddish and in English as early as 1958. The *Women's American ORT Reporter*, the magazine of this fast-growing national organization, appeared in 1966. By the early 1970's, Jewish feminists were mimeographing *Lilith's Rib* (1974), and by 1976, the quarterly *Lilith* had already made its appearance. *Lilith* represents the rather limited circle of the more militant feminists. Thus, by the third quarter of the twentieth century, practically every one of the diverse groups among Jewish women had a journal which spoke for it. American Jewish women of today are articulate, aggressive, often eloquent.

General Surveys of the History of American Jewish Woman

Isaac Markens wrote the first general history of American Jewry in 1888. There was to be no attempt to write even a few pages on the

American Jewess till about 1891, when Nahida Remy published *Das Juedische Weib* ("The Jewish Woman"). Her future husband, Professor Moritz Lazarus, the German psychologist, expressed the hope in his introduction, 1891, that her work would serve as "a mirror to proud consciousness of Jewish women" (Louise Mannheimer [trans.], *Nahida Remy's, "The Jewish Woman"* [Cincinnati, 1895], p. 12). It was then translated from the German into English (1895). Though the American data in this book is sparse, there is at least an attempt to enumerate the notable American Jewesses. In 1918, Leon Huehner (Huhner) republished from the *American Hebrew* an article which had already been issued in a slightly condensed form by the Council of Jewish Women. Huehner's fifteen-page sketch, *The Jewish Woman in America*, limited itself primarily to women of the eighteenth and nineteenth centuries. Allen Tarshish, in his unpublished Hebrew Union College doctoral disertation, "The Rise of American Judaism: A History of American Jewish Life from 1848 to 1881" (Cincinnati, 1937–39), addressed himself briefly to the Jewess of the middle nineteenth century. His source-based conclusions are valuable. In 1970, the historian Anita Libman Lebeson wrote *Recall to Life: The Jewish Woman in* America (South Brunswick, N.J., 1970). This book, a series of biographies and comments on women's national organizations, is in reality the first substantial approach to a history of the American Jewess. It is very useful. Three years later, Elizabeth Koltun edited *The Jewish Woman: An Anthology*. This is the anthology published by *Response* mentioned above. Actually, the data and appended bibliography in Koltun's book do not add much to our knowledge of the American Jewish woman. It was this same Ms. Koltun who, in 1976, published *The Jewish Woman: New Perspectives* (New York, 1976). This latter cooperative book, like the special *Response* issue, contributes little that is new to the history of the Jewess in the United States. *The Jewish Woman in America* (New York, 1976) by Charlotte Baum, Paula Hyman, and Sonya Michel, is an attempt to write a formal history of the American Jewish woman. Actually, the approach is in a way episodic; specific themes are pursued. The emphasis on literary sources, on fiction, is pronounced. The data until the twentieth century is thin; the contemporary period, the late twentieth century, is very helpful. Norma Fain Pratt published "Transitions in

Judaism: The Jewish American Woman through the 1930's" in the *American Quarterly*, Winter 1979, pp. 681 ff. This is a useful, scientifically conceived study.

The American Jewish Woman in the General Histories of American Jewry

Though the "standard" histories of American Jewry rarely addressed themselves to the women in the community, they are nevertheless useful. The authors could not ignore the national women's organizations and such outstanding persons as Rebecca Gratz, Penina Moïse, Emma Lazarus, and Henrietta Szold. Morris U. Schappes, in *A Pictorial History of the Jews in the United States* (New York, 1958), does genuflect in the direction of the women. As a Marxist historian, he accords women equality. There is a great deal of information, data, and history to be culled from the many city, state, and regional histories of American Jewry and from the congregational and institutional histories that have appeared in relatively large numbers since 1954. That was the year of the Tercentenary Celebration of Jewish settlements in New Amsterdam—New York. Jacob R. Marcus has published "A Selected Bibliography of American Jewish History" (*American Jewish Historical Quarterly*, vol. 51, pp. 97 ff.). Most of the works listed by him contain some data on the American Jewish woman. This Marcus bibliography, however, goes only to 1962; researchers, especially those intent on familiarizing themselves with the literature on Jewish women, will do well to consult Nathan Kaganoff's "Judaica Americana," which has appeared in the *American Jewish Historical Quarterly* (*American Jewish History* since September 1978) vol. 52, pp 58 ff.

Since the early 1960's, many new community histories have appeared. Historians, now, have not neglected the smaller towns, such as Lancaster, Pennsylvania, Vicksburg, Mississippi, New Haven, Connecticut, Nashville, Tennessee, Frederick, Maryland, Charlotte, North Carolina, or the state of Utah. The Jews of New Jersey's Raritan Valley, Burlington, Vermont, and Roosevelt, New Jersey, have found historians. Scholars have continued, of course, to write the history of the larger towns: New York, Los Angeles, Hartford, Brownsville, East New York, and New Lots, all in Brooklyn, New Orleans, Milwaukee, Atlanta, Birmingham, Cleveland, Baltimore. Two books on the California gold rush have appeared, and an exemplary history of Congregation B'nai Jehudah of Kansas City, Missouri, was published in 1972: Frank J. Adler, *Roots in a Moving Stream* (Kansas City, Mo., 1972). All these monographs do not fail to record, to a degree at least, the part that women have played.

Because of the feminist movement, some new works allot more space to the efforts of women; indeed, some of the researchers and authors are themselves women. There is a substantial body of data on women incorporated in the three-volume *Colonial American Jew, 1492—1776,* by Jacob R. Marcus (Detroit, 1970; see Index under "Women"). Hutchins Hapgood's early-nineteenth-century *The Spirit of the Ghetto: Studies of the Jewish Quarter in New York* (New York, 1909) has been supplemented by the massive *World of Our Fathers* (New York, 1976) of Irving Howe. Howe has done full justice to the Jewess of the Lower East Side. In the following works, the sociologist Marshall Sklare, as author and editor, has touched on the role of women in Conservative Judaism, in Orthodoxy, and in upper-middle-class suburban society: *The Jews: Social Patterns of an American Group* (Glencoe, Ill., 1958), *Conservative Judaism: An American Religious Movement* (New York, 1972), *The Jew in American Society* (New York, 1974). Together with Joseph Greenblum he has published *Jewish Identity on the Suburban Frontier* (New York, 1967). In the anthology, *The Female Experience: An American Documentary*, (Indianapolis, 1977), Gerda Lerner has incorporated memoir material of the labor leaders Rose Schneiderman and Theresa Malkiel, and has also reprinted the sad story of Mrs. Jake Sachs as told by Margaret Sanger in *An Autobiography* (New York, 1938), pp. 88—92.

Diverse Sources for the History of the American Jewish Woman

Many American Jewish women turned to the writing of poetry. The library of the American Jewish Historical Society contains the manuscript poems of Grace Nathan (d. 1831). The poems of Penina Moïse were published in her *Fancy's Sketch Book* (Charleston, S.C., 1833) and in the *Secular and Religious Works of Penina Moise*. This latter edition, prefaced by a brief biographical sketch, was prepared by the Charleston Section, Council of Jewish Women (Charleston, S.C., 1911). Lee C. Harby published a biography of Penina in the *American Jewish Year Book*, vol. 7, 1905—1906, pp. 17—31. Another Charlestonian whose poems were admired and published by her family was Octavia Harby Moses, *A Mother's Poems: A Collection of Verses* (n.p., 1915). Others whose poetry was published are Rebekah Hyneman, *The Leper and Other Poems* (Philadelphia, 1853), Adah Isaacs Menken, *Infelicia* (Philadelphia, 1870), Minna Kleeberg, *Gedichte* (Louisville, 1877). Her husband's eulogy throws some light on the history of this gifted woman: L. Kleeberg, *Eulogy in Commemoration of the Deceased Poetess, Minna Kleeberg* (New Haven, 1879). Most cherished of all the nineteenth-century Jewish poets was Emma Lazarus *(The Poems of Emma Lazarus* [2 vols., Boston, 1888]). Jessie E. Sampter, the Zionist, wrote several volumes of poetry; her *Around the Year in Rhymes for the Jewish Child* (New York, 1920) is a particularly charming book.

Informative and interesting data for the history of the East European immigrant women will be found in the cooperative work which Charles S. Bernheimer edited: *The Russian Jew in the United States: Studies of Social Conditions in New York, Philadelphia, and Chicago, with a Description of Rural Settlements* (Philadelphia, 1905). Leon Stein has written on *The Triangle Fire* (Philadelphia, 1962) and has edited *Out of the Sweatshop: The Struggle for Industrial Democracy* (New York, 1977). This reader contains a series of essays on the workers in the garment industry.

The vast Yiddish press, literally hundreds of thousands of pages, has not yet been studied with the Jewish woman in mind. Mordecai Soltes, in "The Yiddish Press—An Americanizing Agency," has published some helpful information (*American Jewish Year Book*, vol. 26, 1924—1925, pp. 165-372). More detailed is the unpublished thesis of George M. D. Wolfe, "A Study in Immigrant Attitudes and Problems: Based on an Analysis of Four Hundred Letters Printed in the 'Bintel Brief' of *The Jewish Daily Forward*," thesis presented to the Training School for Jewish Social Work (New York, 1929).

After the World's Parliament of Religions met at the Chicago World's Fair in 1893, the Jews who had participated in the religious discussions published three volumes of minutes and addresses. They are a very important source for the student of American Jewish history. Two of the three volumes concern themselves solely with women. The works published are: *Judaism at the World's Parliament of Religions* (Cincinnati, 1894); *Papers of the Jewish Women's Congress* (Philadelphia, 1894); *Proceedings of the First Convention of the National Council of Jewish Women Held at New York, Nov. 15, 16, 17, 18 and 19, 1896* (Philadelphia, 1897).

Because it had broken with Jewish "canon" law and was committed to acculturation, Reform Jewry was in the vanguard in according a degree of religious equality to women. Among the sources that document this trend are: *The Isaac Harby Prayerbook: Manuscript Form Prepared by Isaac Harby for the Reformed Society of Israelites Founded November 21, 1824* (Charleston, S.C. 1974), pp. 70—73; Barnett A. Elzas, *The Sabbath Service and Miscellaneous Prayers Adopted by the Reformed Society of Israelites, Founded in Charleston, S.C., November 21, 1824* (reprinted New York, 1916), pp. 38, 42, 47—48; Sefton D. Temkin, *The New World of Reform* (London, 1971), the translation of the "Proceedings of the Conference of Reform Rabbis" (Philadelphia, Nov. 1869), pp. 101 ff.; David Philipson, *The Reform Movement in Judaism* (2d ed., New York, 1931), pp. 329 ff.; Liebman Adler, *Sabbath Hours Thoughts* (Philadelphia, 1893), pp. 37—41; Joseph Krauskopf, *The Ascendency of Womanhood* (Philadelphia, 1917); Joseph Leiser, *American Judaism: The Religion and Religious Institutions of the Jewish People in the United States: A Historical Survey* (New York, 1925), pp. 174 ff.; "Report of the Committee on Reform Practice, Rabbi Morton M. Berman, Chairman. Delivered at 41st General Assembly, Union of American Hebrew Congregations, Nov. 13, 1950" (women called to the Torah). Most helpful—and interesting too—are the numerous volumes of responsa written by Solomon B. Freehof. They represent the effort of anti-authoritarian Reform to come to terms with the requirements of rabbinic law. See, for example, Freehof, *Reform*

Responsa for Our Time (Cincinnati, 1977), pp. 216-220. The minutes of the Board of the Hebrew Union College, Cincinnati, 1921, throw light on the efforts of Martha Neumark to be accepted for ordination. The religious views of Sally Priesand, the first American woman rabbi, are reflected in her *Judaism and the New Woman* (New York, 1975).

Unpublished theses frequently supply historical data on the status and behavior of American Jewesses. Women's rights are discussed albeit briefly, in Robert I. Kahn's "Liberalism as Reflected in Jewish Preaching in the English Language in the Mid-Nineteenth Century" (Hebrew Union College doctoral thesis, 1949), pp. 93—95. Some information on women's charitable organizations may be gleaned from Eugene J. Lipman's "A History of Organized Synagogal Philanthropy in the United States" (master's thesis, Hebrew Union College, 1943). Printed copies of *The Constitution of the Female Hebrew Benevolent Society of Philadelphia* (Philadelphia, 1825) are still extant. This is the first Jewish women's organization in the United States. The *Manuscript Catalog of the American Jewish Archives, Cincinnati* (Boston, 1971), vol. 2, pp. 378 ff., lists women's associations under the caption "Ladies Aid Societies." Eleanor F. Horvitz, in the *Rhode Island Jewish Historical Notes*, vol. 7, pp. 501 ff., discusses in detail, "The Jewish Woman Liberated: A History of the Ladies' Hebrew Free Loan Association." Useful too is the work of Paul Swerdlow, "The American Jewess in the Second Quarter of the Twentieth Century: An Attempt to Discover Whether There Is a Typical American Jewess. Her Nature and Characteristics" (master's thesis, Hebrew Union College, 1964).

A careful reading of Isaac Leeser's ten volumes of *Discourses on the Jewish Religion* (Philadelphia, 1866—67) uncovers data that sheds light on the mid-nineteenth-century Jewish woman (cf. vol. 2, pp. 172—176, vol. 10, pp. 242—248). Edgar E. MacDonald, in *The Education of the Heart: The Correspondence of Rachel Mordecai Lazarus and Maria Edgeworth* (Chapel Hill, N.C., 1977), is a very valuable source for an understanding of the thinking and the Jewishness of an early American intellectual. *Ruhamah: Devotional Exercises for the Use of the Daughters of Israel*, a compilation and translation from the German by Rabbi Morris Jacob Raphall (New York, 1852), reflects what was probably an effort to introduce this type of edificatory literature into America. The epitaphs of *The Old Jewish Cemeteries at Charleston, S.C.* (Charleston, 1903), edited by Barnett A. Elzas, are a useful aid in the effort to determine what Jewish husbands thought of their wives—after their death.

In *Three Years in America, 1859—1862* (Philadelphia, 1956), I. J. Benjamin II expressed himself in no uncertain terms on the value of the education received by America's teenage Jewesses (vol. 1, pp. 85 ff.). Bertram Wallace Korn, in his *American Jewry and the Civil War* (Philadelphia, 1951), has several references to the work done by women (see Index under "Women," "Hebrew Ladies"). By the 1890's, a number of rabbis had begun to preach on the new woman and her new opportunities. However, even the most liberal, like E. G. Hirsch and Max Landsberg, preferred, on the whole, to take refuge in adulatory flights of oratory and to relegate women to the area of social service (Emil G. Hirsch, *My Religion* [New York, 1925], pp. 359—371; Max Landsberg, "The Position of Women Among the Jews," in *Judaism at the World's Parliament of Religions* [Cincinnati, 1894], pp. 241—254). The more traditional rabbis like Julius M. Magil lectured on *The Worthy Woman* (Reading, Pa., 1895), content to pay tribute to the hard-working housewife immortalized in Proverbs 31.

Albert I. Gordon, in *Jews in Transition* (Minneapolis, 1949), wrote about the women in his Conservative Minneapolis congregation (see under "Hadassah," "Marriage," "Women"); Polly Adler, once madam in a bordello, solemnly assured her readers that *A House Is Not a Home* (New York, 1953). Benjamin Rabbinowitz, in the *Publications of the American Jewish Historical Society*, vol. 37, pp. 280 ff., describes the beginnings of the Young Women's Hebrew Associaton; *American Jewish Archives* in vol. 25, pp. 65 ff., 96 ff., republished documents retailing the problems of the rabbi's wife and the work which the sisterhoods did on behalf of the blind. Bernard Reisman, in *The Chavurah: A Contemporary Jewish Experience* (New York, 1977), described the communes which Jewish men and women of the 1970's established in their effort to find the spiritual fellowship, the "togetherness," which some had sought in vain in the synagogue.

In short, one is tempted to venture that there is hardly a published work on any aspect of American Jewish life which does not contain some information on Jewish women. Thus one may read a beautiful apostrophe to them and their gracious generosity in Myer Moses, *An Oration Delivered Before the Hebrew Orphan Society on the 15th Day of October, 1806* (Charleston, 1807), pp. 29–31. Malcolm H. Stern has analyzed some pre-1840 intermarriage statistics in *Essays in American Jewish History to Commemorate the Tenth Anniversary of the Founding of the American Jewish Archives Under the Direction of Jacob Rader Marcus* (Cincinnati, 1958), pp. 69 ff. The data on the inter-marriages of a century later were presented by Joseph R. Rosenbloom in Bertram Wallace Korn (ed.), *A Bicentennial Festschrift for Jacob Rader Marcus* (Waltham, Mass., 1976), pp. 487 ff. In *The Pioneers: An Historical Essay* (St. Louis, 1880), the gifted Rosa Sonneschein discussed the St. Louis women's literary society. Thomas Kessner and Betty Boyd Caroli published a study of "New Immigrant Woman at Work: Italians and Jews in New York City, 1880–1905," in the *Journal of Ethnic Studies*, vol. 5, no. 4, Winter 1978, pp. 19–31, and in the same *Journal*, vol. 5, no. 2, pp. 81 ff., the sociologist Abraham D. Lavender wrote on "Jewish College Women: Future Leaders of the Jewish Community?"

The rabbi of Sephardic Shearith Israel in New York City lectured to the ladies of the congregation in 1884 on *The Position of Woman in Jewish Law and Custom* (New York, 1884). The social reformer Sophie Irene Loeb, a professional journalist, published a volume of cute *Epigrams of Eve* (New York, 1913). The *American Jewish Year Book*, vol. 22, 1920–1921, pp. 383–393, reprinted a memoir of the Bureau of Jewish Social Research on "Professional Tendencies Among Jewish Students in Colleges, Universities, and Professional Schools." The period covered is the academic year 1918–19. A statistical study of Jewish collegians for the academic year 1934–35 was made by Lee J. Levinger in *The Jewish Student in America: A Study Made by the Research Bureau of the B'nai B'rith Hillel Foundations* (Cincinnati, 1937). Interesting details on the life of the labor leader Dorothy Jacobs Bellanca are tucked away in the *Amalgamated Clothing Workers of America. Twenty-fifth Anniversary Convention. Report of the General Executive Board and Proceedings of the Thirteenth*

Biennial Convention, May 13—24, 1940, pp. 476—478. Ronald M. Goldstein has assembled interesting cultural and economic data on Jewesses in his "American Jewish Population Studies Since World War II" in the *American Jewish Archives*, vol. 22, pp. 15 ff. Rabbi Victor E. Reichert of Cincinnati executed a tour de force when he published *My Ethical Will: Teenagers' Testaments. Written by the Members of the Confirmation Class of May 25, 1958, of the Rockdale Avenue Temple, Congregation Bene Israel* (Cincinnati, 1958). Rose H. Alschuler incorporated her spiritual testament, "I Believe—Today," in *Bits and Pieces of Family Lore, Presented to Her Son, Daughters, and Grandchildren on Her 75th Birthday, December 17th, 1962* (Chicago?, 1962).

The 1970's are rich, very rich, in exciting source materials on the emancipation of women. Richard Siegel, Michael Strassfeld, and Sharon Strassfeld included a section on "A Guide to Jewish Women's Activities" in *The Jewish Catalog* (Philadelphia, 1973), pp. 252—260. These pages dealt with consciousness-raising, rabbinic law, and women in religious and secular institutions. A bibliography was appended. In *The Second Jewish Catalog* (Philadelphia, 1976), which Sharon Strassfeld and Michael Strassfeld edited, they included material on the life-cycle ceremonies for women. Despite the fact that these two volumes are an introduction to Jewish "spiritual exercises," they fit well into the modern concept of Jewish historiography.

All the documents listed in the following paragraph have been reprinted in Marcus, *The American Jewish Woman: A Documentary History* (New York, 1980). In *The Jewish Presence* (New York, 1977), pp. 46—57, Lucy S. Dawidowicz writes "On Being a Woman in Shul." In 1977, when Rosalyn Yalow recieved a Nobel Prize, she had to submit an autobiographical sketch to the Prize Committee. It is an important and interesting statement. That same year, Susan Brandeis Popkin, a great-granddaughter of the Supreme Court justice, delivered a bat mitzvah address. Unlike the justice, she was a religionist. In "Susie's Story, Read at the Nuernberg-Fuerth Grand Reunion, July 7—9, 1978, at Grossinger's, Catskills, New York," Mrs. Werner (Lisl) Weinberg described how her infant daughter Susie miraculously survived the Holocaust. In late 1978, the *Message* of Congregation Beth Yeshurun of Houston, Texas, published a sermon of Rabbi Jack Segal, "Should We Have Women in the Conservative Rabbinate?" The answer was an enthusiastic yes. This address was republished in the *Jewish Post and Opinion*, January 19, 1979, pp. 3—4.

Biographical Reference Works for the American Jewess

Given the present state of American Jewish historiography, biographical reference books are still the prime source for a knowledge of the Jewish women of this country. This of course will slant any historical study toward "notables," but the balance can be redressed, in part, at least, by chronicling the problems of the female garment workers in the metropolitan centers. Missing, unfortunately, are the female masses, the housewives of an extended middle class. Future research will have to devote itself to this large and important group.

The latest edition of the American Library Association's *Guide to Reference Books* and its supplements will introduce the student to the standard biographical works. Jewish women will be found in all of them. Indispensable are the volumes of A. N. Marquis Company, *Who Was Who in America*. Here one can find biographies of deceased notables from 1897 to the present. References to contemporary notables or their life histories are chronicled in H. W. Wilson Company's *Current Biography Yearbook* and *Biography Index*. Very useful are *American Authors, 1600—1900* (ed. by Stanley J. Kunitz and Howard Haycraft [New York, 1938]) and their *Twentieth Century Authors* (New York, 1942). The volume on *Twentieth Century Authors: First Supplement* (New York, 1955) has been edited by Stanley J. Kunitz and Vineta Colby. Basic for any study of female writers is the extensive series of *Contemporary Authors* of the Gale Research Company. They are invaluable if one is interested in the careers of women like Marie Syrkin or Barbara Tuchman or Gloria Steinem. The current Marquis volumes on *Who's Who in America* are basic for all research; they may be supplemented by the same publisher's current edition of *Who's Who of American Women*. Very useful too is the *Dictionary of American Biography* and its supplements (New York, 1946 to 1974), and the three-volume *Notable American Women, 1607—1950* (Cambridge, Mass., 1971).

Biographies of the following Jewesses are found in the *Dictionary of American Biography* and its supplements: Mary Antin, Sophie Braslau, Ruth Mack Brunswick, Claribel Cone, Etta Cone, Rose Eytinge, Jennie Maas Flexner, Alma Gluck, Emma Goldman, Rebecca Gratz, Emma Lazarus, Sophie Irene Simon Loeb, Florence Prag Kahn, Clara Damrosch Mannes, Adah Isaacs Menken, Penina Moïse, Belle Lindner Israels Moskowitz, Maud Nathan, Alla Nazimova, Ernestine Louise Siismondi Potowski Rose, Rosika Schwimmer, Gertrude Stein, Rose Harriet Pastor Stokes, Henrietta Szold, Lillian D. Wald, and Fannie Bloomfield Zeisler. In the three volumes of *Notable American Women*, the following Jewish women are included: Mary Antin, Nora Bayes, Dorothy Jacobs Bellanca, Ruth Jane Mack Brunswick, Claribel Cone, Hannah Bachman Einstein, Rose Eytinge, Jennie Maas Flexner, Rebecca Franks, Carrie Bamberger Frank Fuld, Love Rosa Hirschmann Gantt, Alma Gluck, Emma Goldman, Josephine Clara Goldmark, Rebecca Gratz, Anna Held, Ida Henrietta Hyde, Florence Prag Kahn, Bertha Kalich, Lizzie Black Kander, Emma Lazarus, Florence Nightingale Levy, Irene Lewisohn, Sophie Irene Simon Loeb, Clara Damrosch Mannes, Adah Isaacs Menken, Penina Moise, Belle Lindner Israels Moskowitz, Maud Nathan, Alla Nazimova, Jessica Blanche Peixotto, Phoebe Yates Levy Pember, Julia Richman, Ernestine Louise Siismondi Potowski Rose, Jessie Ethel Sampter, Margarethe Meyer Schurz, Rosika Schwimmer, Hannah Greenebaum Solomon, Gertrude Stein, Frances Stern, Florine Stettheimer, Rose Harriet Pastor Stokes, Henrietta Szold, Lillian D. Wald, Louise Waterman Wise, and Fannie Bloomfield Zeisler.

America's Jewish biographical compendia began in 1905 with vol. 6, 1904—1905, of the *American Jewish Year Book*, which published "Biographical Sketches of Jews Prominent in the Professions, Etc., in the United States," pp. 52 ff. The following year, "Biographical Sketches of Jewish Communal Workers in the United States" appeared in vol. 7, 1905—1906, pp. 32 ff. It was almost a generation later before the first Jewish biographical directory in English was printed: this was *Who's Who in American Jewry, 1926* (New York, 1927). Later editions by various compilers and publishers appeared in 1928, 1935, 1938—39, and 1980. These volumes, all more or less standard, also contained biographies of women. However, several years earlier, vanity biographical books were already printed by enterprising businessmen. Among them are two volumes of *Distinguished Jews of America* (New York, 1917—18). Most of the biographies here are of East European immigrants. The volumes seem to be *Frauenrein;* as yet, immigrant women were nonpersons. A few Jewesses are mentioned in *American Jews: Their Lives and Achievements* (2 vols., New York, 1947—58). Still another vanity enterprise is *The Israel Honorarium* or *The American Israel Honorarium* (Jerusalem, 1968). The series of *Who's Who in World Jewry,* begun in 1955, are not "mug books." Obviously all these biographical works must be supplemented by the three large-scale Jewish encyclopedias mentioned above.

Since the feminist revolt, a number of biographical works have appeared emphasizing the role of women in society. Inasmuch as some present-day Jewesses have high visibility in the women's movement, most of these books have no choice but to include a number of them. The following works all carry information on Jewish female achievers; the list is by no means complete. June Sochen, *Movers and Shakers: American Women Thinkers and Activists, 1900—1970* (New York, 1973) tells the story, among others, of Emma Goldman and Rose Pastor Stokes. In Caroline Bird's *Enterprising Women* (New York, 1976), there are accounts of careers of successful women such as Ida Rosenthal, Tillie Lewis, Sylvia Porter, and Katharine Graham. Jeane Westin, in *Making Do: How Women Survived the '30's* (Chicago, 1976), records the experiences of Leah Parnes and Lillian Cantor Dawson (pp. 141—144, 274—277).

In *We Were There: The Story of Working Women in America* (New York, 1977), pp. 293 ff., Barbara Mayer Wertheimer portrays in some detail the careers of Jewish women who were pioneers in the garment industry unions. In "Organizing the Unorganizable: Three Jewish Women and Their Union," which is found in *Labor History,* vol. 17, pp. 5—23, Alice Kessler-Harris discussed in detail the work of the union organizers Pauline Newman, Fannia Cohn, and Rose Pesotta. The latter is the only one of these three women to write a formal autobiography (Rose Pesotta, *Bread Upon the Waters* [New York, 1944]). It describes her travails as a labor organizer in the 1930's. Winifred G. Helmes edited *Notable Maryland Women* (Cambridge, Md., 1977). This book contains biographies of quite a number of Jews. A similar collection of biographical vignettes has been assembled by Barbara Stuhler and Gretchen Kreuter in *Women of Minnesota: Selected Biographical Essays* (St. Paul, 1977). Sydelle Kramer and Jenny Masur are the editors of *Jewish Grandmothers* (Boston, 1976). This is a collection of oral interviews with foreign-born East European Jewesses who have spent their adult lives in this country. These detailed sketches offer much useful information for the social and economic historian. The most helpful of all these books which delineate the careers of Jewesses is Cecyle S. Neidle's *America's Immigrant Women: Their Contribution to the Development of a Nation from 1609 to the Present* (New York, 1975). At least twenty immigrant Jews are described by her.

There are several biographical works which limit themselves entirely to Jews. All of them include women. The earliest is Henry Samuel Morais's *Eminent Israelites of the Nineteenth Century* (Philadelphia, 1880). The American Jewesses whose lives he sketched are Rebecca Gratz, Rebekah Hyneman, Minna Kleeberg, and Emma Lazarus. The latter three were poets. It is worth noting that Morais was acquainted only with the earlier writings of Lazarus, for Emma had as yet not entered into her pronounced Jewish phase. In *Three Outstanding Women* (New York, 1941), Dora Askowith described the careers of Mary Fels, Rebekah Kohut, and Annie Nathan Meyer. Of the twenty-five *Autobiographies of American Jews* (Philadelphia, 1965) compiled by Harold U. Ribalow, six are of women: Mary Antin, Rebekah Kohut, May Weisser Hartman, Irma Lindheim, Anzia Yezierska, and Marie Syrkin. The last taught at Brandeis, edited the *Jewish Frontier,* and wrote a biography of Golda Meir. Greta Fink, in *Great Jewish Women: Profiles of Courageous Women from the Maccabean Period to the Present* (New York, 1978), described the following Americans: Rebecca Gratz, Ernestine Rose, Hannah G. Solomon, Henrietta Szold, Lillian Wald, Emma Goldman, Helena Rubinstein, Gertrude Stein, Louise Nevelson, Dorothy Schiff, and Golda Meir.

There is a constantly increasing body of biographical material enriching our knowledge of the American Jewess. Leo Hershkowitz and Isidore S. Meyer, in *The Lee Max Friedman Collection of American Jewish Colonial Correspondence: Letters of the Franks Family, 1733—1748* (Waltham, Mass., 1968), have prepared a definitive scholarly edition of the letters of Abigail Franks to her son Naphtali in London. The *Letters of Rebecca Gratz* (Philadelphia, 1929), edited by David Philipson, gives us an insight into the thinking, the accomplishments, and the Jewishness of the best-known Jewess of the antebellum period. There is no definitive biography of this very interesting person. However, two graduate theses chronicling her career are on deposit in the Hebrew Union College Library in Cincinnati: Leonard I. Beerman's 1949 master's thesis, "Rebecca Gratz: An Analysis of the Life and Activity of the Foremost Jewess of the Nineteenth Century as Reflected in Hitherto Unpublished Source Materials," and the 1957 doctoral thesis of Joseph R. Rosenbloom, "And She Had Compassion: The Life and Times of Rebecca Gratz." The collection of Rebecca Gratz letters in the American Jewish Archives is very large. They are all copies.

The biographies of Isaac Mayer Wise, the organizer of Reform Jewry's basic institutions, are important because Wise assumed a liberal stance toward women as early as the 1840's. His liberalism is reflected in David Philipson and Louis Grossman, *Selected Writings of Isaac M. Wise* (Cincinnati, 1900), pp. 397—399, and in James G. Heller, *Isaac M. Wise: His Life, Work, and Thought* (New York, 1965), see the Index under "Woman's Suffrage" and "Women." The poet Emma Lazarus was a younger contemporary of Wise. Her work and influence is chronicled in two biographies: Heinrich Eduard Jacob, *The World of Emma Lazarus* (New York, 1949) and Eve Merriam, *Emma Lazarus: Woman With a Torch* (New York, 1956). Neither is in any sense definitive. Emma Lazarus merits further study if only to evaluate her place in American literature and to explain why she has captured the imagination of twentieth-century American Jewry. A comparative study of Emma Lazarus and her contemporaries, Nina Morais and the two Nathan sisters, Maud and Annie, might well be rewarding. The following three monographs are helpful in understanding the literary work and aspirations of Emma Lazarus: Ralph L. Rusk (ed.), *Letters to Emma*

Lazarus in the Columbia University Library (New York, 1939), Morris U. Schappes, *Emma Lazarus: Selections from Her Poetry and Prose* (2d. ed., New York, 1947), Schappes, *The Letters of Emma Lazarus, 1868—1885* (New York, 1949). Harriet Lane Levy's *920 O'Farrell Street* (Garden City, N.Y., 1947) is a charming account of a late-nineteenth-century San Francisco family. In all probability there is here a modicum of fiction interwoven with the facts. Mrs. Levy was an aunt of Albert A. Michelson, the Nobel Prize—winning physicist.

There is a substantial number of biographies of American Jewish women. Most of them have been written in the twentieth century. The Hebrew Union College Library collection of biographies and autobiographies of American Jewesses will total one hundred at least. They are listed in the *Hebrew Union College—Jewish Institute of Religion Dictionary Catalog of the Klau Library, Cincinnati* (Boston, 1964—65). In writing *The American Jewish Woman, 1654—1980*, the author, Jacob R. Marcus, consulted numerous biographies of women whose work extended into the twentieth century. Among the memoirs which he found helpful were Simon Litman, *Ray Frank Litman: A Memoir* (New York, 1957). This is the story of a female protorabbi. Marcia Davenport, in *Too Strong for Fantasy* (New York, 1967), describes her mother's beginnings as an opera and concert singer. Her mother was Alma Gluck. Marvin Lowenthal's *Henrietta Szold: Life and Letters* (New York, 1942) is primarily a documentary, prefaced by a brief biography. The life of Jennie Franklin Purvin, a Chicago communal worker, civic social reformer, and activist, was summed up in a few pages by Neil Kominsky in his *Jennie Franklin Purvin: A Study in Womanpower* (Cincinnati, 1968). An anonymous curriculum vitae of Sophie (Sophia) Moses Robison, the brilliant social scientist, is outlined in a typescript deposited in the American Jewish Archives. The literature on the Israeli prime minister, Golda Meir, an American by training, is impressively large.

One is tempted to assert that there is hardly an aspect of the human experience which is not reflected in autobiographical accounts written by Jewish women of this country. The sad experiences of a Christian convert to Judaism are poignantly recounted in *Henry Luria; or, The Little Jewish Convert: Being Contained in the Memoir of Mrs. S. J. Cohen, Relict of the Reverend Doctor A. H. Cohen,*

Late Rabbi of the Synagogue in Richmond, Va. (New York, 1860). Phoebe Yates Levy Pember, in *A Southern Woman's Story* (New York, 1879) and in the *American Jewish Archives*, vol. 13, pp. 44 ff., portrays her problems as the matron of a Confederate hospital. In Glenn G. Boyer (ed.), *I Married Wyatt Earp: The Recollections of Josephine Sarah Marcus Earp* (Tucson, Ariz., 1976), this San Francisco Jewess tells of her life with her husband, a legendary figure in Western lore. In an autobiographical account in the *American Association of University Women Journal,* June 1938, pp. 226—236, Iowa-born Ida H. Hyde recounts how she became the first woman to earn a graduate degree in Germany. This is a document of prime historical importance.

The following autobiographies testify eloquently to the sharp differences that characterized Jewish women in the decades that straddled the nineteenth and twentieth centuries. *My First Seventy Years* (New York, 1935) is Florentine Scholle Sutro's account of her life. She moved in circles of wealth and culture. Her family originally came from San Francisco. Another San Franciscan was Amy Steinhart Braden. In an unpublished oral interview she speaks of her family and career as a social worker: "Child Welfare and Community Service: An Interview Conducted by Edna Tartaul Daniel" (University of California, Regional Cultural History Project [Berkeley, 1965]). Moving east to Chicago, one encounters Jennie R. (Mrs. Henry M.) Gerstley, a lovely human being, a communal worker. A copy of her unpublished reminiscences is found in the American Jewish Archives. One of the several Cohens in Cincinnati, in the latter part of the nineteenth century, was a tailor. The life of this German Jewish family is depicted in some detail in Sarah M. Wartcki, *My Mother's Memories of Her Childhood* (Cincinnati, 1976). Mary Antin was an immigrant, a gloriously happy one who, in *The Promised Land* (Boston, 1912), proudly proclaimed that America was the best of all possible countries. Mary Antin lived well within the ambit of traditional Americanism; in *Living My Life* (2 vols., New York, 1931), Emma Goldman, the anarchist, rejected much that Antin held dear. Rebekah Kohut, who spent most of her life in New York City, was a Hungarian immigrant who became a communal worker and educator. Her three following autobiographies offer valuable insights into the life of a woman who had "made it": *My Portion: An Autobiography* (New York, 1927), *As I Know Them: Some Jews and a Few Gentiles* (Garden City, N.Y., 1929), *More Yesterdays: An Autobiography, 1925—1949* (New York 1950). Rebekah Kohut knew Maud Nathan and, very probably, her sister Annie Nathan Meyer, the founder of Barnard *(Barnard Beginnings* [Boston, 1935]). Maud was the author of *Once Upon a Time and Today* (New York, 1933). These two sisters were Sephardis, nominally Orthodox Jews observing the Sephardic rite. The others listed above, Ashkenazim, were Orthodox, Conservative, Reform, nonobservant, and even atheistic Jews. What did they all have in common? They were born Jews.

Hannah G. Solomon, the founder of the National Council of Jewish Women, has told her story in *Fabric of My Life* (New York, 1946). It is complemented by her granddaughter's oral interview now in the American Jewish Archives ("Interview with Mrs. Philip Angel, of Charleston, W. Va.," conducted by Gerald Kane, April 20, 1970). By the first two decades of the new century, East European women began to make their presence felt as labor organizers and communal workers among the immigrants. The many tribulations of these leaders are mirrored in the following works: Rose Schneiderman and Lucy Goldthwaite, *All for One* (New York, 1967), Mrs. Gustave Hartman, *I Gave My Heart* (New York, 1960), "Oral History Interview with Pauline Newman, International Ladies' Garment Workers' Union, Conducted by Barbara Wertheimer" (Ann Arbor, Mich., 1978). This interview is on deposit in the Institute of Labor and Industrial Relations, University of Michigan—Wayne State University, Ann Arbor, Michigan. Totally removed, economically at least, from struggling heroines like Schneiderman and Pauline Newman were the two very successful writers, Edna Ferber and Fannie Hurst. Their experiences are set forth in Ferber's two volumes, *A Peculiar Treasure* (Garden City, N.Y., 1960) and *A Kind of Magic* (Garden City, N.Y., 1963), and in Fannie Hurst's *Anatomy of Me: A Wonderer in Search of Herself* (Garden City, N.Y., 1958). A woman who lived in a world of her own was Maimie (May) Pinzer. The early years of this daughter of East European immigrants unfold themselves vividly in her letters published in *The Maimie Papers* (Cambridge, Mass., 1977). They were edited by Ruth Rosen and Sue Davidson. For a brief period Maimie lived on the fringes of society as a prostitute.

With the advancing decades of the twentieth century, the American Jewish woman still refused to fit into any fixed pattern. The golden thread of continuity is invisible. Gloria Steinem's grandmother, a successful politician, has been described in the following work: Elaine S. Anderson, "Pauline Steinem, Dynamic Immigrant," in Marta Whitlock (ed.), *Women in Ohio History: A Conference to Commemorate the Bicentennial of the American Revolution* (Columbus, 1976). Belle Fligelman Winestine was a Montana suffragist (*Montana: The Magazine of Western History*, vol. 24, July 1974, pp. 70–78). Irma L. Lindheim of New York, scion of a"good" family, turned to Zionism in a *Parallel Quest: A Search of a Person and a People* (New York, 1963); Belle Lindner Israels Moskowitz became a power in New York State politics (Julius Henry Cohen, *They Builded Better Than They Knew* [New York, 1946], pp. 245 ff.); Esther Bengis, *I Am a Rabbi's Wife* (Lakewood, N.J., 1936), wrote of her struggle to survive as the wife of the congregation's minister. In *My Caravan of Years: An Autobiography* (New York, 1945), Goldie Stone of Chicago tells the reader how she helped weld the city's two disparate communities, the "German" and the "Russian." From New York to the Pacific Coast, wherever Lucy Robins Lang wandered, this left-winger devoted herself to the working masses (*Tomorrow Is Beautiful* [New York, 1948]). And Gertrude Stein? One can describe her as an expatriate whose cultural, artistic, and literary influence touched many. Actually she defies explanation; she has supplied autobiographical data in Gertrude Stein, *The Autobiography of Alice B. Toklas* (New York, 1934), *Everybody's Autobiography* (New York, 1937), and in *Wars I Have Seen* (New York, 1945). The struggles of East European immigrant women to cope with America's spiritual, cultural, and economic challenges were Sisyphean. They are reflected in the writings of two authors: Leah Morton (Elizabeth Gertrude Leven Stern), *I Am a Woman—and a Jew* (New York, 1926), and Anzia Yezierska, *Red Ribbon on a White Horse* (New York, 1950).

By the 1960's and 1970's, women were obviously making a place for themselves in a man's world. Dorothy Fields became a successful lyric writer (Max Wilk, *They're Playing Our Song: From Jerome Kern to Stephen Sondheim—The Stories Behind the Words and Music of Two Generations* [New York, 1973]). Caroline K. Simon's curriculum vitae, on file in the American Jewish Archives, documents that she was secretary of state for New York, 1959—1963. Minnie (Mrs. Charles S.) Guggenheimer raised the money to keep the Lewisohn Stadium Concerts going for a generation (Sophie Guggenheimer Untermeyer and Alix Williamson, *Mother Is Minnie* [Garden City, N.Y., 1960]). The struggles of a scientist to make a career for herself even if it meant a disruption of the traditional family structure is reflected in Ruth Weiner's "Chemist and 'Eco-Freak'" (*Annals of the New York Academy of Sciences*, vol. 208 [March 15, 1973], pp. 52—56 Problems such as hers loom ominously on the horizon of tomorrow's generation.

It is taken for granted that students conversant with the critical method in the social sciences will not take any biography at face value. Let every researcher in the field of American Jewish history never forget the moron's boast: "I know it's true; I seen it in a book."

Research on the following themes would certainly prove profitable: Rebecca Gratz as Reflected in Her Letters (there is more than one large collection); Rachel Mordecai Lazarus, Early American Jewish Intellectual; Jewish Women as Presidents of Congregations; The Nineteenth-Century "Ladies' Aid" as a Consciousness-Raising Instrument; The Changing Goals of the Conservative and Reform Sisterhoods; The Early Programs and Goals of the National Council of Jewish Women; The Contemporary Goals of the National Council of Jewish Women; The Influence of Hadassah on the American Jewish Woman; The Acceptance of Women of East European Origin into the Older American Jewish Women's Societies and Associations; The Americanization of the Central European Jewess; The Americanization of the East European Jewess; the Economic Activities of the Jewesses of the Middle and Lower-Middle Classes; A History of the Jewish Woman as Reflected in the Local English-Jewish Newspapers of Los Angeles (or any major American city whose backfile of Jewish newspapers is still extant); The Landsmanshaften of New York City's East European Jewesses; A Comparative Study of the Attitudes Toward Jewish Women as Reflected in the Socialist and Bourgeois Yiddish Press; Acculturation and Assimilation of the Mordecai Women as Reflected in the Mordecai Papers; The Experiences Encountered by Women as Rabbinical Students in America's Rabbinical Seminaries; An Analysis of the Contents and Possible Influence of Rosa Sonneschein's magazine, the *American Jewess*, 1895—1899; A Study of the Careers of Female Graduates of Jewish All-Day Schools; The Careers of German Jewish Female Émigrés in the United States after 1933; The Participation of Women in the Field of Jewish Critical Scholarship; The Young Women's Hebrew Association: Success? Failure?; A Study of Notable American Jewesses as Reflected in the Obituaries of the New York newspapers, 1920—1963.

Obviously the field of research into the history of the American Jewish woman is wide open.

Index

Compiled by Robert J. Milch, M. A.